A Matter of Hours

Harper's Ferry Today

The town as seen from about one mile downriver. Loudon Heights (Virginia) on the left and Maryland Heights on the right. Photo by Robert A. M. Schick.

A Matter of Hours

Treason at Harper's Ferry

Paul R. Teetor

Rutherford • Madison • Teaneck
Fairleigh Dickinson University Press
London and Toronto: Associated University Presses

Associated University Presses, Inc.
4 Cornwall Drive
East Brunswick, N.J. 08816

Associated University Presses Ltd
69 Fleet Street
London EC4Y 1EU, England

Associated University Presses
Toronto M5E 1A7, Canada

Library of Congress Cataloging in Publication Data

Teetor, Paul R., 1919–
    A matter of hours.

    Bibliography: p.
    Includes index.
    1. Harpers Ferry (W. Va.)—Capture, 1862,   2. Miles,
Dixon Stansbury, 1804–1862.   I. Title.   II. Title:
Treason at Harper's Ferry.
E474.61.T43   973.7'336   80-65575
ISBN 0-8386-3012-X   AACR2

Printed in the United States of America

Contents

Acknowledgments

The author thanks the following for permission to quote copyright material from the indicated sources: Mr. James B. Blackford for quotation from W. W. Blackford's *War Years with Jeb Stuart;* Mrs. Jack Brussel for reproduction of a map from Wood and Edmonds's *Military History of the Civil War, 1861– 1865;* The Devin-Adair Company for quotation from Otto Eisenschiml's *Vermont General;* G. P. Putnam's Sons for quotation from Edward Hungerford's *The Story of the Baltimore & Ohio Railroad, 1827–1927;* Mrs. Nancy Cockrell for quotation from W. T. Poague's *Gunner with Stonewall;* the University of North Carolina Press for quotation from Henry Kyd Douglas's *I Rode with Stonewall.*

The author acknowledges gratefully all the assistance he has received over more than a decade from the ever-helpful employees of the National Archives, the Library of Congress, the National Park Service, the Maryland Historical Society, and other institutions devoted to the preservation of our national memories. Among the dozens of individuals to whom warm thanks are due I can single out only Colonel Elbridge Colby, distinguished military historian and writer; Colonel R. Clarke Smith, the author's mentor both at law and in war; Dr. Harry Pfanz, Chief Historian of the National Park Service and authority on Harper's Ferry in the Civil War; William D. Snyder, longtime friend and architect of the Index to this work; Charles Ben Brotherton, who typed the manuscript; and Katherine Schindler Teetor, my wife, to whom this book is lovingly dedicated.

A Matter of Hours

1
Overview

To most Americans the name *Harper's Ferry* conjures up either or both of two images. It is one of the beauty spots of Appalachia: a great, green gap where the Potomac and Shenandoah rivers join to force a passage through the Blue Ridge on their way down to the sea. It is perhaps even more famous as the site of John Brown's ill-fated raid on the U.S. Arsenal on the eve of the Civil War, in order to secure guns and ammunition with which to arm and free the blacks of the Southern States.

For Civil War buffs, however, Harper's Ferry has a third claim to fame. Here it was that on the morning of Monday, September 15, 1862, after a three-day siege, without even awaiting an enemy assault and with a relieving Union army under General George B. McClellan only hours away, the Post Commander, Colonel Dixon Stansbury Miles, precipitately surrendered his garrison of some ten thousand Union troops to a besieging Rebel force with an effective strength of only twelve thousand men* under the Confederacy's General Thomas "Stonewall" Jackson. Moreover, the fall of Harper's Ferry permitted 8,000 Rebels under General Lafayette McLaws, that had been trapped by the relieving Union army on the Maryland side of the Potomac River, to escape capture by crossing a pontoon bridge to Harper's Ferry on the Virginia (now West Virginia) side and from there march north with Stonewall Jackson to join General Robert E. Lee at nearby Antietam.

*Jackson also had another 8,000 troops on the Maryland side of the Potomac and 4,000 on the Virginia side of the Shenandoah but because of the intervening rivers none of these troops were readily available for an assault on Harper's Ferry or its western front, Bolivar Heights.

These two events—the surrender of Miles's 10,000 Union troops and the escape of McLaws's 8,000 Rebels—together shifted the balance of manpower at the great and bloody battle of Antietam two days later by 18,000 men, in both cases to Lee's advantage. Since the armies involved at Antietam were of estimated magnitudes of 35,000 men (Lee) and 70,000 (McClellan),[1] it is plain that a shift of 18,000 in the balance of manpower could have had a significant impact on the outcome of that battle. Indeed it is very possible—although not certain, of course in view of McClellan's penchant for procrastination—that an increase of 18,000 in McClellan's manpower advantage could have made the difference between the stalemate that developed at Antietam and a clearcut victory for the Union which an eminent authority has said "might well have ended (the Civil War) two and a half years sooner (than it did)."[2]

Our interest here, however, is not in the effect which the surrender of Harper's Ferry had on the outcome at Antietam but in a controversy concerning the necessity for the surrender that has continued unresolved for a century and a quarter. That controversy turns on whether, as a contemporary military court of inquiry officially found, Colonel Miles's behavior before and during the siege represented only "incapacity amounting almost to imbecility,"[3] or whether, as we shall here conclude from intensive review of the court's record and additional postwar sources which were not available to the court of inquiry, Miles's acts and omissions can better be explained by *a deliberate purpose on his part to deliver up Harper's Ferry to the Rebels, one way or another.* This is a charge of treason.

2
Miles's Military Career

The man who surrendered Harper's Ferry to Stonewall Jackson was a forty-year veteran of the regular army and one of the top-ranking officers in the country's military service. When the Civil War broke out, whether out of loyalty or because his prospect for glory looked better in the Union army, Dixon Miles had elected to stand with the Union when many if not most Maryland and other border-state officers were leaving to join the new army of the Confederate States of America and pressing Miles to do the same. Unfortunately for Miles, the first major battle of the war had, as we shall see, ruined his career and brought him to exile in the relatively obscure post of Harper's Ferry. There, like bitter Benedict Arnold at West Point, Miles could ruminate on what must have seemed to him the ingratitude of the Federal Government for a border-state soldier's loyalty. To understand how all this had come about requires detailed knowledge of the man and his background.

Miles was Maryland gentry. Born in the lush green hill and dale country of northeastern Baltimore County in 1804, he was totally orphaned by the age of four and was brought up at "Stansbury's Prospect," the home of his uncle and namesake, Major Dixon Stansbury.[1] The Stansburys were a well-known Maryland clan (descended from a 1658 immigrant)[2] and had played a prominent role in the military life of the state. During the War of 1812, young Dixon Miles's distant kinsman, General Tobias Stansbury, was in command of the state's 11th Brigade,[3] while his own guardian (Major Stansbury) was fighting the British in the West with Williams's Regiment and being surrendered by General Hull at Detroit.[4] What if any, reaction young Dixon Miles may have had to widespread (although apparently unjustified) talk about treason on Hull's part we do not know.[5]

13

As for Dixon Miles's own father, Captain Aquila Miles, whose tombstone in the graveyard of St. James Episcopal Church near Sweet Air, Maryland, describes him as "a tender husband and an indulgent parent," all we really know of him, aside from his early death, is that he was a professional soldier and probably came from adjoining Harford County, Maryland, although it is not impossible that he came from Edgecumb County in up-country South Carolina's "Ninety-Six District," home of the great secessionist prophet, John Caldwell Calhoun.[6] (Interestingly, Miles later named one of his sons, also buried in St. James's graveyard, John Steuart Calhoun Miles.) In view of the military tradition on both sides of his family it is not surprising to find young Dixon Miles seeking appointment to the Military Academy at West Point at the early age of fourteen.[7] Writing a letter of recommendation to Calhoun, who was then secretary of war, Maryland's Senator Samuel Smith and Baltimore Congressman Peter Little referred to "the respectable standing" of Major Stansbury and his half brother, Major Thomas Talbott (who joined in supporting young Miles's application)[8], although it is clear from a later comment that Stansbury was "not wealthy"[9]. On June 24, 1819, at the age of fifteen, Dixon Miles entered West Point.[10]

His career at the academy was not impressive.[11] During his first year his class rank was fifty-ninth out of eighty-six in French, seventieth out of eighty-six in mathematics and sixty-fifth out of eighty-six in general order of merit. As a result of this deficiency he was turned back from the Class of 1823 to the Class of 1824. His repeat of the first year went much better (top third in all respects) but thereafter his grades relapsed generally to the point where he ranked only twenty-seventh out of the thirty-one cadets who graduated in 1824. His conduct record, however, was "creditable," with relatively few reported delinquencies and those only such usual ones as tardiness at formations, improper conduct, throwing snowballs, etc. On July 1, 1824, Dixon Miles became a second lieutenant in the U.S. Army and started down the long road to seniority and authority.

During the two decades from 1824 to 1846, Miles served in garrison in newly acquired Florida (1825); on frontier duty at Ft. Gibson in the then Indian Territory which is now Arkansas (1825–28); at Jefferson Barracks, Missouri (1828); then back for another, longer tour at Ft. Gibson, Arkansas (1828–36), where he was soon made adjutant of the 7th Infantry Regiment (1830).[12] On February 5, 1833, he was married in Baltimore's Old Christ Episcopal Church to twenty-one-year-old Sarah Ann Briscoe of another large Maryland clan.[13] The writer has been unable to establish either her parentage or relationship to others of this generally Southern-oriented family,[14] particularly Col. James T. Briscoe, who would become a leading figure among the secessionists in Maryland's Civil War Legislature.[15]

Miles took his bride back with him to Ft. Gibson, where he was promptly promoted to first lieutenant (1833).[16] In February, 1835, came the couple's first child, named for his father, who died at Ft. Gibson in November of the same year.[17] In 1836 Miles brought his wife back to Baltimore, where he remained on recruiting duty for three years (1836–39).[18] Here, in May 1836, was born their first daughter, May,[19] later to marry one of Miles's young officers, Lawrence W. O'Bannon, who, at the start of the Civil War would defect to the Confederacy to become chief quartermaster for Rebel General Bragg[20] and, briefly, for General Lee.[21] Here, too, was born in February 1838 their second son, John Steuart[22] Calhoun Miles, who would die when not yet three years old, in December 1840.[23]

From 1839 to 1845, Miles was on quartermaster duty as a captain in Florida, first in the so-called Seminole War (1839–42) and then in Pensacola Harbor (1842–45).[24] During this tour he apparently left wife Sarah and little May at home in Baltimore[25] and in that place was born, in May 1841, the first son that would survive to maturity: Dr. Benjamin Briscoe Miles, a surgeon[26] to whom, at the age of twenty-one would fall the miserable duty of representing his father's honor at the sessions of the Harper's Ferry Commission.[27]

In 1846, when the United States annexed Texas, Captain Miles managed a reassignment from his post as assistant quartermaster at Pensacola to take command of the Seventh Infantry Regiment in General Zachary Taylor's new watch on the Rio Grande.[28] Miles had not long to wait for the war for which he had been a quarter-century preparing.

When Mexican General Arista foolishly crossed the Rio Grande and precipitated war by attacking Taylor's troops on May 8–9, 1846, at Palo Alto and Resaca de la Palma, Miles was on his feet sixty consecutive hours directing his Seventh Infantry,[29] and winning a brevet majority "for gallant and distinguished conduct in the defense of Ft. Brown, Texas."[30] When, on July 6, 1846, Taylor began his own advance southward to Monterrey, the leading city of northern Mexico, it was Miles, with three companies of his Seventh Infantry, who led the advance by steamer upriver to occupy Camargo, where the American army would move inland to Monterrey.[31] Miles arrived at Camargo on July 14, 1846, summoned the Alcalde, and took formal possession of the town.[32]

It was two months later, however, on the approaches to Monterrey itself, that Miles most distinguished himself. Federacion Ridge, some 400 feet high and hosting two artillery redoubts, was one of Monterrey's major outer defenses.[33] On September 21, 1846, American General Worth sent 300 Texans up the steep, rock-hewn hillside, but an obvious disparity in numbers soon decided Worth he had better send Miles and his Seventh Infantry to the support of the Texans. One historian states simply: "Miles found a direct path to the summit and arrived in time to support C. F. Smith's assault on the redoubt. It fell easily."[34] Another puts it more colorfully: "Miles had not only the voice of a trumpet but the eye of a hawk and, striking at once upon a direct line of march, he promptly reached the main ridge. . . ."[35]

By the next day the American attack had reached to the fortified ruins of an old bishop's palace (called "the Obispado").[36] Other American units had seized a nearby strongpoint (Independencia Ridge) early in the morning and the Fifth and Seventh Infantry Regiments then worked themselves into position to enfilade any force moving from the Obispado.[37] By afternoon the Mexican commander deemed his position too critical to remain on the defensive.[38] When a Mexican attack collapsed in a murderous American crossfire, the Mexicans streamed back into the Obispado.[39] However, Miles's Seventh Infantry was so close on their heels that the two forces cleared the walls together and the Mexicans fled on to Monterrey without a fight.[40] A few days later the Mexicans evacuated Monterrey.[41]

Back in Baltimore the *American* reported proudly on Miles's conduct at the Battle of Monterrey, where, "at [the] head of [his] column, he scaled heights and won for his country the fortress known as the Bishop's Palace."[42] On September 23, 1846, "for gallant and meritorious conduct in the several conflicts at Monterey, Mexico," Miles won his brevet lieutenant colonelcy.[43] Clearly Miles's rise from captain to lieutenant colonel in the first four months of the war was merited.

Although Miles and his Seventh Infantry were among the nine regiments transferred from Taylor's Northern Mexico command to join General Winfield Scott in his expedition against Vera Cruz during March 1847 (preparatory to marching on Mexico City itself), no deeds of special note are attributed to Miles in these movements. By mid-May we find him once more at home in Baltimore, enjoying the role of war hero. At a public dinner at the Exchange Hotel he was presented with an "elegant" sword and an equally elegant toast:

> While the companions of his youth are welcoming him back with grateful emotions to the scenes of his childhood, a louder voice proclaims the soldier's reward—a nation's gratitude for the soldier's services.[44]

In late May he was writing his old friend and West Point classmate, Assistant Adjutant General Lorenzo Thomas, in Washington, seeking permission to stay in Baltimore until a detachment of recruits was ready to sail for Vera Cruz, "as I prefer remaining with my family to having a delay in Newport [News] or New Orleans.[45] He was still in Baltimore in mid-July when the pupils of Central High School presented him with a "handsome" sash for his "handsome" sword.[46] On August 7, 1847, the American commander at Vera Cruz, who was eagerly awaiting the arrival of his replacement, reported impatiently that Colonel Miles had not yet reported.[47] but by the eleventh, Miles had arrived and assumed command of the city of Vera Cruz, a position he occupied until December 23, 1847.[48]

Miles's last duty in Mexico was to command 1,200 troops guarding 500 wagons and a large number of pack mules traveling west from Vera Cruz to Santa Fe, New Mexico, in January 1848.[49] Unfortunately, the train was too extended to protect it adequately and its richness drew guerrillas like ants to a picnic. Near its destination, guerrillas drove off some 250 to 300 mules carrying civilian-owned goods.[50] Comparison of this incident with Miles's conduct at Monterrey suggests that he was stronger on personal courage than on military management.

In the post–Mexican War army, when smart young men like Captain George B. McClellan were leaving for more challenging and lucrative civilian work, Dixon Miles, now a senior officer, preferred to stay on military duty. Between 1848 and 1851 he was stationed first in garrison at East Pascagoula, Mississippi, and then on frontier duty in the Indian Territory (Ft. Gibson and Ft. Washita).[51] In March of 1849 we find him home in Baltimore, heading the executive committee for "The Grand Civic and Military Ball for the Benefit of the Poor," sponsored by distant cousin Elijah Stansbury, then mayor of Baltimore.[52]

In April 1851 he achieved permanent rank as lieutenant colonel of the Third Infantry, which was then spread over New Mexico, guarding the white settlers against the Indians[53] and keeping the peace between two very different white cultures, the Mexican refugees who had settled in the fertile Mesilla Valley and the "Anglos," now moving in from Texas in the wake of the Mexican War.[54] From 1851 to 1856, with time out in 1854 for conducting recruits from the East to New Mexico, Miles was in command of Ft. Fillmore, located at Brasitos, opposite Mesilla, on the Rio Grande (about forty miles northwest of El Paso, Texas).[55] Newly built and named in honor of then President Millard Fillmore, this installation housed some 250 men, the third largest army garrison in the United States (after New York City and Vancouver).[56]

From John Russell Bartlett, the American member of the Mexican Boundary Commission then trying to determine whether the Mesilla Valley belonged to Mexico or the United States under the confused provisions of the Treaty of Guadalupe Hidalgo, comes a description of life at Ft. Fillmore in September 1852:

> The barracks at Ft. Fillmore are as yet quite rude, being mere jackals, that is, built of upright sticks filled in with mud. They were hastily put up, but it is the intention of Col. Miles to have more substantial buildings of abode erected forthwith. . . .
>
> . . . We passed a few days very agreeably at Ft. Fillmore, partaking of the hospitality of Col. Miles and his officers. The visit, too was rendered doubly agreeable by the society of four American ladies, belonging to the families of the officers, who had had the courage to accompany the army on its toilsome march of three months across the plains. These were the only American ladies I had met between San An-

tonio and The Pacific Coast and were, I believe, the only ones in this portion of the frontier.[57]

Whether one of these four ladies was Miles's wife we cannot tell. We do know that she had remained at home in Baltimore, pregnant, when Miles first left for New Mexico in the spring of 1851.[58] In 1856, however, Miles's eldest daughter, May, then twenty, was married and records show that it was at Ft. Fillmore,[59] to one of Miles's younger officers, South Carolinian Capt. Lawrence O'Bannon. O'Bannon would, as noted earlier, join the Rebels in 1861 and become quartermaster general of the Confederate Trans-Mississippi Department.[60]

Less happy was Miles's relationship with another of his ranking officers, Captain (Brevet Major) Israel B. Richardson, a Vermonter, who apparently developed a strong dislike of Marylander Miles and his ways. Although Richardson later denied under oath entertaining any "prejudice or unfriendly feeling" and could not recall ever having threatened in O'Bannon's presence to "do Miles an injury" when occasion offered,[61] Miles insisted that Richardson was "manifestly actuated by malicious feeling engendered in former years in New Mexico,[62] and we, too, think it not improbable that there was some degree of bad feeling between the two men. This is significant because it was Richardson, by then a Union colonel, who would prefer charges of drunkenness against Miles after the fiasco of Bull Run I, in the process destroying forever whatever chance Miles had for high command during the rest of the Civil War.[63] (Late in 1855 Richardson resigned from the army[64] to go into business in Michigan, whence he returned to fight on the Union side when war broke out in 1861.)

During 1853, Miles played a role in the developing crisis over the U.S.–Mexican boundary that had resulted from reference to an inaccurate map in the Treaty of Guadalupe Hidalgo. When Congress rejected the Bartlett Commission's proposed compromise boundary thirty-two miles north of the treaty-map line, the governor of Chihuahua proclaimed Mexican ownership of the disputed Mesilla Valley and led 800 Mexican troops into the area.[65] The American territorial governor, William Carr Lane, on his own initiative, proclaimed U.S. sovereignty in the same area and demanded immediate enforcement of his proclamation by the Third Infantry commanders, Colonel E.

V. Sumner (at Santa Fe) and Lieutenant Colonel Miles (at Ft. Fillmore).[66] Although Miles presumably acted on Sumner's orders, he (Miles) became the target of a bitter letter from Lane, vigorously asserting the superiority of civilian authority over that of the military and decrying that "some 250 U.S. troops who are unemployed and are within 5 miles of the scene of action fold their arms in frigid tranquility and thereby sustain the enemies of their country."[67] Sumner and Miles, however, had correctly anticipated that the policy of the Pierce Administration would be to avoid a renewed struggle with Mexico and secure peaceable possession of this 45,000 square miles. This was accomplished by what would become known as the "Gadsden Purchase" (for 10 million dollars, later in 1853).[68]

Throughout the late 1850s the Third Infantry was stationed at various points in New Mexico: Ft. Thorn at Santa Barbara (1856–57); Ft. Fillmore again (1857–58); and finally Albuquerque (1858–59).[69] During this period Miles participated in two important military expeditions against the Indians.

He commanded the southern column in the Third Infantry's victory over the Coyotero Apaches on the Gila River on June 27, 1857.[70] It appears, however, that it had been arranged for the regiment's French-born commander, Col. B.L.E. Bonneville, to ride beside Miles at the head of the right wing, while young Capt. Richard Ewell (later to become a top-ranking Confederate commander) led the left wing.[71] It was Ewell's dragoons that really broke the Apaches[72] and Bonneville's battle report to the department commander in Santa Fe, Brevet Brigadier General John Garland, was full of praise for the captain:

> "Much praise is due to every officer, particularly to Captain Ewell, who was my active man on all important occasions.[73]

After crediting Ewell with the work of a real deputy, Bonneville dutifully added a somewhat ambiguous commendation for the official deputy:

> Colonel Miles was everything I could wish—the same gallant veteran.[74]

Garland apparently took the commendation as intended to say merely that Miles gave Bonneville and Ewell no trouble, because Garland's own report to the adjutant general, Lorenzo Thomas, in New York, commended Bonneville's prosecution of the campaign ("with energy and perseverance") and took special note of the conduct of Captain Ewell ("whose gallantry and sound judgement I have had occasion to note in former reports") but omitted completely any mention of Miles.[75]

The following year (1958) Miles finally won a place in the limelight, as commander of the so-called Navajo Expedition. Relations with the mighty Navajo nation had reached a "critical condition of affairs," as Garland explained to Army Headquarters in New York:

> These Indians have assumed a boldness in their forays of late which forces upon me the necessity of opening a campaign against them with not less than 1000 men; they are understood to number 2500 warriors.[76]

There was apparently some question in some minds as to whether Dixon Miles was really up to the command of such an expedition, but Garland finally concluded that Bonneville had had his day of glory on the Gila; that Colonel Loring had had his on the so-called Utah Expedition against the Mormons; and that "it was but just to allow Colonel Miles his with the Navajos."[77] General Garland soon regretted his decision.

In early August Garland advised Bonneville that the Department was about to put in motion into the Navajo country as large a force as could be collected and with it a company of "Guides and Spies" to be organized by Bonneville in the Albuquerque area.[78] Garland stressed that "in organizing this company I desire the greatest secrecy to be observed as to its destination."[79] He doubted that the expedition could take the field before September 1[80] and in no event before the safe arrival of reinforcements and supplies at Ft. Defiance, where Miles was now waiting to take off.[81] Soon thereafter, however, Garland's hopes for an orderly departure were dashed.

Some time previously an army officer's servant had been murdered by an Indian, and in late August the Indians brought Miles the dead body of a Mexican boy recognized as a captive among them as the murderer of the officer's servant.[82] Decrying this as an attempt to deceive him, Miles immediately took the field with a column of about three hundred men.[83] His advice to Garland on September 3, 1858, that the Navajos had forced his hand evoked the following prompt letter of censure from Garland's adjutant:

> Colonel.
> I am directed by the Commanding General to acknowledge the receipt of your letter of the 3rd instant, covering the report of Captain McLane, R.M.R., and to express his surprise and regret that the movement against the Navajos should have been thus prematurely, inauspiciously commenced and to say that it was well known to Captain McLane and yourself that the General was exceedingly anxious operations should not commence until the safe arrival of reinforcements and supplies at Ft. Defiance. This ill-timed attack has not only defeated the General's intentions but has placed in jeopardy the supply trains and re-inforcements now en route for Fort Defiance and I am further instructed to say that your contemplated offensive operations, based upon Captain McLane's affair, do not meet the approbation of the Department Commander.[84]

Whether Garland would have retained Miles in command of the Navajo Expedition is a good question, but on September 15, 1858, Garland departed for "the States," leaving Miles's immediate superior, Colonel Bonneville, commanding the 3rd Infantry, in command of the Department of New Mexico.[85] French-born Bonneville was apparently more sympathetic with Miles than Garland had been and more adroit at "handling" Miles personally. Bonneville later (October 19, 1858) explained to the Adjutant General of the Army in New York:

> On assuming command of the Department (9/16/58) I found Lieut. Col. D.S. Miles, by order of General Garland, charged with our relations with the Navajo Indians, to prosecute a vigorous campaign, and that Major E. Backus would be sent with a second column to cooperate and assist him. Under these circumstances to supercede Colonel Miles now would imply disapprobation and would be unjust to an old and faithful soldier [on] whose success I have already repeatedly to comment.[86]

Within a week after assuming command of the Department, Colonel Bonneville had occasion to write Miles his "regret" that Miles had not personally attended a recent council meeting, noting diplomatically that "whatever talent might be around you, the government had a claim to your personal attendance and your long experience upon this particular occasion."[87] In the same letter Bonneville agreed with Miles that "the murder of the Mexican captive and the offering him as the murderer is an outrage. . . . You were right in pressing the demand by taking the field against them."[88] "However," the diplomatic Bonneville explained, "your movement is in advance of the preparations that have been made."[89] He further explained that while it was Miles's duty to "press the matter by active operations," nonetheless "I must insist that you allow no opportunity of negotiating to escape, the moment they manifest a sincere desire to comply with your demand."[90] Finally, Bonneville cautioned: "In case the murderer should be given up, you will send him in with the witnesses, to be delivered to the civil authorities for trial."[91]

Apparently encouraged by Bonneville's sympathetic views, Miles promptly sought to have the Garland censure letter stricken from his record but Bonneville sidestepped the request:

> In regard to the censure of the late commanding officer of the department, it is an act of my predecessor over which I have no control.[92]

On the merits Bonneville again agreed with Miles:

> My instructions to you of the 23rd instant informed you that on account of the brutal murder of the Mexican captive you were justified in offensive measures and my regret is that you did not seize on 15 or 20 of the perpetrators.[93]

However, Bonneville doubted the need to raise a "volunteer force" urged by Miles,[94] and again warned that "you are a long way ahead of us."[95] Finally, with reference to a civil trial for the murderer if the Indians should deliver him up, it appears that Miles was still insisting on handling it his own way. However, Bonneville repeated his warning that it would not be proper for Miles to himself do summary justice; he *must* send the murderer to Albuquerque for trial by the civil authorities.[96] Headquarters obviously felt that it had to keep a short tether on this field commander.

Eventually the Navajo expedition reached deep into Indian

territory and invaded the Navajos' great natural fortress, the Canyon de Chelly in northeastern Arizona. Miles's day-to-day decisions in the course of the expedition are of some interest. When an Indian from the Canyon who was picked up "evidently spying out our line of march" seemed from his appearance to be of too much importance to release but it was "embarrassing" the troops too much to retain him, Miles "reluctantly" gave the order to have him shot as a spy.[81] On the other hand, an old Indian captured in the Canyon was not killed and was found useful in getting surrounding Indians to stop shooting into the expedition's camp during nighttime as a result of threats that the Indian would be hanged if the shooting did not stop.[98] Two captured Indian women and three children were released unconditionally; Miles explained: "I could not kill them and they were too great an encumbrance to retain."[99]

In terms of its punitive purpose, Miles reported, the expedition was a success, killing two hundred Indians (Miles's estimate) and capturing over thirty Indians, fifteen thousand sheep and three hundred horses.[100] However, Miles apparently had some anxious hours, because he warned in his report to Bonneville that what with the scarcity of grass, the total lack of wood, and the constant danger from Indian sharpshooters firing down from the rim of the Canyon, "no command should ever again enter [the Canyon de Chelly]"[101]

Bonneville was "gratified" at Miles's report of the success of the scout and the manner in which it had been conducted and added:

> As an additional evidence of my approval, your report will be sent to the lieutenant general commanding the army [Winfield Scott].[102]

Four months later, on January 19, 1859, Dixon Miles was promoted to the rank of full colonel[103]—one of only twenty-two colonels in the nation's thirteen-thousand-man army—and was reassigned, after furlough in Baltimore,[105] to Ft. Leavenworth, Kansas, to command the Second Infantry,[106] one of the eight infantry regiments that made up the U.S. Army on the eve of the Civil War.[107]

Colonel Dixon S. Miles (1804–62)

Forty-year veteran of the regular army who surrendered Harper's Ferry to Rebel general T.J. (Stonewall) Jackson on September 15, 1862. Photo in possession of the National Park Service.

3

Fiasco at Bull Run

The beginning of the Civil War in April 1861 found Dixon Miles and two companies of his Second Infantry at Ft. Kearney in mid-Nebraska, whence he was quickly ordered to bring his troops east. The march to Omaha took eight days; from Omaha they then traveled south by steamer down the Missouri River, running a gauntlet of Confederate soldiers and artillery at St. Joseph, Missouri, and reached Ft. Leavenworth, Kansas, by the end of April, in time to avert the capture of that installation by Missouri Rebels.[1]

By early June, Miles was at Carlisle Barracks near Chambersburg, Pennsylvania, with elements of his Second Infantry, to help put together a force under Maryland's Major General Robert Patterson to counter a Rebel force gathering at Harper's Ferry less than fifty miles south. Miles was given command of a brigade made up of elements of his own Second Infantry, elements of his old Third Infantry, and three regiments of Pennsylvania volunteers.[3] Aside from one regular cavalry unit, all the other four brigades at Chambersburg were made up entirely of volunteers.[3] Though still a colonel, Miles was now an acting brigadier general commanding an important military unit, with excellent prospects for further advancement.

By mid-June the Confederate evacuation of Harper's Ferry and troop movements in the vicinity of Washington had led the War Department to order Miles's brigade to the nation's capital.[4] Their movement by train on June 19, 1861, took Miles through Baltimore, where it was necessary to change stations. The march of his troops, whose appearance was described as "hardy" and discipline as "excellent,"[5] seems not to have evoked any mob violence such as had greeted the Sixth Massachusetts Infantry only a few weeks earlier. There were, however, no bouquets for Baltimore's erstwhile popular war hero, Dixon Miles. Instead, an editorial in the pro-Southern Baltimore *Republican* now bitterly attacked Miles's decision to remain with the Union army as the product of a base desire for higher command and disloyalty to the people of Maryland who had done so much for him.[6] The editorial referred particularly to Miles's ingratitude for an 1860 resolution of the legislature awarding him a magnificent gold sword for his Mexican War service. (Interestingly, that resolution, No. 5, Acts of 1860, had been sponsored by one Oscar Miles, a wealthy, slave-holding state senator from strongly secessionist St. Mary's County, whose relation, if any, to Dixon Miles is not, however, established.[7])

In a pseudonymous letter to the editor of the Baltimore *American* from a friend of Miles quoting a letter just received from him,[8] it was pointed out that Miles had as yet had no promotion or even the prospect of one and was moved only by devotion to "the best interest and glory of his country," intending to "perform his whole duty in defense of his country's laws, his country's unity, his country's dear-old flag." (Miles's language.) As for the sword (which was not yet finished), Miles was quoted as saying that he would not accept a sword voted by the prosecession legislature unless the vote were ratified by the next legislature, to be elected in the fall of 1861.

That the diatribe of the *Republican* against Miles for his "disloyalty" to Maryland was not untypical of Baltimore feeling in the last days of the struggle for control of this critical border state[9] is confirmed by a dispatch published in the New York *Herald* on the very date (July 1, 1861) when Baltimore's pro-Southern police commissioners were finally arrested and imprisoned in Ft. McHenry:

> The bitterness of the Rebels in Baltimore is manifested even in social life. Not content with abusing Colonel Dixon S. Miles—a veteran of the regular army—for continuing to defend the flag under which he has fought for thirty-seven years, some of those who were old and once valued friends have instituted a social persecution of his family and lose no opportunity to insult them, although Mrs. Miles is a most estimable lady, whose society has hitherto been courted by

these same people. They are invoking for themselves a heavy retribution when the time shall come, as it surely will, that sympathy with treason shall be a mark of infamy.[10]

Regardless of how painful life must have become for the Miles family in Baltimore during these troubled times, Miles's rejection of pleas to join his son-in-law (now a Confederate quartermaster) and others of his old friends and relatives in the new Confederate ranks[11] seems to have served him well in Washington. Nor was he really bereft of friends in high enough places to aid in his bid for a top command in the burgeoning Union army.[12] On July 6, 1861, Miles, although still a colonel, was given command of a new division, not fully made up, in General Irwin McDowell's Army of the Potomac.[13] He thus became an acting major general just in time to participate in that capacity in the first great battle of the Civil War.

No sooner was Miles in command of a division than he began striking out on his own without regard for the policy of his army commander, General Irwin McDowell. The following message to Miles from McDowell's adjutant dated July 15, 1861 (as McDowell was cautiously beginning to move his army toward Manassas), illustrates the short tether on which McDowell quickly found he must keep Miles:

> It has just been learned that you have given Colonel Blenker orders to advance with his brigade this evening. The general commanding directs that you make no move whatever until you receive further orders and that you take pains to see that there is no move made by either of your brigades until instructions are received from these headquarters.[14]

Sunday, July 21, 1861, was a beautiful sunny day, and much of Washington drove out to see the new Union army send the new Confederate army back to Richmond. Through most of the day the Northerners did appear to be winning,[15] but Col. Thomas Jackson's Confederate troops held like the "stonewall" by which he would ever thereafter be known, and late in the afternoon the Harper's Ferry Rebels arrived to turn the battle into a Union rout. Responsibility for this debacle rested partly on Northern editors like Horace Greeley who had been continually crying "On to Richmond"; partly on the new Lincoln administration, which felt some such positive action had to be taken; and partly on the Generals—old Winfield Scott and his field commander, Irwin McDowell—who gave in, against their better judgment, even though they were not yet really ready for an offensive. Ironically, however, none of these suffered the terrible retribution that befell Dixon Miles for his part in Bull Run I, which was, in fact, zero.

Being held in reserve at nearby Centreville, while all the fighting went on elsewhere, his Fifth Division hardly fired a shot in anger all day. When the Rebels failed to pursue the fleeing Yankees after the unexpected Confederate victory, there was nothing much left for the Fifth Division to do but wait for the fleeing Union troops to pass through them and then plod their own weary way back to the environs of Washington. In sum Miles had won no victory, but he had suffered no defeat either. His career could hardly have been hurt by Bull Run but for one thing that happened: he was formally accused of drunkenness on duty during the battle.

His accuser was none other than onetime Major—now Colonel—Israel B. Richardson, of New Mexico memory, whose brigade of Michigan volunteers was temporarily assigned to Miles's command during the Battle of Bull Run.[16] Although this arrangement apparently worked for a few hours, tactical disputes as to the best positions for the reserve became serious in late afternoon when the main Union army came fleeing from the field of battle.[17] Whether Miles's or Richardson's proposed defensive position was really better is still an open question and ordinarily it would make no difference, since Richardson's duty was obviously to follow his superior's orders, whatever he might think of them. About 7:00 P.M., however, one of the Michigan regimental commanders reported to Richardson that Miles was drunk and Richardson leaped at this opportunity to disobey Miles's orders, immediately rearranging his units as he thought best.[18] Infuriated when he found out what was happening, Miles threatened to arrest Richardson but the latter said he would pay no attention to any further orders from Miles.[19] The commanding general, McDowell, was called to the scene of this altercation and, rightly or wrongly attributing the manifest confusion of the Union forces in this area to Miles, McDowell assumed the immediate command himself.[20] Four days later, on July 25, 1861, Miles's division was broken up.[21]

On the same day Richardson's formal battle report publicly accused Miles of drunkenness during the battle.[22] Miles promptly struck back in two ways. Firstly, in a letter to the editor of the Washington *Star* he astutely tried to convert the issue into one of Northern-states/Border-states suspicions:

> Perhaps no one has ever before been hunted with more assiduous, malicious, vituperation and falsehood, since the battle of Bull Run than myself. My name, I am told, has been a by-word in the streets of Washington and its bar-rooms for everything derogatory to my character. *It was stated I had deserted to the enemy; I was a traitor, being from Maryland, a sympathizer;* gave the order to retreat; was in arrest, and now, by Col. Richardson's report, drunk. (Emphasis added.)[23]

Secondly, Miles asked for a court of inquiry into Richardson's charge of drunkenness and McDowell promptly granted the request, noting that the charge had been made "very publicly" and that he himself had found "much confusion" in the ranks when he came upon the scene.[24]

A court of inquiry presided over by Brigadier General William B. Franklin (who would later unsuccessfully lead McClellan's task force to relieve Miles at Harper's Ferry) heard some two dozen witnesses describe Miles as drunk at Bull Run while some two dozen others swore equally positively that he was sober.[25] Like ancient Anglo-Saxon litigants and their blood-kin compurgators, accuser Richardson and defender Miles each drew most of his supporting witnesses from his own retinue— Richardson from the Michigan regiments and Miles from the New Yorkers. Almost all the witnesses on both sides were officers, but Miles's supporters, with only three exceptions, were all company grade or lower, whereas Richardson's supporters were more typically field grade and even general officers (McDowell himself testifying against Miles). Indeed, Richardson's counsel in his final argument went well beyond the record in this respect:*"Many of these [accusing] witnesses are army officers and have known Colonel Miles long and well"* (emphasis added).[26]

Examination of Miles's witnesses followed a regular, almost wooden, pattern. Miles had been seen to ride erect in his saddle. His voice was clear and distinct. In the witnesses' opinion Miles was neither drunk nor under the influence of alcohol. In a number of instances the witness had observed Miles only from some distance (up to 150 feet) but there were a goodly number of witnesses whose testimony cannot be said to have been incredible on its face.

The accuser's witnesses had more variegated and perhaps more believable stories. A few examples (among many) will be helpful.

Captain Richie (Miles's aide): Miles was not too much under the influence of liquor to perform his duties but Richie did see the Colonel drink: "I can't say how often; I think that I could safely say several times."[27]

Colonel Richardson (Second Mich.): "From the time that Colonel Stephens had been speaking to me [reporting that Miles was drunk] up to this time I had noticed more particularly the actions and conduct of Colonel Miles and I came to the decided opinion that he was intoxicated, so much so as to be unfit for duty. I came to this conclusion from observing his actions and his manner of talking, more particularly. His voice was guttural and his language incoherent, and he had a difficulty to maintain his seat in his saddle."[28]

Colonel Daniel McConnell (Third Mich.): "I don't think he [Miles] was [in a condition to do duty]; I think he was intoxicated. . . . He was reeling in his saddle, very unsteady; his language, tones and utterance was thick; his general conditions was like an intoxicated man."[29]

Lt. Col. Stevens (Third Mich.): "I considered him [Miles] to be drunk. . . . My reasons were from the manner in which he inquired what regiment it was; at that time he was reeling about in his saddle, his speech quite incoherent, so that we could not readily understand him without paying particular attention; his face was very much flushed and his look indicated drunkenness; also it seemed very hard for him to understand what we said to him; for instance, when I informed him whose regiment it was and who commanded the regiment, he would seem to understand that it was Colonel O'Donnell's or Major Donnell's."[30]

Colonel Walrath (Twelfth New York): ". . . he (Miles) had on two hats and in my opinion he was intoxicated. . . . I should not think he was fit to take the command, this is my opinion, from intoxication. . . . He talked like it and his dress, having two hats on and appearance of his face at that time."[31]

Major Barry (artillerist on McDowell's staff): "I thought Colonel Miles at that time [sunset] was laboring under excitement that was produced by drink; that was my impression. . . . About sunset of the 21st July General McDowell directed me to collect the artillery and post it in a commanding position at Centreville. I had posted one battery and was in the act of posting the second, when Colonel Miles rode up and asked, in an angry and vexed manner or tone, who was moving those guns, or words to that effect. I replied that I was. He rejoined that I had no right to do so, and must not interfere with his arrangements. I replied that I was only carrying out General McDowell's orders, when he replied, in an exceedingly angry manner, that he would not have his arrangements intefered with by anybody. As Colonel Miles knew me very well personally, and also knew what my official position was that day, those circumstances, combined with his excited manner, gave me the impression he had been drinking." Barry concluded that he did not think Miles was in a fit condition to command.[32]

Captain Vincent (Miles's adjutant): Before sunset he saw Miles drink no more than twice, but Miles was under the influence of liquor and was "in a measure unfit to perform his duties as commander."[33]

Captain McKeever (adjutant in Heintzelman's Division): He believed Miles to be intoxicated because of "his appearance, his manner, his behavior towards me personally, his conversations and the fact that his breath smelled strongly of liquor." McKeever further testified that he had asked Miles for help in stopping the fugitives from Heintzelman's Division and warned of danger that the Rebels would intercept the retreat of the Union troops in the rear. "He [Miles] put his hand on my shoulder and pushed me aside, saying 'I know all about the fight—you can't give me any information,' or words to that effect. I think he also added, 'I have something else to attend to.' And his Adjutant General, Captain Vincent, appealed to him in my presence to give some orders to his division; he declined doing so. . . . In my opinion he was unfit to command the troops at that time."[34]

Captain Baird (adjutant of the Thirty-eighth New York, later a key figure in the loss of Maryland Heights during the siege of Harper's Ferry): "It was my impression that he [Miles] was intoxicated . . . [because he] was talking rather loudly and gesticulating violently; his general appearance made that impression on me."[35]

Colonel D'Utassy (Thirty-ninth New York, later one of Miles's brigade commanders at the siege of Harper's Ferry): "I could not say [whether Miles was intoxicated or under the influence of liquor]; I scarcely believe I saw him for just one moment." He added that Miles's orders were judicious and military and that he (D'Utassy) "noticed nothing out of the way as regarded his voice."[36] (Although D'Utassy, a gentleman of something less than the highest probity, as we shall see later, apparently preferred not to throw stones at his commanding officer, the major of D'Utassy's regiment, some thirty years later, recalled Miles's behavior at Bull Run rather differently:

"It was now about noon, and I received an order to join Repetti [another officer of the Thirty-ninth] at Blackburn's Ford. As we were marching briskly along the road, we were met by General [*sic*] Miles and his staff. He seemed to be very drunk. He called out: 'Halt! What have you got there?' 'The left wing of the Garibaldi Guard.' 'Where are you going?' 'To join the Colonel and the rest of the regiment.' ''Bout face and march to the battlefield. Damned quick, too!' There were two roads to the battlefield, diverging just outside the village—as plainly seen from my former position. I galloped ahead, overtook Miles and said, 'General, which road shall I take?' 'Follow your nose, G——d d——n you!' I never saw him again. . . ." The Major then concluded that "Miles' condition, or his treachery, brought us a heavy trial. . . ."[37]

General McDowell: "I noticed in Colonel Miles' manner during the time that I have related that we were near each other, his manner, I mean his language and tone of voice towards me was not becoming in him or respectful to me as the commander of the army. On my return to Centreville from the troops and passing by him some little distance off, I observed his manner as he sat on his horse and thought it stolid or stupefied, and seemed to confirm in me the information I had received that he was under the influence of intoxicating liquor."[38]

Dr. Todd (Twelfth New York): "It was my impression that he [Miles] was [intoxicated]; upon a cursory glance it is not an easy matter to distinguish intoxication from eccentricity or peculiarity of manner. . . . Perhaps the most important reason was his unsteadiness on his horse, and another the very incoherent manner of speaking; it may be attributed to some other cause beside intoxication; those were considered in my mind, sufficient in addition to this general appearance. . . . His manner or tone of voice was perfectly monotonous; the command I heard given [to the Twelfth New York] was this: 'You are now where I want you; lay there, damn you and die there.' . . . I considered him entirely unfit [to command] at that time."[39]

Dr. Woodward (medical director on Miles's staff): A sometime specialist in the treatment of inebriates, Dr. Woodward testified that he had been treating Miles for several days for a dysenteric diarrhoea.[40] He had prescribed for Miles before the day of the battle "several remedies," including opium and quinine pills and brandy, which he administered personally, a tablespoon at a time (although conceding that he had once seen Miles drink some besides what Woodward gave him).[41] It was Dr. Woodward's opinion, however, that Miles was *not* drunk and that if he had been, he (Woodward), riding constantly beside Miles, would "certainly" have readily detected any intoxication.[42]

On October 29, 1861, the Court of Inquiry made a unanimous report:

Statement of Facts

1. That Colonel I. B. Richardson was justified in applying the term drunkenness to Colonel D. S. Miles' condition about 7 o'clock P.M. on the 21st of July last.
2. That the evidence is clear that Colonel Miles had been ill for several days before July 21st last; was ill on that day; that the surgeon had prescribed medicines for him, and on the day of the battle, had prescribed small quantities of brandy.
3. The Court, however, considers his illness a slight extenuation of the guilt attached to his condition about 7 P.M. on July 21st last.

Opinion

The Court is of the opinion that evidence cannot be found sufficient to convict Colonel Miles of drunkenness before a court-martial; that a proper court could only be organized in this army with the greatest inconvenience at present; and that it will not be for the interests of the service to convene a court in this case.

The Court is therefore of the opinion that no further proceedings in the case are necessary.[43]

To understand what happened next it is necessary to know something about the man who was counsel for Miles throughout his ordeal. This was Reverdy Johnson, easily the greatest lawyer in Maryland and, after Daniel Webster's death in 1850, deemed by many the greatest lawyer in America.[44]

A Whig senator from Maryland during the Mexican War and attorney general for President Zachary Taylor,[45] his name is found on one of the briefs in most of the important cases heard by the U.S. Supreme Court during the 1850s, notably as prevailing counsel in the Dred Scott case.[46] Although he presumably believed slavery was not right,[47] he literally detested the abolitionists, because of what he foresaw as the ultimately disruptive effect of abolitionism on the Union.[48] With the demise of the old Whig Party in the middle fifties, he became a Douglas Democrat and advocate of "squatter sovereignty."[49] When Lincoln was elected president and the South began seceding from the Union, Johnson, essentially a "Southerner,"[50] became a Maryland delegate to the ill-fated Peace Congress at the Willard Hotel in Washington, which unsuccessfully proposed slavery-guaranteeing amendments to the Constitution, in the hope of holding the Southern states in the Union.[51] On the other hand, when the Confederate attack on Ft. Sumter signaled the failure of all such efforts, Johnson categorically and apparently sincerely took the position of a Constitutional Democrat. As his biographer wrote:

> After Lincoln's election and the secession of South Carolina, Johnson without a moment's hesitation took his place among the foremost advocates of union and opponents of secession. This position he never left. At the close of the war he stated that he never had referred to the Confederates but as "traitors, rebels or insurrectionists." No man could have been fiercer than he in his denunciation of that "mischievous heresy of secession."[52]

That Lincoln himself had great confidence in Johnson is clear. It was Johnson to whom Lincoln turned in 1861 to answer Chief Justice Taney's opinion in *Ex parte Merryman*, 17 Federal Cases 144, Case #9487 (1861), denying the president's right to suspend the writ of habeas corpus in wartime,[53] and it was Johnson again to whom Lincoln turned in 1862 for a special emissary to monitor and report on abolitionist General

Ben ("The Beast") Butler's controversial military occupation of New Orleans.[54] After Maryland had sent Johnson back to the U.S. Senate early in 1862, Lincoln referred to Johnson as "a very excellent Union United States Senator."[55]

On the other hand it is equally clear that Johnson's essentially "Southern" background remained a powerful influence on his course of action. He eventually supported McClellan vigorously against Lincoln in the Presidential campaign of 1864,[56] and his warm professional relations with such noted Southern clients as Jefferson Davis and Robert E. Lee safely survived the war.[57] As his biographer puts it: "He possessed a marvelous power of making and keeping friends in both political camps."[58]

Consistent with his essentially "Southern" background, throughout the Civil War Johnson frequently exerted himself to free imprisoned persons suspected of disloyalty, especially those living in Maryland (sometimes with and sometimes without pay). He also appeared as counsel for the accused in some notable military trials during the war.[59] One was the drunkenness trial of Dixon Miles.

No sooner was the "opinion" of the Miles Court of Inquiry released than Johnson pounced on the gross logical inconsistency between it and the "statement of facts." If there was really probable cause for a court-martial, the court of inquiry had no business letting Miles go scot free, he argued, with more logic than practicality.[60] Hence the finding of drunkenness must be disregarded and the opinion that "evidence cannot now be found to convict Colonel Miles" must control. In short, Miles was completely vindicated. This conclusion was embodied in a twelve-page printed "review of the Proceedings of the Court of Inquiry and Legal Opinion on the Evidence in the Case of Colonel D. S. Miles, U.S.A.," published on December 20, 1861, over the signature of Reverdy Johnson, former attorney general, and R. H. Gillett, former solicitor of the U.S. Treasury. The sour grapes of losing litigants and their lawyers being a fairly common phenomenon, one might not expect much attention to be paid to this pamphlet, but such was not the case. Moore's *Rebellion Record,* the leading contemporary documentary history of the Civil War, actually treated Reverdy Johnson's "opinion" as the one that counted:

> The Court of Inquiry in the case of Colonel Miles, charged with being intoxicated at the battle of Bull Run, honorably

acquitted him of the charge. The decision is furnished in a report of Reverdy Johnson and R. S. Gillett, in which they declare that the bulk of the evidence produced on the trial goes to show that the charges are entirely false.[61]

Something of the same Alice-in-Wonderland quality attaches to the next act of the drama. It will be recalled that in July 1861 Miles had announced he would not accept the sword voted him by the Maryland legislature in 1860 for his Mexican War service, unless the new legislature to be elected in the fall of 1861 confirmed the state's desire to so honor him. The new legislature elected under the supervision of what was virtually a Northern army of occupation was, not surprisingly, controlled by the Unionists, including new member Reverdy Johnson.[62] Early in the session Miles was accordingly summoned to Annapolis to receive his jeweled sword.

On February 7, 1862, the presentation was made by Governor Bradford in the Hall of the House of Delegates in the presence of both houses and the judges of the Court of Appeal.[63] Both the presentation and acceptance speeches were "remarkably well delivered," and each was "frequently interrupted by applause," according to the Baltimore *American*.[64] The problem which some might see in presenting a hero's sword to a soldier just found guilty of drunkenness on duty was no problem at all to Governor Bradford. He, following Reverdy Johnson's lead, chose simply to disregard the actual finding of drunkenness and substitute the acquittal which all right-thinking Marylanders apparently agreed had to be the verdict:

> The claim to this gift of your State has been still further delayed, as I am aware, by another trial through which you have been more recently called to pass, a trial far more painful to a soldier like yourself than the severest conflicts of the battlefield. Your friends have sympathized with you in that proceeding and looked with earnest anxiety to its result.
>
> That result, as officially proclaimed in the opinion of the court charged with the investigation of the subject, shows that there is nothing existing for which you should be further called upon to answer. This, therefore, in the judgment of all fair and honest minds ought at once to return you to the honorable position you had ever antecedently maintained. But if, from the somewhat anomalous form of the opinion [i.e., the categorical finding of drunkenness] there should still

linger in the minds of any the slightest doubt of your inno-
cence or the faintest stain upon your honor, there, sir, is the
instrument with which to wipe it out. Able and eloquent as
may have been your forensic advocate [Reverdy Johnson],
here is an advocate even more eloquent and efficient than he.
Take it, sir, and wield it in the cause of the Union and the
Constitution. Unsheathed for such a purpose and used as
you know how to use it, you may rest assured, as we do, it will
achieve for yourself a personal triumph as satisfactory and
complete as will be the ultimate triumph of your country over
the misguided, demented host now threatening its destruction.[65]

Miles's acceptance speech, in the same flowery Victorian
prose, was more happily concerned with the "glorious victories
our arms achieved in a foreign land" and with "sustain[ing] the
proud name won in the days of yore for Maryland, whose sons
were ever foremost in the battle, crimsoning the battlefield with
their blood," etc., etc. The closest he came to any mention of his
recent trial was a reference to his nearly thirty-eight years of
"arduous" service, followed by "personal enmity and unjust
aspersion."[66] There was also an assurance in closing that "when
this blade is drawn from its scabbard, it will be, as his Excellency
supposes, in a worthy cause in defense of our common country
and for the glory of my beloved state.[67]

Even discounting the powerful influence of Reverdy Johnson
on the Maryland legislature, which would shortly return him to
the U.S. Senate,[68] the sword episode makes it clear that most of
Maryland's Constitutional Democrats rallied to Dixon Miles's
support with such passionate disregard for the fact of his
drunkenness as might suggest that the patriotism of all Constitutional Democrats was somehow at stake in Miles's ordeal.
Be that as it may, it appears that the same trial which convinced
the Army establishment that Miles was unfit for any major
command simultaneously convinced the border-state Marylanders—whose support was Lincoln's constant concern—that
Miles had been unfairly put upon and at least deserved another
chance. This confronted the War Department with a difficult
question: what to do with Dixon Miles?

4

The Command of
Harper's Ferry

No one really knows now how Miles came to be assigned to command of the Harper's Ferry–based "Railroad Brigade." That unit was chiefly concerned with fighting off the Rebel guerrillas (commonly called "bushwhackers") that infested the line of the Baltimore & Ohio Railroad, one of the Union's three great East-West lifelines.[1] Putting the old Indian fighter in such a job, particularly in an area so close to his loved and loving Maryland, made some sense, but it is unlikely that common sense had much to do with the decision.

While Miles's assignment (between March 8, 1862, and March 29, 1862)[2] was officially made by General McClellan as Commander of the Army of the Potomac, McClellan was then largely preoccupied with preparation for his imminent Peninsular Campaign and there is no evidence that the assignment was really his personal choice (although Horace Greeley later had no hesitation in placing the blame squarely on McClellan's shoulders).[3] It is a fair speculation—although *only* a speculation—that Miles's assignment to the command at Harper's Ferry was more likely the handiwork of Reverdy Johnson,[4] this time almost certainly working together with John W. Garrett, another Maryland Constitutional Democrat. As the president of the Baltimore & Ohio Railroad, Garrett was the man most concerned with who commanded the "Railroad Brigade." Fortunately, from Miles's viewpoint at least, Garrett had as Southern sympathies as Johnson, even though, like Johnson, his overt loyalty to the Union had earned him the full confidence of the Lincoln administration. Writes the official historian of the Baltimore & Ohio:

> Like many of the important citizens of Baltimore at the outbreak of the Civil War, he had found much sympathy in his heart with the cause of the South. . . . Mr. Garrett, at that time, made no secret of his own personal feelings. 'Our Southern friends', was his way of speaking of the leaders of the Confederacy in its beginning weeks and months. . . .
> . . . Yet in the long run—and in fact the time was not long in arriving—he proved to be a mighty friend indeed of the North. At no time—even at the beginning—did he, by outer action or expression, show the slightest disloyalty to the Union. . . .
> . . . [While] one of John W. Garrett's regular tasks became the releasing of his somewhat rash friends from prison, after they had been there long enough to repent of their hasty words . . . Garrett became not only a strong adherent of the North and the Union, but a large power in helping it through to eventual victory. In this a fortuitous circumstance aided greatly. His friend Edwin M. Stanton of Ohio became, under Lincoln, Secretary of War and, by the very nature of his position, a tremendous force in the Lincoln Cabinet. The ties that bound Garrett to Stanton were more than those of friendship alone. The lawyer from the mid-West had been general counsel of the Ohio Central Railroad, which, at the beginning of the Civil War days, already was being merged into the parent Baltimore & Ohio structure. Garrett liked Stanton. And Stanton not only liked Garrett but he had an abounding faith in him. Hence his willingness to comply, whenever it was possible, with Garrett's wishes and suggestions.[5]

On the other hand, despite the Lincoln administration's apparent willingness to give Miles command of the Railroad Brigade at Harper's Ferry as a concession to the desires of Maryland's Constitutional Democrats, it is clear that Lincoln and Stanton were not prepared to place their reliance on Miles alone if and when Harper's Ferry should find itself in real trouble.

Real trouble came soon—a virtual dress rehearsal for next fall's siege—when Stonewall Jackson led 15,000 of his "foot-cavalry" down the Shenandoah Valley in late May of 1862 to within sight of Bolivar Heights, the western defense perimeter of Harper's Ferry.[6] Jackson's real purpose was to frighten Lincoln into denying McClellan vital reinforcements for his Peninsular Campaign to take Richmond, and in this Jackson succeeded brilliantly.[7] As Jackson's troops threatened Harper's Ferry, the whole North quavered and Lincoln and Stanton— who were personally directing all military moves from Washington, in McClellan's absence—immediately sent an up-and-coming West Point–trained young brigadier of unquestioned Union loyalty named Rufus Saxton to take command of Harper's Ferry in the emergency. Saxton, in fact, did a magnificent job.[8]

In contrast to the "most demoralized condition" his aide later reported finding on their arrival,[9] Saxton inspired his 7,000 Union troops to work like beavers improving their defenses. He had hundreds of them hauling a battery of extremely heavy naval (Dahlgren) guns up the steep slopes of Maryland Heights to a strategic site from which to bombard the advancing Rebels.[10] As Jackson approached Saxton's outer defense line (Bolivar Heights) Saxton realized he had not the number of troops needed to defend that long front and wisely pulled his main force back to a much shorter river-to-river defense line in front of Camp Hill, just west of Harper's Ferry itself.[11] Simultaneously he sent the rest of the troops thus released to the crest of Maryland Heights to protect the great new naval guns emplaced on its forward slope against a rumored attack from the rear of the Heights.[12]

Late on the third day two fierce Rebel assaults on the new inner defense line were driven back, and the following dawn revealed that Jackson's men had silently folded their tents and stolen away.[13] With two merging Union armies (McDowell and Frémont) closing in on his rear, Jackson had concluded to waste no more time on Harper's Ferry.[14] Rebel deserters quoted Jackson as saying: "Fifty thousand men could not now take Harper's Ferry."[15] Thirty years later (1893) Congress belatedly recognized Rufus Saxton's feat by voting him the nation's highest military award, the Medal of Honor, for "distinguished gallantry and good conduct" in the defense of Harper's Ferry in May 1862.[16]

How Miles conducted himself during these three days of thrust by Jackson and parry by Saxton is nowhere recorded, except that Saxton's battle report when it was all over routinely listed Miles's name among a dozen to whom "great credit is due."[17] In any event, as soon as the threat from Jackson was lifted, Saxton and the others moved on, leaving Miles once more the ranking officer at Harper's Ferry. Indeed, his position was actually improved shortly thereafter when command of the Union Army's Middle Department, headquartered in Baltimore, in June fell to 78-year-old Major General John Wool, hero of both the War of 1812 and the Mexican War.[18]

As a regular army officer himself, Wool had little use for the volunteer civilians and militiamen overrunning the Union army, reserving his confidence for regulars like Miles. Testifying later before the Harper's Ferry Commission, Wool conceded that he was personally acquainted with Miles and that he had not thought Miles had "the capacity to embrace so large a command as he [Miles] had there [at Harper's Ferry]":

> . . . but he appeared to be very zealous and he was one of the best officers I had. Indeed, he was the only one I could place there, the *only regular officer* [emphasis added]. I do not know that I had one that would answer his purpose, unless it was General Morris, who commanded at Ft. McHenry.[19]

That Wool's confidence in Miles was not really as reluctant as his later testimony suggests is indicated by an order of August 28, 1862, actually *expanding* the jurisdiction of Miles's "Railroad Brigade" as far west as Cumberland, Maryland.[20] Regardless of who bears the blame for originally putting Dixon Miles in command of Harper's Ferry, it is clear that General Wool must bear some responsibility for keeping him there and even increasing his responsibilities. Wool, although a native of upstate New York, had endeared himself to the Baltimore "Secesh" sympathizers and alienated what Wool called the "Jacobins" of that city by a number of actions, including a clampdown on arrests based on mere suspicion of disloyalty, and refusal to administer a loyalty oath to all Baltimore citizens, as requested by the Unionist upper branch of the city council.[21] By year-end, Wool had to be reassigned to New York City.[22]

That, then, was how things stood at the end of the relatively quiet summer of 1862: quiet because the great battles were all being fought far to the south, around Richmond, and military action in the Shenandoah Valley was for the nonce limited to colorful but fairly minor skirmishes involving cavalry, both regular and irregular ("bushwhackers"), on both sides. Illustrative of this guerrilla warfare, which went on more or less continually along the upper Potomac, is this dispatch to the *New York Times* from Harper's Ferry on August 28, 1862, just before the storm of full-scale war would again envelop it;

Yesterday the village was filled with painful rumors to the effect that [pro-Union] Virginia cavalry numbering one hundred men, had been surrounded by a large band of guerrillas at Waterford [a pro-Union Quaker village in northern Virginia], about 16 miles from here, and cut to pieces, only five escaping. The Captain, for whom the Richmond authorities had offered a reward of one thousand dollars, was reported as among the prisoners. Such was the statement brought by one of the members who, being on picket duty, had escaped. All of the cavalry here [at Harper's Ferry] were sent immediately in pursuit. Toward night a dispatch was received from Capt. Means announcing that he was safe at Point of Rocks. This occasioned great joy inasmuch as the worst fate was anticipated for him and the immense number of the company who had previously deserted from the rebel service into which they were impressed. About 10 o'clock in the evening our cavalry returned, reporting that Capt. Means' men fought the rebel force until their ammunition gave out, with the loss of one killed and several wounded. None were taken prisoners. The bodies of six dead rebels were found.

This was at first supposed to be part of White's [Confederate] cavalry force but it has since been ascertained that they were bushwhackers. These "irregular fighters" are overrunning this part of the State. We hear of their operations in every direction and during the past week they have become unusually bold.

Last Friday a party of them suddenly darted into Smithfield [now Middleway], a small village some twelve miles from here and captured seventeen out of twenty [Union] cavalry who were stationed there. One of them who escaped has shown me a splendid Colt revolver which he obtained from the rebels in the melee. Several of the prominent citizens of the place, who are known to have aided in their capture have been seized, brought here and imprisoned in the engine house. There is a poetic justice in confining such characters in this place [where John Brown was captured].

On the same day the train of cars on the Winchester (& Harper's Ferry Rail) road were destroyed about sixteen miles from here—the attacking force consisting of about sixty mounted guerrillas. Obstructions were placed on the track in front and, as soon as the train stopped, in the rear, to prevent a back movement. These, together with a volley fired by the enemy, brought it to a halt. Mr. Lacor, the Express agent, was seriously injured. He has since been conveyed to Baltimore. Four soldiers on board were seized and three in citizen's clothing released. Capt. D'Utassy, brother to the Colonel of the Garibaldi Guard, effected his escape in an ingenious manner. Seeing the enemy by the roadside as the train approached, he immediately doffed his military coat and belt, buttoning up his linen duster closely around him and thus passed as a private citizen. One of the rebels seized his equipment lying in the corner, remarking with an oath, that he had secured one Yankee uniform. As all the cars were in flames, they detached the engine from the tender, placed revolvers to the head of the engineer, and threatened to blow his brains out if he did not send his machine adrift. They then decamped with their prisoners. Fortunately, the engine did not run off the track but sped on in safety until the motive power was exhausted. Such is the true version of the affair.[23]

Then, in the last days of August 1862, as McClellan was bitterly complying with an order from Lincoln to quit the Peninsula and return his army to Northern Virginia, Stonewall Jackson dealt a stunning surprise blow to General Pope's Union Army of Virginia, which was waiting in vain for McClellan at Bull Run II.[24] Suddenly the way was open for a Confederate invasion of the North and Robert E. Lee immediately grasped his unexpected opportunity. On the fourth of September 1862, Lee's legions began fording the upper Potomac, enthusiastically singing "Maryland, My Maryland." The northermost crossing was near Point of Rocks, only nine miles down river from Harper's Ferry.

5
Invasion

A dispatch of September 3, 1862 from General Lee to President Davis explained that the objective of Lee's first invasion of the North was simply to permit Marylanders to throw off the Union yoke and join the Confederacy.[1] A dispatch of the following day expanded his vision to include possible entry into Pennsylvania,[2] but his immediate objective, after crossing the Potomac, remained only to occupy Frederick, the principal city of Western Maryland. Moving northeast from the fords of the Potomac in almost a straight line along the Monocacy River, Lee's troops by Saturday the sixth occupied Frederick, where Lee's proclamation exhorting Marylanders to join the cause of the South was published on the morning of Monday, September 8.[3]

Throughout the succeeding days the Northern papers were wild with excitement as to whether Lee's real purpose was to capture Washington from its (largely defenseless) rear, to attack equally near Baltimore, or to move on more distant Philadelphia.[4] Most logical were predictions that Lee's purpose was to capture the large Union garrison at nearby Harper's Ferry, only a few miles upstream on the Potomac, now completely cut off by the invading Rebels from the Union army around Washington.[5] Although the Rebel army, as it turned out, passed Harper's Ferry by on its way to Frederick, Miles's reaction to the strong possibility of attack, as the Rebels poured across the Potomac, is significant because it reveals a pattern similar to what would occur when the attack was made directly against Harper's Ferry a week later.

On September 2, Captain Means's guerrillas ("Loudon

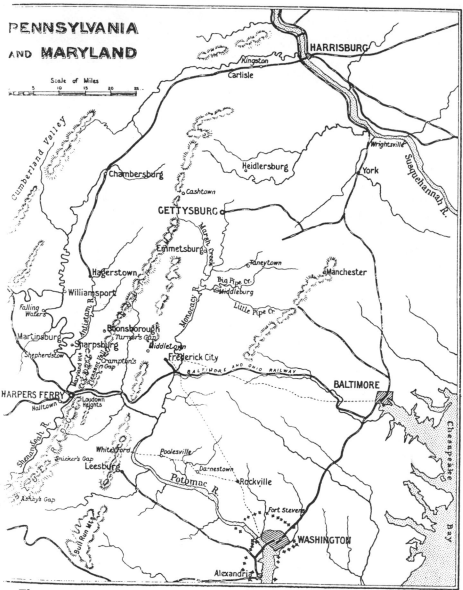

***Theatre of Operations and Potential Targets of Lee's Maryland Campaign,
September 1862***

Map of parts of Maryland and Pennsylvania taken from Wood and Edmonds's *Military History of the Civil War,* reproduced by courtesy of Mrs. Jack
Brussel.

County Rangers") and the 1st Maryland cavalry of the Potomac Home Brigade ("Cole's Cavalry") had been cut to pieces at Leesburg, on the Virginia side of the river, by an unexpectedly strong force of Rebels.[6] On the third, Colonel Miles sent Means back to Leesburg to learn what forces were converging there.[7] From a nearby mountain, through his spyglass, Means counted some forty regiments and sixty-odd pieces of artillery coming into Leesburg.[8] When he reported his news back to Miles next day, however, the latter, who had earlier in the day wired General in Chief Halleck and Department Commander Wool his conviction that reports of enemy infantry in Leesburg and the Shenandoah Valley were "unfounded,"[9] flatly refused to believe it: "It is a damned no such thing," he told Means.[10] Means concluded that Miles had "taken too much to drink," since "that was the first time Colonel Miles treated me so abruptly in my life."[11] However, there was virtually[12] no other testimony before the Harper's Ferry Commission that any of Miles's troubles at Harper's Ferry were due to drinking. Indeed, Means himself conceded that Miles's condition did not manifest itself in either confusion of ideas or excitement, but "he seemed to be stubborn, nothing else. In the fix he was in then, he would not believe anything you would tell him.[13] There is no record that Means's intelligence was passed on to higher headquarters, and a few hours later Miles reported to Wool that Cole's Cavalry had found no enemy in nearby parts of Loudon County.[14]

It was later the same day (Thursday the fourth) that the first large units of Rebel infantry (as distinguished from screening cavalry) began crossing the Potomac, chiefly at White's Ford, Cheek's Ford, and Noland's Ferry, all near the mouth of the Monocacy River.[15] Noland's Ferry was only three miles down river from Miles's southernmost outpost, at Point of Rocks, itself only a dozen miles down river from Harper's Ferry. At Point of Rocks, trouble-shooter Means confirmed that pickets of the 87th Ohio Infantry were encountering the enemy about three miles to the South.[16] On this basis the commander of the 87th, Colonel Banning, at about 5:00 P.M., telegraphed Miles that the main body of Rebels was crossing the river.[17] For seven hours, while Means watched the Rebels crossing at Noland's Ferry by the thousands, there was no reply from Miles.[18]

Meanwhile, the evidence shows, at 8:30 P.M. Miles was relaying to Halleck and to Wool Banning's report that the enemy had passed the Potomac in force, south of Point of Rocks, and was advancing on him.[19] At 10:00 P.M. Miles further informed Halleck and Wool that Banning had estimated that the enemy already had thirty-thousand men across the river and that he (Banning) had abandoned his outpost at Noland's Ferry.[20] However, Miles informed his superiors, he had ordered Banning to halt his retreat (apparently at Point of Rocks) and obstruct the road and had informed Banning that he (Miles) would support him.[21] Shortly thereafter Wool wired Miles to reinforce Banning "if it can be done without danger to your position and if it be true that the enemy is advancing on him."[22] An hour later (11:00 P.M.) Wool specified that Miles send Banning his major and remaining two companies of the 87th Ohio to report to Banning at Point of Rocks next morning.[23] Consistent with Wool's direction, about midnight Miles finally wired Banning that he would be reinforced at daylight.[24]

Daylight, however, brought no reinforcements.[25] At Banning's request Means now headed back to see Miles, with a pause for breakfast at Knoxville with Colonel Maulsby of the Potomac Home Brigade, commanding Harper's Ferry's close-in defenses along the Potomac.[26] Means later testified: "I went up and saw Colonel Miles but he would not believe anything I said or that there were any soldiers over the river, or any danger."[27]

In this disbelief—assuming it was sincere—Miles could have been supported by a report made sometime during the day by Cole's Cavalry, just returned from Point of Rocks, that all reports from there in regard to the enemy were false and that none but cavalry had passed over the Potomac.[28] Relaying this intelligence to Wool, Miles added his own opinion that *I don't believe there is any danger*" (emphasis added).[29] Either Means's report or something else[30] soon thereafter shook Miles, however, because at 9:00 A.M. he wired Wool, repeating his previous night's estimate that thirty thousand Rebels had crossed at Noland's Ferry and explaining why he had omitted to send Banning reinforcements:

> If Colonel Banning had more troops than are with him it would embarrass his retreat, *which he must do before this force.* He can retreat and obstruct their advance, and such are his orders. I cannot safely detach from here until I know the intentions of the enemy at Charlestown. Three brigades is the force, I am told, in the Valley assigned to attack this place and Martinsburg. (Emphasis added.)[31]

A repetitive wire sent about an hour later concluded:

As Banning's force would be cut off if he staid [sic] longer, I have ordered him to retreat slowly. (Emphasis added.)[32]

By noon Wool was convinced by his own staff's on-site investigation that a large force of Rebels was, indeed, now on the Maryland side of the Potomac and, apparently, that Harper's Ferry was a target.[33] Sometime during Friday the fifth he sent this important message to Miles:

The position on the heights ought to enable you to punish the enemy passing up the road in the direction of Harper's Ferry.[34] Have your wits about you and do all you can to annoy the rebels should they advance on you. Activity, energy and decision must be used. *You will not abandon Harper's Ferry without defending it to the last extremity.* (Emphasis added.)[35]

It may be that the last sentence of Wool's wire effectively slowed down Miles's plan for Banning to retreat upriver from Point of Rocks. No records now available reveal the timing or tenor of Miles's order—assuming he gave one—to Banning. Nor is there even a reliable indication as to when the retreat actually occurred, except that a late Saturday cutoff can safely be assumed. This is because on the morning of Sunday, September 7, President Garrett of the B & O messaged Secretary of War Stanton that at 10:00 P.M. the previous night (Saturday the sixth) a dispatch had been received via Wheeling from Berlin (modern Brunswick), five miles east of Harper's Ferry, to the effect that the Union troops at Point of Rocks had fallen back to Berlin "as a precaution."[36]

It further seems probable—although the source is a poor one[37]—that on Saturday the sixth Banning retreated, in steps, all the way from Point of Rocks to Berlin, to Knoxville, and finally to Sandy Hook (located just across the Potomac River from Harper's Ferry).[38] Although Miles's aide portrayed these successive withdrawals as made "before superior numbers" at Berlin and an enemy "in large force . . . advancing toward Knoxville," the same source noted that Miles later in the day successfully sent back and recovered a limber-to-howitzer, equipment and ammunition left by Banning at Berlin[39]—a feat seemingly inconsistent with the idea that a horde of rebels was breathing down Banning's back.

In any event we now know that Lee had no intention—*at that time*—of capturing Harper's Ferry; that his line of march to Frederick was in a different direction: substantially a straight line northeast along the Monocacy River, passing no closer than a dozen miles to Harper's Ferry; and that any fighting between the Rebels and the defenders of Harper's Ferry must have been little more than incidental skirmishes. Why, then, was Banning pulled back from Point of Rocks—and then from Knoxville—under such circumstances?

Two examples on Saturday the sixth illuminate the pattern of Miles's orders. To Banning, while still at *Berlin* (Brunswick), Miles wrote: "Defend your place *as long as you can.* . . . If you have to fall back, stop at Sandy Hook; that place is to be defended at all hazards" (emphasis added).[40] To Maulsby, then still at *Knoxville,* Miles wrote: "The position at Sandy Hook is to be held, if it takes half of the force at this post, and you will not abandon it. The cannon you ask for are with Colonel Banning, who will deliver them to you *when he is obliged to retreat as far as Sandy Hook*" (emphasis added).[41]

It should be noted that in each case the order was to stand fast, but in each case the possibility of retreat was already visualized as the likely outcome of events. Moreover, while Miles made it plain that an order to retreat would be permissible, it would not be Miles who would give the actual order; that responsibility was carefully delegated. No doubt such orders could be the result of an honest, innate defeatism—but they could also be a deliberate method of coaxing defeat with a minimum of responsibility on Miles. And all in a situation where retreat was clearly unnecessary. In any event, this was a pattern which would be followed in more crucial decisions to come.

Equally significant is Miles's handling of his Frederick garrison when it became apparent that Frederick was Lee's target. This was a lonely company detached to guard quartermaster stores and medical supplies for the large army hospital there. Late on the night of Friday the fifth, the company commander, Captain Faithful, was notified by Miles to destroy all quartermaster and commissary stores and join his regiment under Maulsby in Knoxville.[42] It is unnecessary to speculate on whether such drastic action was really required; events quickly demonstrated that it was not.

Captain Faithful simply disregarded Miles's order and set his men to work feverishly loading quartermaster and commissary stores into hurriedly commandeered railway cars to be drawn to Baltimore by an equally hurriedly commandeered small engine.[43] He then gathered in enough public and private wagons to send a stock of costly hospital stores and 275 convalescents off to Gettysburg.[44] All this done, Faithful marched his men off to join Maulsby at Knoxville, where they arrived early in the afternoon of Saturday the sixth, only to find Knoxville bereft of soldiers, Maulsby having retreated to Sandy Hook—as Miles had anticipated would be "necessary."

Thus ended the brief excitement at Harper's Ferry as Lee's troops crossed the Potomac River only a few miles to the south, during the first two days of the Maryland campaign. When Lee reached the Frederick area, it began to appear that the Ferry was not Lee's target, at least for the nonce. Meanwhile, however, Miles had accomplished a remarkable feat. Unlike the previous May, when Saxton had been sent up by Lincoln to take charge during the crisis, this time Miles had not been replaced in command. And that despite the fact that an able brigadier general named White happened to become available at this very time and place. The White story is important.

6
Miles vs. White

Born in upstate New York in 1816, Julius White[1] had moved to the Midwest at the age of twenty, living thereafter at various times in Missouri, Wisconsin, and finally in Illinois.[2] There he built a successful insurance agency (Northwestern) in the city of Chicago and a respectable home in the even newer suburb of Evanston, where the new college (Northwestern) founded by his friend Dr. John Evans was setting a high moral and intellectual tone.[3] Always active in politics, White had at one time served in the Wisconsin legislature. When his downstate friend and sometime lawyer, Abraham Lincoln, became a candidate for president of the United States, White took an active role in his campaign. Indeed, it was from White's porch that Lincoln watched Evanston's enthusiastic torchlight parade in his honor.[4] When Lincoln was elected president, one of the top federal patronage jobs in Chicago (collector of customs) fell to Julius White.[5]

When the startling news of Bull Run I awakened the North to the sad fact that rebellious Richmond was not about to fall in ninety days, it was Julius White, young Frances Willard long remembered, who stood up on the cushion of his pew after church the next Sunday and in a voice of intense earnestness called for a "war meeting" the following evening in the same church.[6] Resigning his lucrative post as collector of customs, White proceeded to raise a regiment, the 37th Illinois Volunteers (commonly known as the "Frémont Rifles") and was appointed colonel of the regiment in September 1861.[7] Despite his civilian background, White worked hard at his new military job in the tough fighting in southwestern Missouri and in the

52

Brigadier General Julius White (1816–90)

Chicago politician and friend of Lincoln who outranked Colonel Dixon Miles
but allowed him to retain command of Harper's Ferry and surrender it to
Stonewall Jackson. Photo by Mathew Brady, reproduced by courtesy of the
National Archives.

Spring of 1862 was promoted to brigadier general for gallant conduct in the severely contested Battle of Pea Ridge, Arkansas.[8] When the top Union brass in the West (Halleck and Pope) came east at Lincoln's call in the summer of 1862, with them came Lincoln's old friend White.[9]

Late in July, White was assigned to command of the 3,000-man Union garrison in Winchester, Virginia, key to the Shenandoah Valley.[10] Young Captain Ripley of the 9th Vermont Infantry noted White's arrival favorably in a letter home:

> Gen. Piatt has been superceded by Gen. Julius White, a Volunteer, and a pretty able man we begin to think. He is prompt, precise and energetic, and knows what he is about.[11]

Unfortunately, the calm of the Shenandoah Valley while the Peninsular Campaign raged in southern Virginia was broken late in August by the guns of Bull Run II.

General Halleck, fearful for the exposed Winchester garrison just beyond the Blue Ridge, in the wake of Bull Run II sent his chief of staff, General George W. Cullum, to Winchester to confer with White on what to do if a large Rebel force should spill over into the Valley.[12] Whether Cullum also visited Harper's Ferry on this particular trip is not established but in any event, shortly after Cullum's return to Washington,[13] Halleck, on Tuesday, September 2, wired White the following peremptory order:

> You will immediately abandon the fortifications at Winchester, sending the heavy guns under escort by rail to Harper's Ferry. If this cannot be done they should be rendered unserviceable. Having sent off your artillery, you will withdraw your whole force to Harper's Ferry.[14]

At the same time, Halleck also wired Miles at Harper's Ferry explaining that White had been ordered to evacuate Winchester.[15]

White and his troops arrived at Harper's Ferry in the late afternoon and early evening of Wednesday, September 3,[16] as the Rebel army was converging on Leesburg preparatory to crossing the Potomac. Since White officially outranked Miles, a question naturally arises as to why White did not succeed to the command of Harper's Ferry—as would be automatic today—at least for the duration of the crisis.

As noted above, the man with immediate responsibility for the command of Harper's Ferry since June had been old General Wool in Baltimore. Asked subsequently by the Harper's Ferry Commission whether he considered Miles a better officer for the command of Harper's Ferry than White, General Wool declined to answer: "That would be a very difficult question to answer under the circumstances."[17] The fact is that the seventy-eight-year-old general not only had, as we have seen, a strong prejudice in favor of regular army officers,[18] but that in this particular situation he had unquestionably been duped by Miles. A series of wires between Wool and Miles on September 4, 1862, the day after White arrived at Harper's Ferry,[19] while Miles had Means spying out the strength of the enemy gathering around Leesburg,[20] reveals an extremely misleading, if not positively false, representation by Miles which must have quickly confirmed all Wool's natural mistrust of a civilian soldier like White. Consider the following (all on the fourth):

> *Miles to Wool:* "I am convinced that the various reports of infantry coming up to Leesburg and through Manassas Gap into the Valley of the Shenandoah are without foundation of truth . . ."[21]
> *Wool to Miles:* "I have received your dispatch stating that the report about the advance of the enemy, as before reported, is unfounded. *I understand that Winchester has been abandoned without the approach or presence of any enemy and that it has not been occupied by the rebels.* Answer immediately." (Emphasis added.)[22]
> *Miles to Wool:* "*General White abandoned Winchester night before last,* and with his troops arrived at this post yesterday afternoon. *No enemy that I can hear of in the Valley of the Shenandoah, nor do I know if Winchester is occupied by him.*" (Emphasis added.)[23]

To omit any mention of the fact that White had abandoned Winchester pursuant to a peremptory order from Halleck—a fact of which Miles had personal knowledge—could hardly have been more deceptive under the circumstances.

Wool's response was prompt and predictable. At 10:30 he wired Miles:

> General White will either repair to this place or join the Army

of the Potomac; but his troops and supplies will remain at Harper's Ferry until further orders, and you will dispose of them as circumstances may require.[24]

Shortly thereafter, still on the fourth, for unstated reasons Wool countermanded his Baltimore-or-Army-of-the-Potomac assignment and ordered White to repair to Martinsburg, West Virginia (some twenty miles northwest of Harper's Ferry), to

take command of the troops at and near that station, instead of repairing to this city, as previously directed. You will adopt the most active and energetic measures to protect and defend that place and the [rail]road occupied by troops under your command. The most sleepless energy is expected.[25]

The last wire of the series (to Miles) confirmed that he (Miles) was to retain all the troops now at Harper's Ferry.[26]

Astonished and chagrined, citizen-soldier White promptly departed for Martinsburg the next day (Friday the fifth) but as promptly on his arrival sent off a wire to Halleck's chief of staff, Cullum:

I reported my arrival at Harper's Ferry to Gen. Halleck and shortly afterward I received orders from Major General Wool to repair to this post, leaving my command and six other regiments under Colonel Miles at Harper's Ferry, very much to my astonishment and regret. I respectfully ask to be restored to my command, if consistent with the public interest.[27]

When Cullum replied that "no order from General Halleck has been given to you to go to Martinsburg,"[28] next day (Monday the eighth) White made one more attempt to break out of his prison. He wired Halleck privately, reciting the history of his misadventures (including Wool's order to turn over his command to Miles), and asked flatly to be relieved of his command at Martinsburg.[29] Halleck's reply the same day held out hope only for the future; in the present crisis White must stay put:

In moving from Winchester to Harper's Ferry you came under the orders of General Wool. It is not proper at present to change the General's dispositions. Probably some different assignment will be given you as early as possible.[30]

The fact is that the night before the White-Halleck exchange Halleck had—for better or for worse—committed himself to leaving Miles in command at Harper's Ferry. As McClellan rode out of Washington on the afternoon of Sunday the seventh to lead the Army of the Potomac north from Rockville, Halleck had wired Miles:

> Our army is in motion. It is important that Harper's Ferry be held to the latest moment. The Government has the utmost confidence in you and is ready to give you full credit for the defense it expects you to make.[31]

We may question how much "confidence" Halleck really had in Miles, but it is plain that Halleck, with the true bureaucratic spirit, was not about to assume responsibility for changing Wool's choice of commander at Harper's Ferry. Miles's poisoning of Wool's mind against civilian-soldier White thus bore significant fruit. Next day (Monday the eighth) Miles responded to Halleck's wire: "Thanks for confidence. Will do my best. Enemy advancing from Winchester. . . ."[32] And with White safely out of the way, on Tuesday, September 9, Miles now in full command of all the troops at Harper's Ferry, including White's as well as his own, reorganized his entire force into four brigades to defend the four areas of the Harper's Ferry complex which Miles apparently considered most important.[33]

7

The Union Right: D'Utassy's 1st Brigade

The 1st Brigade, made up of three New York infantry regiments (D'Utassy's 39th, Segoine's 111th, and Sammon's 115th) and one battery of Indiana light artillery (Von Sehlen's 15th), was assigned to defend the right of the Union line along Bolivar Heights, a ridge about two miles west of the village of Harper's Ferry, running north and south between the Potomac and Shenandoah Rivers at an elevation of about two hundred feet above the rivers.[1] To lead the 1st Brigade, Miles selected Col. Frederick G. D'Utassy, one of the few officers who had been willing to testify for him at his Bull Run drunkenness trial.[2] D'Utassy commanded the 39th New York, better known as the Garibaldi Guard, a colorful polyglot New York City regiment composed of four companies of Italian-Americans, two German, one French, one Hungarian, one Swiss, and one of miscellaneous Americans.[3] Their dress uniform was a conglomeration of an Italian black felt hat with cluster of drooping dark green cock feathers, a Hungarian hussar jacket of dark blue with scarlet and gold trimmings, and French trousers with double broad red stripes down the outer seams.[4]

D'Utassy, the man who put the colorful unit together and led it for its first two years, was an Austrian Jew, born Strasser, son of a horse dealer in Vienna and Pest.[5] He had fled to America about the time of Kossuth's Revolution of 1848, but whether as a fugitive from justice or from injustice was never clear.[6] Once safely in America he translated "Strasser" to its Hungarian equivalent, "Utassy," threw in a "de" for euphony and set up as a teacher of modern languages to the nouveau riche of New York.[7] Despite a slight stature, unlovely face, and absence of antecedents, his tact and insinuating address, added to his undoubted proficiency in all European languages except Russian, quickly made him a great success.[8] When the Civil War broke out he was a natural candidate to organize and command the military "melting pot" that was the Garibaldi Guard.

D'Utassy later told the Winchester Commission that he had been soldiering here and in other parts of the world since 1843,[9] but the real extent of his military experience and proficiency is an open question. His *reputation*, in many respects, was not bad. Thus, shortly after the Harper's Ferry fiasco, General Daniel Tyler wrote: "My impression is that Colonel D'Utassy is too good a soldier to have compromised himself at Harper's Ferry."[10] The *reality*, however, was apparently something else. His first major, a lonely WASP in the Garibaldi Guard, wrote much later:

> It is an old saying that a good colonel makes a good regiment; and we did not feel that we had altogether escaped the opposite of this condition. D'Utassy gave great personal attention to our supplies, and the men were well fed and well clad; but beyond this he did little. In matters of discipline he was practically useless.[11]

The attention paid by D'Utassy to supplies and similar housekeeping and financial matters was, in fact, ultimately sufficient to attract the attention of the War Department's Secret Service.[12] By early 1863 investigators learned that D'Utassy and his original brigade commander, General Blenker, together with subordinate cavalry and artillery commanders, were in the habit of stealing horses from Virginia farmers and forwarding them to the stables of a man named Pourtales in Alexandria, when they would be sold or spirited away. These parties, including Pourtales, would then divide the spoils among themselves.[13]

In the spring of 1863 D'Utassy was court-martialed and convicted of several specific offenses.[14] These included the sale of government-owned horses and conversion of the proceeds to his own use at Roach's Mill, Virginia, in mid-October 1861, and again at Hunter's Chapel, Virginia, about February 10, 1862.[15] At the same time he was found guilty of opening two private letters sent to one of his lieutenants at Winchester, Virginia, in the summer of 1862; also of selling an appointment as major of the 39th New York to one of his captains for $180 at Roach's Mill, Virginia, about August 1, 1861. Finally he was convicted of corruptly receiving $3,265.40 from the Government on November 27, 1861, by presenting false accounts for alleged recruitment expenses in April and May 1861.[16]

For these offenses—all of which had, of course, occurred before the siege of Harper's Ferry—D'Utassy was later (1863) cashiered and sentenced to confinement at hard labor for one year.[17] We see him last in Sing Sing Prison in March 1864, seeking early release—still insisting that he had been innocently convicted and still the master of high-flown mid-Victorian phraseology. In a "Memorandum of Points" he proposed to send to President Lincoln, D'Utassy wrote, among other things:

> [Point]#17: That I have a dearly beloved and aged mother, whose honored head is bowed down, and whose heart is almost broken on the verge of the grave—Shall my appeal for mercy, not to say *justice*, be in vain? Shall I have to add to the infamy heaped upon me and my family the gnawing worm of conscience, that, though involuntarily, I have become a matricide?[18]

Then Col. Frederick D'Utassy of the Garibaldi Guard fades permanently from view.

As it turned out, D'Utassy's competence or incompetence as a military leader never really made much difference to the result of the siege of Harper's Ferry. This was because the steep natural topography of D'Utassy's part of Miles's Bolivar Heights line virtually defended itself. Stonewall Jackson recognized this and, as we shall see, he never made more than a feint against the almost impregnable Union right under D'Utassy.

8
The Union Left: Trimble's 2nd Brigade

Quite different was the situation on "the left" of the Union line along Bolivar Heights, where Miles positioned his new 2nd Brigade, composed of Colonel Trimble's 60th Ohio, Sherrill's 126th New York, and Stannard's 9th Vermont infantry regiments and Potts's battery of light artillery (detached now by Miles's order from Ford's 32nd Ohio infantry).[1] It was "the left" only in the sense that it was left of D'Utassy's 1st Brigade. In fact, the troop positions of the 2nd Brigade extended no farther south along Bolivar Heights than the Charlestown Pike (running east-west from Harper's Ferry and Bolivar to Halltown and Charlestown). This thus left largely unprotected, except for a handful of pickets, the mile-long portion of Bolivar Heights extending south from the Charlestown Pike to the Shenandoah River. It is only fair to add that the terrain from the pike south to the river is protected by very steep and heavily wooded cliffs and ravines, so that a proper defense would not have been difficult. That would require some troops, however, and while the 3rd Infantry of the Potomac Home Brigade [sometimes hereafter "3rd Maryland (PHB)"] and some of Ford's 32nd Ohio were positioned here after the Maryland Heights debacle, Miles never did assign his 2nd Brigade anything like adequate manpower to defend the wild southern sector of Bolivar Heights.

The man selected by Miles to defend this Achilles' heel was Colonel William H. Trimble of the 60th Ohio. Trimble was a relatively undistinguished son of a distinguished Ohio pioneer

61

family who have been described as "men of integrity, industry, intelligence and sobriety."[2] They were a part of the Scotch-Irish stock that migrated to Pennsylvania in the eighteenth century, then moved south into Virginia's Shenandoah Valley and eventually across the Appalachians to Kentucky, finally in the early nineteenth century crossing the Ohio River to nearby Highland County, deliberately freeing their slaves as they moved into free country.[3] There Grandfather James laid the foundation of the family's prosperity by clearing a 1,200-acre farm tract near Hillsboro.[4]

Uncle William Allen Trimble served notably in the War of 1812, was surrendered by Hull at Detroit, and parlayed his local military renown into a seat in the U.S. Senate, where he died in 1821 at the early age of thirty-five.[5] Father Allen Trimble was perhaps the most distinguished of the clan, serving as Republican governor of Ohio from 1826 to 1830.[6] A lifelong champion of such humanitarian causes as common schools, penitentiary reform, and progressive agriculture,[7] ever-popular Trimble closed his public career ingloriously at the age of seventy-two in 1855 by accepting a Whig/Know-Nothing splinter-group draft to run unsuccessfully for governor against rising abolitionist Republican, Salmon P. Chase, whose platform, Trimble feared, would lead to "a dissolution of our glorious Union."[8] In this final fiasco, it should be noted, Allen Trimble did *not* have the support of either of his sons, Dr. Carey A. Trimble, soon to be a congressman from nearby Chillicothe,[9] or William H. Trimble, who would command the 2nd Brigade at Harper's Ferry.

The latter grew up on the family acres in Highland County, married the strong-willed daughter of one of his father's important political allies,[10] and himself took hesitant steps in the family political tradition as a state legislator for three years.[11] However, he never achieved significant political position and it seems a good question whether his command of the Highland County–based 60th Ohio Volunteers reflected his family's traditional local position more than his own capacity for personal leadership.

When one reads his testimony before the Harper's Ferry Commission,[12] Trimble comes across as a diffident person and one less sophisticated than most of the other regimental commanders. Although fifty-one years old at the time, he referred to himself as a "young"[13] officer and prefaced his criticisms of Miles by such phrases as these:

> I took some pains to avoid forming an incorrect opinion of Colonel Miles, because I felt it was better to doubt my own judgment than to doubt the capability of my superior. . . .
>
> I do not know as I have sufficient military judgment to form a correct opinion and estimate of a military commander. . . .[14]

Although Harper's Ferry was not the first battle in which Trimble had been under enemy fire, he seems to have reacted to the enemy bombardment there unduly sensitively ("It was perfectly terrific").[15] This may, however, have been due in part to the news that his much younger brother, Charles, had just been killed at the battle of Bull Run II, only days before.[16]

On Friday the fifth of September, when Miles appointed Trimble to command the 2nd Brigade, the latter immediately took Colonel Stannard of the 9th Vermont—probably the best soldier at Harper's Ferry—and together they examined the southern sector of Bolivar Heights to see what was necessary for its defense.[17] Both "thought it a weak point and it was generally so regarded."[18] As a result of their examination they recommended to Miles the cutting down of a belt of forest only about a half mile from the Union front, in which the enemy could conceal themselves, as well as the cornfields between the forest and the Union front line.[19]

Miles examined the weak points of the southern sector on Tuesday, September 9, but refused to agree to either proposal.[20] Moreover, he flatly rejected the suggestion that defensive works be extended along Bolivar Heights from the Charlestown Pike to the Shenandoah River.[21] The enemy could never plant artillery on Loudon Heights or on the table lands beneath the Heights (from which to bombard this southern sector), he asserted, and the ground in the ravines on the left flank running from the turnpike to the Shenandoah was "impassable."[22] In sum, the patently indefensible left flank was not to be made defensible, even though, in fact, almost a week would pass before battle would be joined at this critical point. One of Stannard's junior officers later wrote:

> We were put into camp at one point where the Charlestown

Pike crosses Bolivar Heights, this being the only important crossing of the Heights from the North and West. Now was the time when we would have been glad to dig day and night; *but in spite of all the pressure put upon him by the officers of higher rank, Colonel Miles would not allow it, ridiculing the anxieties of the garrison* (emphasis added). . . . This was the talk of every Company mess of the Ninth Vermont. The dullest soldier sitting there could foresee the inevitable result. Bitter criticism and growing distrust of his [Miles's] loyalty were to be heard on all sides.[23]

9

Maryland Heights: Ford's 3rd Brigade

The 3rd Brigade organized by Miles on Friday, September 5, was given the mission of defending Maryland Heights' fifteen-hundred-feet-high bluffs, which are on the Maryland side of the Potomac, across from the village of Harper's Ferry.[1] Much smaller than any other of Miles's brigades, the 3rd was made up only of Ford's 32nd Ohio Infantry and one (Steiner's) battalion of the 1st Infantry Regiment of the Potomac Home Brigade, plus McGrath's company of the 5th New York Heavy Artillery (to man the big naval guns halfway up the Heights) and two cavalry units, Corliss's Rhode Island and Russell's 1st Maryland Battalions, which, however, used Maryland Heights more as a basis for their reconnaissance activities than for anything else.[2] Command of the 3rd Brigade went to Colonel Thomas H. Ford of the 32nd Ohio[3]—next to Miles the most controversial figure at Harper's Ferry. No one ever questioned either his loyalty to the Union or his conviction that slavery was wrong, but he was not, as the Harper's Ferry Commission later found, a competent military leader.[4]

Ford was born in Virginia in 1814, but his family crossed the mountains to northern Ohio when he was a boy.[5] His formal schooling was sparse and he was largely self-educated.[6] He was engaged for some years in farming but not very successfully.[7] When the Mexican War broke out in 1846 he raised one company of the 3rd Ohio Regiment, which served about a year with Zachary Taylor's Army of the Rio Grande.[8] He was wounded in action, but most of his duty consisted of guarding

Colonel Thomas H. Ford (1814–68)

Ohio politician and leader of the "Know Nothing" party who evacuated Maryland Heights when Colonel Dixon Miles refused to reinforce Ford's inadequate defense force. Photo taken from E. Z. Hays's *History of the 32nd Regiment (Ohio Veteran Volunteer Infantry)*, reproduced by courtesy of the Library of Congress.

wagon trains.[9] (What, if any, contact he may have had with Capt. Dixon Miles in Taylor's army we do not know.) Sometime after his return to Ohio he decided to move into the city of Mansfield in Richland County and study law.[10]

His record at the bar during the early 1850s is complex. He was apparently a powerful and admired orator but lacked the application essential to a successful law practice.[11] He became a partner, successively, of eight other Mansfield practitioners.[12] Among his colleagues at the Mansfield bar were several distinguished lawyers, including John Sherman, future U.S. senator and father of the nation's antitrust law, as well as brother to the great general.[13] Senator Sherman later described Ford as "a gentleman of experience and ability."[14] Another competitor, in an assessment of the members of the Mansfield bar, had this to say of Ford:

> Ford was a man cast in nature's largest mold; a man of imposing personal presence and possessed of great natural gifts as an orator. Some of his efforts upon the stump have rarely, if ever, been excelled. . . . None knew him intimately who did not become attached to him. He had faults, but they were *faults of the head and not of the heart.* (Emphasis added.)[15]

And again:

> [In 1850–51] Thomas H. Ford was at his best and was a man of great natural powers, but was *indolent and careless* and did not make the mark he might have made at the bar. (Emphasis added.)[16]

Not too surprisingly, by the mid-1850s Ford was engrossed more in politics than in the law, and in the peculiar politics which characterized the State of Ohio in the years immediately preceding the Civil War he made a considerable mark. His vehicle was the American Party, commonly called the "Know-Nothings." This was primarily an anti-Catholic, anti-immigrant movement which achieved brief power in various states during the 1850s, while the old Whig Party was dying and the new Republican Party was aborning.[17]

In Ohio the eventual fusion of the Know-Nothing movement into the antislavery Republican Party was in considerable part the work of Tom Ford. At a meeting of the Know-Nothings' national council in Philadelphia in June 1855, when the majority voted to adopt a pro-Southern slavery plank, Ford, the leader of the Ohio delegation, delivered an antislavery speech which Greeley's New York *Tribune* acclaimed as "the great effort of the debate."[18] Although impromptu (like all Ford's speeches), it must have been an inspiring performance and gave Ford a national reputation.[19] More important, it won Ford the nomination for Lieutenant Governor of Ohio, as a fusion running mate of Salmon P. Chase, the new Ohio Republican Party's candidate for governor.[21] Despite the bolting of a minority of Know-Nothings, which backed former Governor Allen Trimble (father of Colonel William H. Trimble) for the governorship,[22] the Chase/Ford ticket was elected in 1855 and Ford became lieutenant governor of Ohio.

By 1857, however, Ford's political prospects had declined as rapidly as they had risen, largely because the absorption of most Know-Nothings into the Republican Party in Ohio had destroyed the independent political strength of the Know-Nothing lodges.[23] As a result of Chase's policy of "conciliation without abandonment of principle,"[24] the Ohio Republicans in 1857 were able to exclude the Know-Nothings, including Ford, from their ticket and yet carry the election.[25] With bitterness Ford wrote Chase: "Every living man, connected, however remotely, with the American [i.e., Know-Nothing] organization in Ohio is dead with the Republicans."[26] As the critical national election of 1860 approached, Ford understandably opposed Chase's almost successful bid for the presidential nomination ("against anybody that has ever seen him"),[27] but it is clear that Ford's own elective ambitions were now largely dead and he remained a simple Mansfield lawyer until the outbreak of the Civil War.

It was President Lincoln's call for 300,000 three-year volunteers to save the Union in the wake of the disaster at Bull Run I in July 1861 that set Tom Ford to organizing a volunteer regiment which would become the 32nd Ohio Infantry.[28] Most of the men came from Mansfield, although some came from farther afield.[29] Among the latter was Ford's major, Dr. Sylvester Hewitt, a Mt. Gilead physician, who was extremely well liked by all who knew him,[30] but apparently no more a master of the military arts than Ford, as would become painfully plain at Harper's Ferry.

There is conflicting evidence as to the value of the regiment's training. A local historian reported that while in camp near

Mansfield "strict military discipline was enforced by the Colonel, who was determined the soldiers should be well-drilled."[31] To the contrary, Whitelaw Reid, then editor of the Cincinnati *Enquirer,* wrote: "The 32nd had been hurried to the field without discipline of any kind—in fact it was hardly organized."[32]

Be that as it may, by early Fall the 32nd was learning to fight by actually fighting in the battle of Cheat Mountain and other actions in West Virginia.[33] During the severe winter weather it encamped at Beverly, West Virginia, where it was reorganized and disciplined.[34] Came spring, and the 32nd found itself marching up and down the Shenandoah Valley with Frémont, in pursuit of the elusive Stonewall Jackson and participating in the unfortunate defeats of Cross Keys and Port Republic.[35]

By the time the 32nd went into camp at Winchester during the summer of 1862 it was thus a fairly well seasoned outfit—except for its colonel who, because of sickness and for other reasons, seems to have missed most of the 32nd's battles.[36] His chief ailment was a fistula, which required sixty days' leave and an operation, as a result of which he rejoined the 32nd in Winchester almost unable to ride a horse and frequently confined to bed by the swelling.[37] Indeed, Ford apparently tendered his resignation at this time but General White refused to accept it.[38] Ford was at the head of his regiment when it marched into Harper's Ferry from Winchester late on Wednesday, September 3.

10
The Strategic Importance of Maryland Heights

The assignment which Miles gave Ford two days later to defend Maryland Heights[1] was probably the most important assignment at Harper's Ferry short of overall command. This was so because it is the highest land in the area. Compared with Maryland Heights' peak altitude of almost fifteen hundred feet, Loudon Heights (across from Harper's Ferry on the Virginia side of the Shenandoah) reaches a maximum altitude of little over twelve hundred feet; Bolivar Heights and Camp Hill (west of the village of Harper's Ferry) are both much lower (about five hundred feet in altitude); and the village of Harper's Ferry itself at river level is only about three hundred feet above sea level. Sufficiently long-range guns, such as the nine-inch ("Dahlgren") guns installed by General Saxton on the forward (i.e., southern) slope of Maryland Heights, could reach the plain between Camp Hill and Bolivar Heights and, although with considerable inaccuracy, even the Bolivar Heights line itself.

The strategic importance of Maryland Heights had been recognized early in the War by Stonewall Jackson. While the Confederates had brief control of Harper's Ferry from late April to early June 1861, Jackson wrote Lee:

I have finished reconnoitering the Maryland Heights and have determined to fortify them at once and hold them, as well as the Virginia [Loudon] Heights and the town, be the cost what it may. Two pieces of field artillery [12 pounders]

70

should be placed on the Virginia [Loudon] Heights and a larger number of six-pounders on the Maryland Heights. Heavier ordinance could be advantageously employed in defending the town. The heights west of Bolivar must be strengthened. I am of the opinion that this place should be defended with the spirit which activated the defenders of Thermopylae, and, if left to myself, such is my determination.[2]

Jackson, however, was not left to himself. His dispatch of troops shortly thereafter to Maryland Heights was promptly counter-manded by Lee on political grounds (possible antagonism of the State of Maryland, then still a likely candidate to join the Confederacy).[3] On May 21, 1861, Jackson was replaced in command of Harper's Ferry by General Joseph E. Johnston, who substituted a strategy of mobile defense from Winchester for Jackson's plans to fortify Harper's Ferry. In mid-June, in fact, Johnston abandoned Harper's Ferry.[4] Jackson thus never had a chance to implement his plan to fortify Maryland Heights.

During Jackson's Valley Campaign, in May 1862, as we have seen, Rufus Saxton had had his men haul two mighty naval guns halfway up the forward (southern) slope of Maryland Heights to play upon Jackson's troops advancing from Bolivar Heights to Camp Hill, where Saxton on second thought had chosen to rest his main defense.[5] At the same time we saw Jackson sending a force up the Potomac to cross it, return downriver and take the guns of Maryland Heights from the rear[6]—a plan aborted by Jackson's need soon thereafter to leave Harper's Ferry when it became apparent that he could capture it, if at all, only at the risk of being himself trapped by two Union armies (Frémont's and McDowell's) gathering to his west.[7]

Having gone through this May 1862 dress rehearsal, Miles had to be aware of the problem of protecting the heavy guns on Maryland Heights, and his awareness is confirmed by an order he gave for a fact-finding expedition soon after Saxton's departure. In June or July 1862 he directed Capt. Eugene McGrath of the 5th New York Heavy Artillery, who was in command of the artillery on the Heights, and Major John Steiner, commanding a 150-man detachment of the 1st Maryland Infantry (PHB), guarding the artillery, to look into the problem.[8]

These two examined steep-sided Elk Ridge for five or six miles to the north, as far as Solomon's Gap, the first saddle in the ridge and thus the first place where access to the ridge could be had relatively easily from the floor of the valley.[9] Both McGrath and Steiner reported in writing that it was necessary, in order to protect the forward slope of Maryland Heights, where the big guns were located, against attack from the rear, to have artillery and protective infantry at the peak of Maryland Heights and also at Solomon's Gap.[10] Miles told McGrath he had ordered both men and guns (four thirty-two-pounders and two twenty-four-pounders), and for two weeks McGrath got everything in readiness to arrange the new artillery on Solomon's Gap but, inexplicably, nothing ever came of it.[11]

During August the Middle Department commander, old General Wool, came up from Baltimore to inspect the defenses of Harper's Ferry. Unsatisfied, he ordered abatising on Camp Hill and entrenchment on Bolivar Heights, while at the peak of Maryland Heights he ordered Miles to build a blockhouse.[12] To implement the last, after his return to Baltimore (August 28, 1862) Wool specifically detailed an engineer, Major Robert Rodgers (son of Maryland's great naval hero Commodore John Rodgers) to report to Miles at Harper's Ferry

for duty in the construction of a blockhouse above the battery [on Maryland Heights] in order to protect it from a flank movement of the enemy and prevent them from taking possession of the heights.[13]

Despite the importance obviously attached by General Wool to fortifying the peak of Maryland Heights, when Rodgers arrived at Harper's Ferry sometime between August 28 and September 6,[14] Miles "gave no countenance" to the idea.[15] He refused to permit construction of the blockhouse, despite the ready availability of building materials sufficient to erect such a blockhouse there in "a very short time," Wool later told the Harper's Ferry Commission.[16] It must have been sometime *after* September 8, 1862 (when Miles sent Rodgers off to Washington with "dispatches")[17] that Rodgers returned to Baltimore and reported Miles's strange behavior.[18] By that time there was no direct wire communication between Harper's Ferry and Baltimore,[19] which may or may not explain why Wool did nothing more about Miles's flat-out disobedience of his orders.

Although Wool's concern for a blockhouse, and that of McGrath and Steiner for a battery at Solomon's Gap, was immediately to protect the heavy guns on the forward slope of Maryland Heights against attack from the rear, at the highest level of the Union command it was felt—as Miles well knew—that Maryland Heights was not just a controlling gun position but *the ultimate stronghold of the whole Harper's Ferry complex*. The evidence of this crucial fact, most of which somehow never got into the record of the Harper's Ferry Commission, must be explained in detail.

General McClellan tells in his memoirs of being visited by Secretary of State Seward, his next-door neighbor and sole remaining supporter in Lincoln's cabinet, late one evening shortly before he (McClellan) left Washington for the front.[20] This visit had to be on the fourth, fifth, or sixth of September 1862, when the Rebels were crossing the Potomac and marching to Frederick.[21] Seward was much concerned about the safety of the Harper's Ferry garrison (many of whom were fellow New Yorkers). Together, Seward and McClellan then went to General Halleck's home and got him out of bed. At Seward's request McClellan made a strong argument for ordering Miles either (1) to abandon Harper's Ferry and unite his ten thousand men with McClellan's Army of the Potomac (about to move north from Rockville) or (2) *to remove the whole Harper's Ferry garrison to Maryland Heights until it could be relieved by the Army of the Potomac.*[22]

Halleck did not agree that the Harper's Ferry garrison was serving no purpose where it was and declined to order Miles to join McClellan.[23] Halleck's basic strategy was to make Lee fight for Harper's Ferry, thus slowing down Lee's northward push so that McClellan could catch up with him. Halleck never admitted that such was his purpose in keeping the Harper's Ferry garrison's feet to Lee's fire. In his official report of November 25, 1862, Halleck merely asserted that with most of Lee's army between Miles and McClellan (an imperfect assumption) Halleck could not expose the garrison and its artillery and stores to capture by withdrawing it from Harper's Ferry.[24] However, Halleck's most recent biographer agrees with the present writer that Halleck's real purpose—which obviously could not be stated publicly, particularly after the garrison had been captured—was more probably to hold Lee back until McClellan could catch up with him.[25]

Moreover, McClellan left his midnight meeting with Seward & Halleck under an impression that Halleck was also opposed to the alternative of concentrating the whole Harper's Ferry garrison on Maryland Heights.[26] In this, however, McClellan was wrong. The evidence before the Harper's Ferry Commission included a wire from Halleck to Wool dated Friday, September 5:

> I find it impossible to get this army into the field again in large force for a day or two. In the meantime Harper's Ferry may be attacked and overwhelmed. I leave all dispositions there to your experience and local knowledge. *I beg leave, however, to suggest the propriety of withdrawing all our forces in that vicinity to Maryland Heights.* I have no personal knowledge of the ground and merely make the suggestion. (Emphasis added.)[27]

Testifying before the Harper's Ferry Commission, General Wool could not recall receiving this wire but said he did *not* believe he would have recommended putting the whole garrison on Maryland Heights, because he personally thought the steep-sided Bolivar Heights and Camp Hill positions defensible and (erroneously) believed the covering guns on Maryland Heights had been secured by the building of the blockhouse he had ordered in August.[28]

While Miles thus apparently did not learn through Wool of the top Union command's view that Maryland Heights should be the last stronghold of the Harper's Ferry complex, other evidence (never presented to the Harper's Ferry Commission) makes it clear that *Miles in fact knew this to be the view of official Washington.* It will be recalled that just before Halleck on Tuesday, September 2, ordered General White to evacuate Winchester in favor of Harper's Ferry, Halleck's chief of staff, General George W. Cullum, paid White a visit to examine his works against the possibility of a Rebel attack and consider whether White should retreat to Harper's Ferry.[29] It would have been logical for Cullum to have visited Harper's Ferry on the same trip and in any event we do know that then or some other time Cullum prepared a survey for the defense of Maryland Heights from the east side.[30]

Be that as it may, either at this time or sometime earlier, *Cullum instructed Miles to make Maryland Heights not just a protected gun position but the last stronghold of his defense.* Although General Halleck strangely did not testify to this fact in his October 1862 appearance before the Harper's Ferry Commission,[31] his November 1862 report on the conduct of the war—after McClellan's dismissal—testifies to this very important fact:

> The garrisons of Winchester and Martinsburg had been withdrawn to Harper's Ferry and the commanding officer of that post [i.e., Miles] had been advised by my chief-of-staff [i.e., Cullum] *to mainly confine his defense, in case he was attacked by superior forces, to the position of Maryland Heights,* which could have been held a long time against overwhelming numbers. (Emphasis added.)[32]

(Equally suggestive is the fact that although General White sought a subpoena to have Cullum testify at the hearings,[33] the judge advocate apparently refused; Cullum never testified.)

In the face of this advice from the general in chief's chief of staff "to mainly confine his defense . . . to the position of Maryland Heights," we see Miles now assigning only about one and one-half of ten available infantry regiments and none of three batteries of supporting light artillery to this key position.[34] Nor did the handful of defenders sent over by Miles have even the protection of the permanent type fortification atop the Heights which the department commander had thought important enough to order (and furnish an experienced engineer to construct) but to which Miles "gave no countenance."[35] Plainly the new commander, Ford, was taking on something that even a more experienced and energetic officer would have found extremely difficult to handle.

Ford quickly realized the seriousness of the situation and tried to do something about it. Even before he took his regiment across the Potomac to join Major Steiner's battalion of the Potomac Home Brigade (which had been there all summer), Ford sent Steiner out to reconnoitre Solomon's Gap.[36] There the reconnaissance party found a plateau of six or eight acres of cleared land which seemed like "a commanding and excellent position for a battery of 12 pounders," which would "render Maryland Heights secure from an approach of the enemy from that quarter, which was the only one where the attack could be successfully made and where [the reconnaissance party] expected it."[37]

As soon as he received this report Ford applied unsuccessfully to Miles to keep the light artillery (Potts's battery) which had long been attached to his own 32nd Ohio Infantry but which was now being assigned to Colonel Trimble's 2nd Brigade for use on the "left flank" of Bolivar Heights.[38] When the 32nd Ohio crossed the river, Ford took Potts's battery along, anyway, but Miles sent a messenger who intercepted the battery before it started up the hill and ordered it back to Bolivar Heights.[39] In the days that immediately followed, Ford made repeated urgent requests for supporting artillery. He was eventually promised a battery for the Heights proper, but never for Solomon's Gap.[40] Like the southern sector of Bolivar Heights, the rear of Maryland Heights would remain an open invitation to any attacker of Harper's Ferry.

Ford also made real efforts during the week after taking over Maryland Heights to improve his eleven to fifteen-mile defense perimeter around Elk Ridge[41] by cutting timber and by logging up and otherwise obstructing the roads leading to the troop positions, in order to impede the approach of the enemy and permit their harassment by the Union garrison.[42] His efforts were seriously limited, however, by the apparent inability of Miles's supply officer in Harper's Ferry to supplement Ford's ten axes and supply other necessary tools,[43] all of which may have reflected only negligence by the Miles administration of the post but would not be inconsistent, either, with Miles's plainly *deliberate* disregard of repeated recommendations to post a battery at Solomon's Gap, orders to build a strong fortification at the peak of Maryland Heights, and advice from the general in chief's chief of staff to "mainly confine his defense . . . to the position of Maryland Heights."

That Maryland Heights could become a terrible Achilles' heel was in no way restricted information. On Saturday, September 6, a *New York Times* special correspondent was turned back on a B & O train from Baltimore, which was stopped just short of Frederick by the advancing tide of Rebel invaders. He proceeded to write a jeremiad which, unfortunately, had much truth to it:

A fearful responsibility rests somewhere for the culpable mismanagement of affairs in this Department. Heaven spare the guilty offenders; the outraged North will not. . . . I tremble for the fate of our forces stationed at Harper's Ferry and vicinity. On the Maryland Heights, opposite the village, we have several 100 pounders, which guard the country for miles around.

If, however, the rebels have crossed the Potomac at No-land's Ferry [some 15 miles below] in strong force, as is positively stated, they undoubtedly marched direct up the river, and are attacking the batteries in the rear. Should they do so successfully (the heights on this side are not precipitous but rather easy of ascent) and capture the guns, Harper's Ferry below will be entirely at their mercy. The light artillery planted behind the heavy entrenchments in the rear of the village [i.e., on Camp Hill] will be of no avail.

[After identifying the Union regiments originally at Harper's Ferry and those just arrived from Winchester]: The force therefore at Harper's Ferry is in the neighborhood of 12,000, sufficiently large enough to repel any number of troops that may attack them from in front but useless and lost if the enemy have obtained possession of Maryland Heights. [Then closing on a sombrely humorous note]: The Rebels instead of marching up-stream to carry out the above mas-terly program, may all have gone direct to Frederick. . . .[44]

The Rebels had not, in fact, carried out "the above masterly program" but had marched swiftly past Maryland Heights on the road to Frederick. By Sunday, September 7, it seemed increasingly likely that Harper's Ferry was *not* a target of the Rebel invasion. For the nonce that was correct.

11

Camp Hill: Ward's 4th Brigade

To man Camp Hill—Miles's "inner defense line"—he set up a 4th Brigade, composed of the 12th New York Militia and the 87th Ohio Volunteers (both of which were made up of ninety-day enlistees whose service was up, or about up) together with two batteries (Graham's heavy, and Rigby's light, artillery).[1]

Camp Hill rises steeply from both the Potomac and Shenandoah Rivers near where they converge at the easternmost point of the little village of Harper's Ferry. It then falls off westerly to the plateau of Bolivar. The fortified and entrenched defense line across the western slope of Camp Hill was less than a mile in width from river to river, as contrasted with Bolivar Heights' river to river breadth of some three miles (including the undefended southern sector).

A very good case could have been made for making Camp Hill the main defense line of Harper's Ferry (as Saxton, finding the Bolivar Heights line too thin to defend, had finally decided in May).[2] Assuming, however, that Miles was determined to make his main stand along Bolivar Heights,[3] it made no sense to waste two infantry regiments on the Camp Hill "inner defense line" a mile to the rear of manpower-short Bolivar Heights (unless Miles had a special morale problem with these two regiments of ninety-day men which we do not fully understand).[4]

The man chosen to command the 4th Brigade was the colonel of the 12th New York Militia, William Greene Ward, a silk-stocking citizen soldier from a prominent and well-to-do

New York City family. Nathaniel Greene, the number two general in Washington's Revolutionary army, was a distant relative.[5] Colonel Ward's own grandfather, Samuel Ward, son of a royal governor of Rhode Island, was a colonel in the Revolution.[6] When the Revolution was over, the grandfather moved to New York and began successfully trading to the far parts of the world.[7] Ward's own father, William, youngest son of the Revolutionary War colonel, was a tea importer addicted to lawsuits and Madeira.[8] One uncle (Samuel) was a senior partner in New York's biggest banking house[9] and another (John) was a president of the Stock Exchange.[10]

Two of his cousins were nationally known figures. One was Sam Ward, who married a granddaughter of John Jacob Astor and would become known in post–Civil War days as "the king of the lobby."[11] Even London's *Vanity Fair*—rarely concerned with "our American cousin"—ran a SPY profile of "Uncle Sam". "He is the one man [in the United States] who knows everybody worth knowing, who has been everywhere worth going to and has seen everything worth stepping aside to see. . . . The prince of good livers, a delightful companion, [yet] a man of much experience and observation."[12]

During the first part of the Civil War, Sam was busy regularly forwarding to his old friend, William H. Seward, former governor of New York and now secretary of state, all the confidences he could pick up at the New York Hotel, a secessionist hangout.[13] Despite broad intimation that Sam would be receptive to a major diplomatic post in return for such services, Seward never succumbed and, indeed, seems to have grown cold to his old friend, whose confidences thereupon dried up.[14] This was Sam's contribution to the Civil War.

Very different were the life-values of Colonel Ward's even more famous cousin, Julia Ward Howe, who would be on almost anyone's list of the half-dozen most influential American women of the nineteenth Century.[15] Whisked away from New York to Boston by her idealist-philanthropist husband, Samuel Gridley Howe, poetess Julia Ward became associated with most of the great names of the flowering of New England and with most of the reform movements of her day, including Unitarianism, women's suffrage, prison reform, world peace, and, last but not least, abolitionism.[16]

Indeed, both Howes were important enough figures in the abolitionist world to merit a secret call during the late 1850s from a man named John Brown, who was in Boston drumming up support for an idea that Mrs. Howe reluctantly concluded was "wild and chimerical."[17] She also concluded, however, that Brown was a "very remarkable man" who looked "a Puritan of the Puritans: forceful, concentrated, and self-contained."[18] When later the Howes read the first news of a surprise attack by a small band of unknown men on the federal arsenal at Harper's Ferry, Howe said simply: "Brown has got to work."[19] In her *Reminiscences* Julia Ward Howe wrote: "None of us could exactly approve an act so revolutionary in its character, yet the great-hearted attempt enlisted our sympathies very strongly."[20]

It was those same strong sympathies that led Samuel Gridley Howe to Washington two years later in the fall of 1861 as a member of the President's Sanitary Commission—the Civil War predecessor of the Red Cross—and with him came his poetess wife, Julia.[21] Riding home to the Willard Hotel after attending one of General McClellan's evening reviews of his troops, her companions evoked cheers from Union soldiers as they rode along singing an old camp-meeting hymn with new words about "John Brown's Body" which had got their start in Boston.[22] Someone suggested that Julia write "better words for that stirring tune"—and she promptly did so. By dawn she had rewritten "John Brown's Body" into the more sophisticated "Battle Hymn of the Republic," deemed by many the greatest of all American war songs.[23]

No record tells us whether the 12th New York's young Colonel William Ward, six years out of Columbia College (or his brother John, a recent Columbia Law School graduate and now a captain commanding Company F),[24] were more in tune with cousin Sam or with cousin Julia. The former might well be assumed from the way the silk-stocking Wards poured money (an estimated ten thousand dollars) into their regiment with obvious rewards.[35] (There had even been a court-martial but Ward was acquitted.)[36] It would not have been out of character, however, if the Wards sometimes looked down the steep slope of Camp Hill to the firehouse where old "Puritan of Puritans" John Brown and his followers had shot it out with Colonel Robert E. Lee's detachment of marines—and found themselves humming the strains of cousin Julia's mightly war-song as they waited to see what, if anything, General Robert E. Lee had in store for the garrison of Harper's Ferry.

12
All Quiet at Harper's Ferry

By Sunday, September the seventh, the great bulk of the Rebel army was encamped around Frederick, as a wide-ranging reconnaissance by the 1st Maryland Cavalry under "the Fighting Parson," Major Charles Russell, confirmed on Tuesday the ninth.[1] Although the threat to Harper's Ferry from Lee's invasion force now seemed more remote, Miles was daily reporting to Washington a plethora of other alleged threats to his domain, mostly from the west and north. As far as can be determined, these reports were almost entirely groundless.

Miles had accurately reported to Wool on Friday the fifth that Rebel General A. P. Hill had crossed the Potomac[2] but on Saturday the sixth Miles forwarded to Colonel Banning of the 87th Ohio at Berlin (Brunswick), a half dozen miles downriver from Harper's Ferry, the inconsistent intelligence that A. P.. Hill had fortified Lovettsville, about three miles south of Berlin and inland from the Potomac.[3] The same day (Saturday the sixth) while passing on to White (newly arrived at Martinsburg) the intelligence that Frederick was now occupied by the enemy in force, Miles advised that:

> General A. P. Hill, with his division, is encamped at Lovettsville about seven miles from here, and intrenching. I shall expect by tomorrow he will commence hammering at me.[4]

It is very difficult to see how Miles could have believed and passed on such erroneous intelligence about a situation so close to Harper's Ferry—but he did. In the early morning hours of Sunday, September 7, Miles wired Wool:

81

The enemy is steadily pressing on my pickets from Point of Rocks; has driven them in to Sandy Hook and is getting batteries in position on a plateau opposite. I am ready for them.[5]

Wool promptly advised Governor Curtin of Pennsylvania:

The last report from Harper's Ferry states that the forces that appeared at the Point of Rocks had recrossed to Virginia and that General Hill was fortifying himself at a point 5 miles from Berlin, on the opposite [Virginia] side of the river. I have sent out to ascertain and shall be able to inform you in the course of the morning if the rumors are true.[6]

As of the same evening Wool was still placing credence in this groundless rumor. To President Lincoln's wire "What about Harper's Ferry? Do you know anything about it?[7] Wool replied:

General Hill is menacing Harper's Ferry but with what force is not stated. I think Harper's Ferry will be defended.[8]

The following day (Monday, September 8) the garrison was apparently still under the same impression. A young officer's letter home on that date reads:

A part of Jackson's right wing, A. P. Hill's Corps, is operating a few miles above us on the Shenandoah, but whether they mean us or Martinsburg is uncertain.[9]

About this time, however, someone apparently discovered that A. P. Hill's division was not at Lovettsville or anywhere else south of the Potomac River, for we hear no more thereafter of the Hill rumor. Instead, attention was now centered on an even more exciting and equally groundless rumor.

This was a report that Rebel General Braxton Bragg, a principal Confederate commander in the West, had secretly led his troops eastward across the Appalachian mountains and was even now marching them down the Shenandoah Valley to cooperate with Lee's invasion army. It is some measure of the political and military chaos of the day that responsible Union officials should have given any credence to this rumor. The idea of bringing Bragg's army east over the mountains, however, was not concocted entirely out of thin air.

In the same dispatch (on September 3, 1862) in which Lee informed President Davis of his intention to invade Maryland, he (Lee) had suggested that "should Bragg find it impracticable to operate to advantage on his present frontier, his army, after leaving sufficient garrisons, could be advantageously employed in opposing the overwhelming numbers which it seems to be the intention of the enemy now to concentrate in Virginia.[10] This idea, however, was at most a seed compared with the full-blown rumor.

As the Baltimore *American* reported it, Wool was told by Miles that the latter had received information that a large Rebel army under General Bragg was moving from Winchester (only twenty miles south of Harper's Ferry) to Martinsburg, with the apparent intention of crossing the Potomac at Williamsport and striking off toward Hagerstown and Chambersburg.[11] The fact was—as a series of wires between worried President Lincoln and his Western commanders eventually established—that *Bragg had never left Tennessee.*[12] Moreover, Miles's own cavalry on reconnaissance next day were unable to find *any* Rebel army marching down the Shenandoah.[13] This rumor thus had a short life, but one wonders why Miles should apparently have accepted and passed on such patently erroneous intelligence.

The only *real* fighting in the Shenandoah Valley during these few days was, in fact, no more than a cavalry skirmish at Darkesville, Virginia. Early on Sunday the seventh, newly arrived Julius White found his outposts at Martinsburg attacked by some four or five hundred of Ashby's Cavalry (including part of the 12th Virginia Cavalry).[14] White's Union cavalry promptly took the offensive and during the day chased the Rebels back through Darkesville, where they made an unsuccessful stand, and on to Winchester where the chase ended.[15] It merited a fleeting headline in Northern newspapers[16] and an immediate commendation for White from Secretary of War Stanton.[17]

The Darkesville skirmish, otherwise of small importance, was significant because it severely damaged the already strained relations between White and Miles. In the middle of this half-day-long running battle, victory apparently seemed a good deal less likely to White than it eventually turned out. Totally ignorant of the enemy strength, White urgently messaged Miles to send him a "strong reconnaissance" and added: "I believe you should send up to my support my old brigade."[18] Miles's reply stated that he had heard several days previously that three Rebel brigades would march on Martinsburg, mentioned several irrelevant matters, and simply avoided answering the request for White's old brigade.[49] Rightly angry, White immediately forwarded a copy of Miles's wire to Wool and laid it on the line:

> I send you the above copy of a dispatch from Colonel Miles, Harper's Ferry. His position will not be attacked. I respectfully suggest that he support this post (Martinsburg) with a reenforcement of four regiments of infantry and two batteries. I have but three 6-pounder guns.[20]

Before any answer from Wool had arrived, White learned that his men had beaten the enemy decisively at Darkesville and his bid for help from Miles was thus moot.[21] A showdown that might in the end have been better for the fate of Harper's Ferry was thus averted.

Out of the Darkesville skirmish, too, came additional rumors of a Rebel army in the Shenandoah Valley. Interrogation of some forty-one Rebel POWs taken led White to inform Wool that they claimed to be the advance of a large column newly arrived in Winchester from Leesburg (some said Manassas).[22] This "intelligence," like the Hill and Bragg rumors, served to confuse and upset the Union troops. A frightened White wired Wool that his force was insufficient to meet successfully "any considerable body."[23] White received in reply the following directive from Wool:

> If 20,000 men should attack you, you will, of course, fall back. Harper's Ferry would be the best place I could recommend; but be sure that you have met such a force or any other that would overwhelm you. . . .[24]

The threat that would cause White to retreat to Harper's Ferry was not yet in the Valley, but White would have occasion to remember Wool's words before the week was out.

Finally, there were rumors about the alleged approach of an enemy army from the North, quite similar to those concerning the alleged approach of enemy armies from the West. The former featured Rebel General Loring, an associate of Miles in New Mexico days and now a top Confederate commander in West Virginia. Loring was variously reported—quite without

Colonel Dixon S. Miles (1804–62)

Union commander at Harper's Ferry, attacked by Stonewall Jackson in September 1862; pictured in front of his headquarters by Mathew Brady. Photo reproduced by courtesy of the National Archives.

foundation—as advancing on *Hagerstown* with five thousand troops[25] or on *Martinsburg* with fifteen to twenty thousand troops,[26] both on Monday the eighth. Another variation appears in Miles's report to Halleck on Tuesday the ninth that Loring was marching twenty thousand men from *Leesburg* via *Snickers Gap;* probably, Miles predicted, to *Cumberland* via *Romney,* "but if he comes, I am ready for him."[27] Ironically, on Wednesday the tenth the Washington papers carried long stories, the source of which is unknown, that Miles had fallen upon Loring as the latter tried to cross the Potomac and made the usually clear waters of that river literally run red with the blood of the Rebels[28]—a fittingly fictitious defeat for an utterly fictitious enemy.

By Tuesday and Wednesday (the ninth and tenth) Miles's wires to Halleck[29] and White [30] were reporting, accurately, that there was now no substantial enemy force in the Valley.[31] And with that knowledge and the realization that, for whatever reason, Lee's army in Frederick had chosen to pass Harper's Ferry by, there came some relaxation and confidence. To the correspondents at Harper's Ferry on Wednesday, September 10, Colonel Miles stated that he could hold the Heights against any force.[32] "The enemy never can take them," he asserted.[33] The *New York Times* correspondent agreed. He wrote:

All is perfectly quiet in this neighborhood. The place is occupied by a Union force amply sufficient to hold it against the largest force of the rebels—none of whom, however, have yet shown themselves. You may set down Harper's Ferry as entirely safe.[34]

This special dispatch the *Times* appropriately headlined: "All Quiet at Harper's Ferry."[35]

13
The Rebel Game Plan Changes

On Monday, September 8, Lee made the second of three crucial decisions of his Maryland Campaign. The first, of course, had been the original extemporaneous decision after Bull Run II to enter western Maryland and seek the support of its citizenry for the Rebel cause. The last would be his decision to stand and fight McClellan's pursuing army at Antietam. Between these two occurred the one of interest here: Lee's decision at Frederick—contrary to the most elementary tactical principles—to detach several parts of his army in enemy territory for a bonus capture of Harper's Ferry before heading for Harrisburg and, eventually, Philadelphia, Baltimore, or Washington.

It is important to recognize that Lee's plans did not originally include a siege of Harper's Ferry. When, writing from Dranesville, Virginia, on Wednesday, September 3, Lee gave President Davis his first news of the plan to invade Maryland, Lee stressed only the opportunity to help Maryland throw off the "oppressor's" yoke while the Union armies were still demoralized after Bull Run II.[1] There was no suggestion of trying to capture Harper's Ferry. Nor was there any such thought in Lee's message to Davis on the following day, expanding the invasion plan to include the possibility of entering Pennsylvania.[2]

The same (September 4, 1862) message also reported the evacuation of Winchester by White and expressed an opinion that Miles and White would both retreat into Maryland:

> This will still further relieve our country and, I think, leaves the [Shenandoah] valley entirely free. They [the Union armies] will concentrate behind the Potomac.[3]

On September 5, when reporting that "this army is about entering Maryland," Lee informed Davis that:

> It is not yet certain that the enemy have evacuated the [Shenandoah] valley but there are reports to that effect and I have no doubt that they will leave that section as soon as they learn of the [Rebel] movement across the Potomac.[4]

Lee further advised Davis that he was now abandoning his original supply line to Leesburg from Richmond through Warrenton (east of the Blue Ridge all the way) in favor of a new supply line—less vulnerable to Union attack—from Culpeper Court House down the Shenandoah Valley (i.e., through Luray, Front Royal, and Winchester), and thence over the Blue Ridge into western Maryland.[5]

On the following day (Saturday, September 6) came the first indication that Lee had begun to think of capturing Harper's Ferry. Traveling with one of his two corps commanders, General James Longstreet, on the road to Frederick. Lee heard the sound of artillery fire from the direction of Point of Rocks and Harper's Ferry (apparently a chance encounter between Rebel cavalry and Banning's Union pickets).[6] Lee speculated that the enemy was concentrating his forces from the Valley for defense at Harper's Ferry and asked Longstreet his opinion as to organizing forces to surround and capture the works and garrison there.[7] Longstreet, always more inclined to the defense than the offense,[8] strongly opposed the idea:

> I objected and urged that our troops were worn with marching and were on short rations and that *it would be a bad idea to divide our forces while we were in the enemy's country,* where he could get information in 6 or 8 hours of any movement we might make. The Federal army, though beaten at Manassas, was not disorganized and it would certainly come out to look for us and we should guard against being caught in such a condition. Our army consisted of a superior quality of soldiers *but it was in no condition to divide in the enemy's country.* I urged that we should keep it well in hand, recruit our strength and get up supplies and then we could do anything we pleased. (Emphasis added.)[9]

As Lee made no reply, Longstreet "supposed the Harper's Ferry scheme was abandoned."[10]

Meanwhile, at Harper's Ferry on the same weekend (Friday, September 5, and Saturday, September 6) a strange thing happened. It involved a young Rebel cavalryman named Lt. Milton Rouse, the same that had hijacked the Winchester train late in August and performed other feats of derring-do with his men of the 12th Virginia Cavalry (a "scout," i.e., a "spy" unit).[11] When captured by Miles's cavalry on Friday the fifth he had claimed to be wounded in the thigh and making his way to his father's orchard plantation near Kabeltown, a dozen miles south of Harper's Ferry on the Shenandoah River.[12] After waiting for Miles at his headquarters quite a while in vain, Rouse's captor (cavalry colonel B. F. Davis) yielded to Rouse's vocal complaints about his wound and sent him to the base hospital with a surgeon.[13] Rouse promptly proceeded to escape from the surgeon and it was next morning (Saturday the sixth before Union scouts could find him and bring him back to Miles's headquarters.[14]

Rouse was closeted with Miles for approximately an hour.[15] Miles's aide, Binney, testified before the Harper's Ferry Commission that he (Binney) had come in only during the last part of the conversation between them:

Colonel Miles did everything he could to worm out of him the position of the enemy and what their plans were but he could get no information of any importance at all from him. There was considerable talk with regard to his parole. The young man begged for his parole and gave his word as an officer and gentleman that he would not undertake to take up arms again until he was properly exchanged. He had some conversation in regard to Colonel Davis on account of some insulting language that Colonel Davis had used toward him. He put on considerable airs about his honor and being a gentleman, etc. He was finally paroled, Colonel Miles keeping a copy of the parole. I escorted him outside of the lines.[16]

Naturally there was no testimony before the commission as to what passed between Miles and Rouse during the principal part of this conversation, but the Union garrison had immediately been suspicious. Binney testified:

The next day there was considerable excitement around Harper's Ferry in regard to Colonel Miles having paroled this man and there were some remarks made in regard to it.

There seemed to be quite a feeling of censure against Colonel Miles for it. I reported to Colonel Miles what I heard in that line. He represented that it was not worthwhile to pay attention to it; that at that time there had been nearly 300 Union prisoners who had been taken at Manassas and paroled, who had passed through Harper's Ferry and [been] sent on to Baltimore and he said that if our men were entitled to parole, theirs were.[17]

There is, of course, no comparison between the normal formal exchange procedures usually employed in such cases and Miles's indefensible action in this instance, sending Rouse home *immediately through the front lines*.[18] Most significant for present purposes is the unusual opportunity which Rouse's private interrogation necessarily afforded Miles to communicate directly—if he so desired—with Rouse's superiors, among whom was the young man's recent teacher at Virginia Military Institute, Professor Thomas J. Jackson.[19]

On Monday, September 8, Longstreet came to Lee's tent at Frederick only to find him closeted with Stonewall Jackson.[20] When Lee heard Longstreet's voice he immediately invited the latter to join them. There Longstreet found that a decision to detach a task force to surround and capture Harper's Ferry had virtually been reached.[21] He later wrote:

> The two were discussing the move against Harper's Ferry, both heartily approving it. They had gone so far that it seemed useless for me to offer any further opposition and I only suggested that Lee should use his entire army in the move instead of sending a large portion of it to Hagerstown, as he intended to do. General Lee so far changed the wording of his order as to require me to halt at Boonsboro with General D. H. Hill. . . . This was afterward changed [back] and I was sent on to Hagerstown, leaving D. H. Hill alone at South Mountain [Boonsboro].[22]

More details about Lee's plan were learned the same day by General John Walker. Lee wanted Walker's division to return to the Potomac River and destroy the massive aqueduct that carried the waters of the C & O Canal across the mouth of the Monocacy River.[23] While at the aqueduct Walker would get instructions to cooperate in the capture of Harper's Ferry and, since he would be operating largely independently of the rest of

Lee's army, Lee thought Walker should know the ulterior purposes and objects of the campaign.[24]

Lee explained that the Rebel line of communications from Rapidan Station to Manassas and thence to Frederick was too near the Potomac and liable to be cut any day by the enemy's cavalry. Lee had therefore given orders to move the line back into the Shenandoah Valley, by way of Staunton, Harrisonburg, and Winchester, crossing the Potomac at Shepherdstown.[25] The capture of Harper's Ferry was made necessary, Lee told Walker, "*not* to garrison and hold but because in the hands of the enemy it would be *a break in our new line of communications with Richmond*" (emphasis added).[26]

The expedition was also rendered attractive by the prospect of capturing much materiel of war, an estimated ten to twelve thousand men already at Harper's Ferry and another three thousand at Martinsburg whom Lee thought likely to take refuge at Harper's Ferry in the crisis.[27] There were other, incidental benefits, too. A few days delay for the main Rebel army at Hagerstown would hopefully permit clothing and shoeing the most needy soldiers and enable eight to ten thousand involuntary stragglers and a large number of new recruits waiting at Richmond to join the army, Lee thought.[28]

With his army reconcentrated at Hagerstown after the fall of Harper's Ferry, Lee would then proceed to destroy the Baltimore & Ohio Railroad, march to Harrisburg, and there destroy the long bridge of the Pennsylvania Railroad across the Susquehanna River, thereby disabling that railroad for a long time.[29] "After that I can turn my attention to Philadelphia, Baltimore or Washington, as may seem best for our interest."[30] In response to Walker's readily apparent astonishment at such a daring plan, Lee explained why he expected to be able to do all this without hindrance from McClellan:

> He is an able general, but a very cautious one. His enemies among his own people think him too much so. His army is in a very demoralized and chaotic condition and will not be prepared for offensive operation—or he will not think it so—for 3 or 4 weeks. Before that time I hope to be on the Susquehanna.[31]

Civil War historians have generally agreed with Walker that the reason for Lee's decision to reduce Harper's Ferry was his concern, as expressed in a September 12 dispatch to President Davis, that the Union garrison there, not having evacuated it as anticipated, would be in a position constantly to interrupt his supply line from Richmond as he moved north into Pennsylvania.[32] Moreover, such public reports on the sad condition of affairs at Harper's Ferry as the Baltimore *Republican*'s story on Monday, September 8[33]—which was almost certainly in Lee's hands the same day[34]—could well have helped to make the venture seem attractive.

Nonetheless, as Longstreet had urged upon Lee the preceding Saturday—with what Longstreet thought was at least temporary agreement—to divide an army in enemy country must necessarily involve very great risk. Not even superbly optimistic Robert E. Lee could be entirely blind to the terrible risk involved—as Longstreet was expressly warning him—in violating such an elementary axiom of warfare. In any event it is plain that on conferring with Jackson, Lee learned *something* that changed his tentative judgment of two days previously. Whether Jackson learned from Rouse and conveyed to Lee a message from Miles that Harper's Ferry could be taken without delay, we will probably never really know. But among the myriad suspicions later voiced by Miles's troops after they found themselves unexpectedly surrendered to Stonewall Jackson, none was more acute than that of the 32nd Ohio regimental historian:

> Lee's Antietam campaign was one of the greatest blunders of the war and furnishes strong circumstantial evidence that there was some sort of understanding that Harper's Ferry should be surrendered in time to permit the troops employed in its capture [re-]joining the main army under Lee . . . otherwise Jackson would not have been sent against a position so strongly garrisoned and so susceptible of a prolonged resistance, if defended with skill and courage.[35]

Such circumstantial evidence, standing alone, might not be sufficiently persuasive to support a finding of communication and understanding between Jackson and Miles. However, when viewed in light of a mass of other circumstantial evidence that Miles was determined to see Harper's Ferry fall to the Rebels, Lee's almost incredible decision to divide his army in enemy territory immediately after a proven opportunity for communication between Jackson and Miles becomes a significant cir-

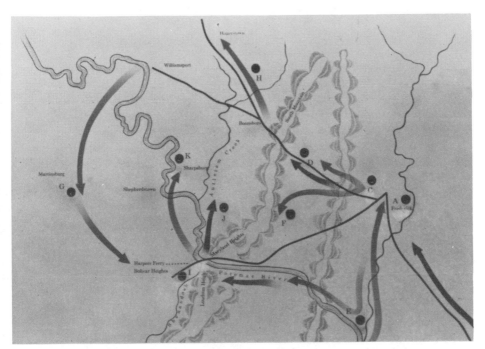

Jackson's Three-Pronged Attack on Harper's Ferry, September 10–15, 1862

Visual aid to understanding of Stonewall Jackson's strategy for surrounding and capturing Harper's Ferry. Note particularly the routes taken from Frederick by Rebel generals McLaws *(F);* Walker *(E);* and Jackson himself *(G).* The escape route of the Union cavalry on the eve of surrender is marked *(I).* Photo by Robert A. M. Schick, courtesy of the National Park Service Visitors' Center at Harper's Ferry.

cumstance which simply cannot be dismissed in weighing the case against Dixon Miles.

On the same day (September 8, 1862) that Lee was reversing his original intention to bypass Harper's Ferry he was also issuing a formal proclamation to the people of Maryland, inviting them to join the Confederacy.[36] However, the response in this western part of Maryland, particularly in terms of enlistments in the Rebel army, was extremely disappointing.[37] Lee did not wait long for a fuller response but proceeded on Tuesday, September 9, to issue his top secret Special Order #191, outlining in detail for his major commanders the complex plan of Operation Harper's Ferry.

The entire Rebel army would leave Frederick on the morrow (Wednesday, September 10), heading northwest along the National Road (now Route Alternate 40) toward Boonsboro, just west of the Blue Ridge, at that point called South Mountain.[38] Jackson's command would form the advance of the army, cross the Potomac at a point of Jackson's choice, seize the B & O Railroad, seize any Union troops left in Martinsburg, and "intercept such [Union troops] as may attempt to escape from Harper's Ferry," all by the morning of Friday the twelfth.[39] Note carefully that Jackson was *not* expected to capture any part of the Harper's Ferry complex; that was to be accomplished by the division of General McLaws (with Anderson's division), which would peel off at Middletown, cut across South Mountain several miles south of Boonsboro (at Burkittsville), and by the morning of Friday the twelfth "would *possess [itself] of the Maryland Heights and endeavor to capture the enemy at Harper's Ferry and vicinity*" (emphasis added).[40]

General Walker (busy, as we have seen, trying to destroy the Monocacy aqueduct) would not return to Frederick but would cross the Potomac into Virginia and move in a roundabout way (through Lovettsville) to take possession of Loudon Heights by the same time (morning of Friday the twelfth); he would then cooperate with McLaws and Jackson "as far as practicable" and "intercept retreat of the enemy."[41]

Finally, Longstreet's command, with the army's trains, and D. H. Hill's division (the army's rear guard) would both simply halt at Boonsboro.[42] (Before leaving Frederick, however, Longstreet's orders were, in fact, amended to continue his march northwest from Boonsboro to Hagerstown to head off a Federal force erroneously rumored to be moving south from Chambersburg, Pennsylvania,[43] an ironic reversal of Longstreet's sole contribution to the plan.)

The most notable thing about Special Order #191 is its indubitable assumption—in striking contrast to what eventually happened—that the surrender of Harper's Ferry would follow naturally from McLaws's seizure of Maryland Heights and that Jackson, after seizing Martinsburg, would have nothing to do but drive the Martinsburg garrison into Harper's Ferry and intercept any Union soldiers fleeing west from the Ferry.[44]

Did this mean that Lee and Jackson believed that a mere bombardment from Maryland Heights (and Loudon Heights)—on the far sides of two broad rivers—would alone bring thousands of Union soldiers in Harper's Ferry to their knees? It cannot be denied that this theory apparently had some currency, as indicated in the subsequent battle report of Rebel General Lafayette McLaws, the man to whom Lee had assigned responsibility for the seizure of Maryland Heights *and* the capture of Harper's Ferry:

> So long as Maryland Heights was occupied by the enemy [wrote McLaws], Harper's Ferry could never be occupied by us. If we [Rebels] gained possession of the heights, the town was no longer tenable to them.[45]

It is almost impossible to believe, however, that two such masters of the military art as Lee and Jackson could have shared this delusion. Jackson, indeed, made it clear in his battle report that "McLaws and Walker being thus separated from the enemy by intervening rivers could afford no assistance beyond the fire of their artillery and guarding certain avenues of escape. . . ."[46] The peculiar feature of Special Order #191 that looked for McLaws, not Jackson, to capture Harper's Ferry would therefore seem to mean only one thing: Lee and Jackson had an unexpressed reason to believe that the seizure of Maryland Heights would somehow become a catalyst for the surrender of Harper's Ferry. The scheme of Special Order #191 thus constitutes another circumstance tending to show possible agreement between Jackson and Miles that Harper's Ferry would fall to the Rebels.

On Wednesday, September 10, the first of Stonewall Jackson's troops left Frederick at 5:00 A.M., and "all day long through Frederick Street sounded the tread of marching feet."[48] The envelopment of Harper's Ferry had begun.

14
Envelopment

It was about suppertime on Wednesday, September 10, when young Lieutenant Colonel Stephen Downey, commanding the Potomac Home Brigade's 3rd Infantry Regiment, came riding hard into Boonsboro, Maryland, with a nineteen-man cavalry reconnaissance party.[1] Downey was a protege and eventual law partner of western Maryland's radical Republican congressman and former governor, Francis Thomas, sponsor of the Potomac Home Brigade.[2] His regiment, which had been a part of Miles's "Railroad Brigade" for a month and a half, was now stationed a few miles west of Harper's Ferry at Kearneysville,[3] whence his troops patrolled the B & O tracks as far east as the Ferry and as far west as Martinsburg.[4]

Tonight Downey was far afield, on the east side of the Potomac, between Sharpsburg and Boonsboro, looking for an approaching Rebel army he knew had to be there. The previous day (Tuesday the ninth) he had somehow learned that the enemy was moving from Frederick to Boonsboro or Hagerstown, but the timing of the rumor was apparently off by a day and Miles had precipitately dismissed Downey's report as "unfounded."[5]

This time, however, Downey struck pay dirt.[6] Riding down the main street of the village of Boonsboro, the little party ran smack into advance elements of Stonewall Jackson's army. Young Downey promptly ordered a charge on the enemy, and the surprised Rebels, reasonably assuming this handful of Yankees to be but the advance of a larger force, turned and started galloping back toward the pass over South Mountain from which Jackson's army was now debouching. Before the ensuing chase and continuing duel could proceed very far, however, the fleeing Rebels were horrified to run into none other than Stonewall Jackson himself, strolling beside the road, lost in meditation. There was nothing else for the Rebels to do but turn on their pursuers in order to protect their leader, and this they did. The logic of numbers belatedly prevailed and Downey's little party, in turn, became the pursued, eventually escaping with none but Downey wounded, and he only slightly.

Returning to his headquarters in the Kearneysville-Shepherdstown area, Downey promptly messaged General White in Martinsburg his important intelligence, and White in turn immediately passed the news to Wool and Miles, although noting that Downey could not say whether the enemy (described only as "in considerable force") was headed for Martinsburg or Hagerstown.[7] Two hours later White forwarded to both Wool and Halleck further intelligence gathered by "Scout" Noakes, just back from Maryland, that at least fifteen thousand Rebels were passing through Boonsboro, with Hagerstown, he thought, their probable destination.[8]

Miles's reaction to the first confirmed news that Lee's army had broken camp in Frederick and was on its way somewhere north or west was puzzling. At 9:00 P.M. (about the same time that he must have received White's relay of Downey's news) Miles wired Halleck:

> Enemy reported advancing from Boonesborough [to Rohrersville].[9] He may intend to pass on to Maryland Heights or the Potomac at Antietam Creek. Troops in position and ready.[10]

Either later that night (Wednesday the tenth) or next morning, Miles received a written report from Downey, no copy of which apparently survives but the tenor of which emerges from Downey's testimony before the Harper's Ferry Commission. Downey testified that after returning from Boonsboro on the tenth he wrote Miles that he had met Jackson's advance in Boonsboro and had learned from a loyal citizen that a strong rebel force of 70,000 men "intended to attack Harper's Ferry."[11] Downey further testified that Colonel Miles, in answer to that letter, "after I had given him all this information, said that he did not think the enemy intended to attack Harper's Ferry."[12] Miles's reply to Downey survives and substantially corroborates the latter's testimony in this respect. After *repri-manding* the young colonel for his "hazardous" dash upon the enemy with only nineteen cavalry men, Miles replied:

> The enemy is scattered between Rohrersville and Boonsborough, foraging I expect. I cannot learn that he has any disposition to advance this way. Should he do so, it will be through Solomon's Gap or across the Potomac.[13]

Miles then explained Downey's proper lines of retreat to Harper's Ferry or Martinsburg in the event that the Rebels moved on either Solomon's Gap or Antietam ford.[14]

By Thursday, September 11, Jackson had left Boonsboro behind and recrossed the Potomac River well to the north, just below Williamsport, Maryland, according to plan but a little behind schedule. Ironically but naturally, this movement was briefly hailed as good news in the North, which wanted to believe it signified a retreat back to Virginia by Lee's invasion force.[15] On the next day (September 12, 1862), Lincoln wired McClellan (whose army had not yet reached Frederick):

> Governor Curtin [of Pennsylvania] telegraphs me: "I have advices that Jackson is crossing the Potomac at Williamsport and *probably the whole rebel army will be drawn from Maryland.*" Receiving nothing from Harper's Ferry or Martinsburg today [Friday the twelfth] and positive information from Wheeling that the [telegraph] line is cut, corroborates the idea that the enemy is recrossing the Potomac. *Please do not let him get off without being hurt.* (Emphasis added.)[16]

Not until the Potomac had been crossed at Williamsport could it have been apparent to an uninitiated observer that Jackson's real goal was Martinsburg, a dozen miles south-southwest from Williamsport. Once the Potomac had been crossed, Jackson sent A. P. Hill's division straight for Martinsburg and directed the rest of his task force to points around that city which effectually left White's 3,000 men just one direction in which to retreat: to Harper's Ferry.[17]

Midday on Thursday the eleventh White sent out a strong reconnaissance of all arms under Colonel Cameron of the 65th Illinois to feel out Jackson's intentions and then wired Miles to send up a train for his materiel by midnight—just in case.[18] By suppertime White no longer had any doubt about what was happening. At 7:30 P.M. he wired Miles:

> As near as I can learn I am being surrounded and shall make immediate preparation to move toward you. If the train has not been sent, let it come at once. Send out a support to Kearneysville [Downey's headquarters] as you proposed. I shall march before daylight. There will be no difficulty in supporting me. What I most want is artillery and infantry *Don't fail me.* (Emphasis added.)[19]

Why Jackson, with a task force of 12,000 men, would permit—indeed, invite—White's 3,000 men to leave their position of peril and join 10,000 other Union troops in a better defensive location is one of the more pregnant questions of the Harper's Ferry campaign. The decision to forgo such an advantage must have been based on a remarkably firm belief that—for some reason—Miles would surrender without any of the fighting which Jackson necessarily knew would be required in a battle with White. And such was, of course, what actually happened. But how Lee and Jackson could have been so sure of a bloodless victory at Harper's Ferry *in advance of the event* is difficult to explain, unless they had good reason to expect the cooperation of Dixon Miles.

Meanwhile, the main prong of the Rebel tweezers—McLaws's movement to Maryland Heights—was progressing slowly but surely, without the excitement that somehow always accompanied Jackson's movements. During Wednesday the tenth McLaws's task force had peeled off from the National Road at Middletown, a half dozen miles northwest of Frederick, and marched another half dozen miles southwest to the little village of Burkittsville, on the east side of South Mountain, where McLaws spent the night.[20]

During the gray morning and rainy afternoon of Thursday, September 11, McGrath and Steiner (Ford's artillery and infantry commanders) and McIlvaine (Miles's chief of artillery) were called to the lookout atop Maryland Heights to see McLaws's troops pouring slowly over South Mountain from Burkittsville into Pleasant Valley far below.[21] All through the day the Rebel movement continued until the valley floor must have seemed crawling with McLaws's 8,000 invaders.[22] Mostly they came over Brownsville Gap, about five miles north of the

Potomac and nearly opposite to a similar gap in Elk Ridge of which we have already heard: Solomon's Gap.[23]

It was just after suppertime that the first Rebel shots of the battle for Maryland Heights were fired.[24] They were merely exploratory, feeling out the handful of pickets Miles had permitted Ford to post at Solomon's Gap. The pickets fled, but with darkness and rain both falling McLaws did nothing more that night. It was nearly midnight on Thursday, September 11, when Miles sent his last wire to the outside world. To Halleck in Washington he reported the start of the battle for Harper's Ferry:

> My eastern front [Elk Ridge] is threatened. My pickets at Solomon's Gap shelled out. The ball will open tomorrow morning. Force opposing me is estimated at ten regiments of infantry with proportionate artillery, before dusk; others have come into camp since. General White will abandon Martinsburg sometime tonight and I expect this will be the last you hear of me until this affair is over. All are cheerful and hopeful. Good-bye.[25]

15
Maryland Heights: Friday

On the following day, Friday the twelfth, McLaws began the actual seizure of Maryland Heights. It was a carefully planned maneuver. The principal thrust would be by Kershaw's and Barksdale's brigades (under Kershaw). They would mount Elk Ridge at Solomon's Gap and then make their way south (Kershaw along the ridge, Barksdale along the east slope) some four to five miles to the main Union "defense positions" on Maryland Heights.[1] Meanwhile Semmes's and Mahone's brigades were to remain on the floor of Pleasant Valley, sealing it off against attack from the north, and also to occupy Crampton's Gap and Brownsville Gap, the only two passes over South Mountain to the east, and Solomon's Gap, the only pass over Elk Ridge to the west.[2]

Wright's brigade was to climb South Mountain at Brownsville Gap and move south, parallel to Elk Ridge, to a point overlooking Weverton on the Potomac River, where it would plant a two-gun battery to control the turnpike, railroad, and canal (which there all wind around the mountain on their way to Harper's Ferry).[3] Cobb's brigade would move south through Pleasant Valley on the west side thereof, that is, along the base of Elk Ridge,[4] keeping in communication with Kershaw above and keeping up to his advance "so as to give support if possible, if it was needed and to serve as a rallying force should any disaster render such necessary."[5] Finally, McLaws himself would move south down the center of Pleasant Valley toward the Potomac River with the rest of his task force.[6]

Kershaw's subsequent battle report[7] provides a concise statement of Friday's events on the main front: Elk Ridge.

On the morning of the 12th Instant I was directed, with
Barksdale's Mississippi brigade and my own [South
Carolina], to move from Brownsville and occupy the Maryland Heights, taking the road by Solomon's Gap to the
summit of Elk Ridge, and thence, along the ridge, to the
point which overlooks and commands Harper's Ferry. At an
early hour the command was in motion and reached the gap
without opposition. At this point, however, the pickets of the
enemy were discovered, and it became necessary to approach
the position carefully, with skirmishers thrown well to the
right and left. This being done, the enemy withdrew his
picket after a few scattering shots. Reaching the summit of
the mountain, skirmishers were thrown well down the
mountain to my right, while the column filed to the left along
the ridge. Captain Cuthbert, Second South Carolina Regiment, commanding the skirmishers on the right, soon encountered a volley from about three companies of cavalry,
but upon the fire being returned the enemy left with some
loss. About a mile farther on, Major Bradley, Mississippi
regiment, commanding skirmishers, reported an abatis
across the line of march, from which he was fired upon by a
picket. Directing him to press forward and ascertain the force
in front, he soon overcame the obstacle without further
resistance. Leaving then the path which at that point passed
down the mount to the right, we filed along the crags on the
ridge. The natural obstacles were so great that we only
reached a position about a mile from the point of the
mountain at 6 o'clock p.m. Here an abatis was discovered,
extending across the mountain, flanked on either side by a
ledge of precipitous rocks. A sharp skirmish ensued, which
satisfied me that the enemy occupied the position in force. I
therefore directed Major Bradley to retire his skirmishers,
and deployed my brigade in two lines, extending across the
entire practicable ground on the summit of the mountain,
the Eighth Regiment, Colonel Henagan, on the right, and the
Seventh, Colonel Aiken, on the left, constituting the first line;
the Third Regiment, Colonel Nance, in rear of the Eighth,
and the Second Regiment, Colonel Kennedy, in rear of the
Seventh, constituting the second line; General Barksdale's
brigade immediate in rear. These dispositions being made,
the approach of night prevented further operations; the
commands rested on their arms in the position indicated.

Granted that Kershaw's slow but relentless advance south
along the spine of Elk Ridge was well planned and executed, it

is plain that his 2,000 men[8] were nevertheless as successful as they were because of the lack of properly organized resistance by the outmanned Union defenders of Elk Ridge.[9] At Solomon's Gap, instead of the artillery fire which Ford had sought in vain from Miles, Kershaw met only a dozen of the 7th Rhode Island "college cavaliers"[10] and two dozen pickets from Ford's own 32nd Ohio Infantry, all of whom, as just seen, withdrew quickly after a few Rebel shells had come their way.

From then until late in the afternoon, when serious resistance was first encountered by the Rebels, they moved steadily southward, along the ridge and west side of the mountain, through heavy growth that made the advance difficult and slow. Across the Potomac on Bolivar Heights the bulk of the Harper's Ferry garrison "watched the lines of thin, blue smoke rise out of the treetops from the Rebel line of battle, now advancing, now hesitating, and now advancing again along [Elk Ridge's] steep and woody slope."[11] To Kershaw's regimental historian it later seemd that "all along the whole distance of five miles we were more or less harassed by them [the Yankees]."[12] It is difficult to isolate identifiable skirmishcs until late in the afternoon. One such skirmish involved a company of Ford's own 32nd Ohio and two companies of Maulsby's 1st Maryland (PHB). All of these three units had been with Ford some time but had been sent up to the "lookout" at the high point of Elk Ridge (Maryland Heights) only the preceding day, when McLaws's troops made their appearance in Pleasant Valley.[13]

A much larger reinforcement came across the river from Bolivar Heights early Friday morning. Late Thursday night Major Hildebrandt, now commanding D'Utassy's 39th New York, was ordered to report to Ford with six of his own companies and two from Colonel Sammon's 115th New York.[14] He reached Ford's headquarters halfway up the hill by 5:00 A.M., and Ford, who apparently had no hesitancy to shuffle units around, sent him on up the mountain with four of his (Hildebrandt's) own companies and two from the Potomac Home Brigade to capture "two" companies of "exhausted" Rebels, that Ford understood were up at Solomon's Gap.[15] Ford's faulty intelligence was soon corrected. At the "lookout" some of the cavalry who had just been driven in from Solomon's Gap warned Hildebrandt that the Rebels were in "heavy force," but he pushed ahead on the narrow road and through the dense woods on either side.[16]

Eventually Hildebrandt's skirmishers encountered heavy Rebel fire, and by the time he decided to withdraw to a better position he had lost a half dozen men.[17] In his retreat position he remained for "a few hours," then returned to Ford's base camp halfway down the hill, where he was ordered back "up on the heights" by Ford, only to be ordered back down again by Ford's executive officer, Major Hewitt.[18] An officer of the 32nd Ohio later testified before the Harper's Ferry Commission that "they [Hildebrandt's six companies] came back and claimed that they were driven in but I did not believe they were."[19] Credible or not, Hildebrandt's command seems to have been Ford's principal force on Elk Ridge most of Friday, as appears from the following message which Ford sent Miles sometime during that day (probably midmorning):

> Our forces, consisting of 400 infantry, under command of Major Hildebrandt, and 50 cavalry, under Captain Russell [of the 1st Maryland Cavalry] are now fighting at Solomon's Gap. The rebels have thrown thirty shells and wounded several men. The rebels are attempting to pass through the gap and our men are resisting.[20]

By late afternoon, as Kershaw's report makes clear,[21] the Rebels had reached the principal Union "fortifications" on Elk Ridge, a slashing and abatis of trees cut down by some of Ford's men during the preceding days, behind which (i.e., just south of it) was a so-called breastwork, stretching across the ridge from a rock ledge overlooking Pleasant Valley. The abatis and breastwork were about a quarter-mile north[22] of a cribbed log structure atop Maryland Heights[23] which was some twenty feet high and was known as "the lookout."[24] The "lookout" was located about two miles north of Captain McGrath's gun position and Colonel Ford's adjacent headquarters.[25] At the abatis the skirmishing became sharper and Kershaw's men found themselves unable to advance successfully into the abatis in the face of opposing Union fire.[26]

In this impasse at the abatis and breastwork, about 4:00 P.M. a 600-man regiment finally arrived to reinforce the Union cause. Unfortunately, that regiment, the 126th New York, was the greenest regiment at Harper's Ferry. Raised in the Finger Lakes country of New York State just three weeks earlier, the newly arrived 126th was under the command of Colonel Eliakim Sherrill, forty-nine-year-old farmer and tanner, a former Whig state senator and U.S. congressman with only a little experience in the peacetime militia.[27] About 10:00 P.M. the night before (i.e., Thursday the eleventh), in response to a Ford plea for reinforcements, orders had been issued to the 126th New York to march at sunrise for Maryland Heights with one day's rations and eighty rounds of cartridges per man. At sunrise, however, as the regiment marched through Bolivar, it was halted and marched back to its bivouac area on the left of Bolivar Heights, where it waited for further orders until about 3:00 P.M. that day.[28]

No source tells us why there was such a strange eight- to nine-hour delay in sending the 126th across the river and up the hill, but a good guess can be made. Conversing with Capt. Russell, Ford told Russell:

> Colonel Miles has sent over here, offering to reenforce me with some raw troops. I would rather do what fighting I have got to do here with the little handful of men which I have confidence in, for I believe they would do me more harm than good.[29]

It seems a fair speculation that Miles initially withheld the 126th New York from Ford, hoping the latter would take responsibility for the action, but that by midafternoon either (1) Miles had decided to wait no longer or (2) Ford had finally given in and agreed to take them. Be that as it may, by the time the sun was only "an hour high" (i.e., near dusk) Sherrill's men were forming a line of battle across the mountain in the rear of skirmishers from the 32nd Ohio,[30] most of whose remaining companies (except those left on the southeast slope under Captain Crumbecker) had now been ordered up the hill by Ford to support the two companies already there.[31] Like the Rebels that they could hear talking in the darkness just a hundred yards or so to the north of them,[32] the green troops from upstate New York rested on their arms all Friday night, awaiting the dawn that would bring them their first taste of battle.[33]

Meanwhile McLaws's force under Wright, moving south along the parallel ridge of South Mountain, had reached Weverton, thus closing off the riverside approach to Harper's Ferry.[34] Others of McLaws's forces, under Cobb and Armistead, moving south along the floor of Pleasant Valley to the Potomac River, stopped short of the village of Sandy Hook,[35] but Maulsby, the Union commander there, was ordered to leave it, retreating almost to the Harper's Ferry bridges.[36] When, on Saturday, the Rebels attempted to round the foot of Maryland Heights and capture the bridges, they were promptly driven back to Sandy Hook by Union artillery at Camp Hill on the other (Harper's Ferry) side of the Potomac.[37]

The same 4:00 P.M. message from Miles that directed Major Hewitt to send most of the rest of the 32nd Ohio up the hill to defend the heights also explained that Maulsby's troops had been withdrawn from Sandy Hook, leaving that point exposed.[38] Accordingly and, as it turned out, significantly, Hewitt was directed by Miles's order to take a bundle of combustibles and leave it upon the "point" of the eastern and southern portion of the mountain and place a guard over it.[39] Although Hewitt no longer had his copy of the order when he testified before the Harper's Ferry Commission, he recalled that:

> the orders were that if we were pressed too hard, to fall back and ignite that combustible as a signal for the batteries on the Maryland and Bolivar Heights both to play upon the Maryland Heights after the men were drawn out of the way under the cover of these guns.[40]

At the same time Hewitt was directed by Miles's order to run a line of pickets (under Captain Crumbecker) up the steep eastern slope of Maryland Heights to the "lookout,"[41] presumably to warn Ford if the Rebels tried to flank the main Union line at the summit by advancing south along the eastern slope of the mountain.

The package of combustibles was, in fact, never used,[42] but the basic strategy which the order enunciated, that is, withdrawing the Union infantry if too "hard-pressed" and substituting an artillery barrage to hold the advancing enemy, would prove to be a disaster on the following day (Saturday the thirteenth). While, as we shall later see, blame can be placed on Ford and Hewitt for the unskilful way in which this strategy was employed, there would seem to be a real question whether such a strategy could have worked well *under any circumstances*. Explanation is called for.

At that time, lacking either radio or telephonic communication, observed fire was the norm. Unobserved fire like McGrath's uphill shots to the summit of Maryland Heights would depend for accuracy on accurate presetting of the tube's elevation (from earlier fire) and, as a practical matter, would also depend on unlikely cooperation by the enemy in staying in the immediate target area. As for the Union batteries across the river on Camp Hill, despite their ability to see the summit of Maryland Heights (and thus to employ observed fire), they suffered a great handicap in that the thousand foot difference in altitude and the mile and a half distance involved made precision fire almost impossible. In either case there would seem to be a substantial danger of hitting Union soldiers about as often as Rebels, unless, of course, the Union soldiers had already retreated so far back as really to have lost the fight. It seems plain from the "combustible" order that Miles was not even thinking of holding the Heights he had denuded of fortifications, artillery, and soldiers in sufficient force to make an effective defense. A contemporaneous event confirms this.

Before the Harper's Ferry Commission, Captain Eugene McGrath, a forty-eight-year old Irish immigrant bootmaker from New York City who commanded the Union artillery on Maryland Heights,[43] testified that it was probably Friday when Miles visited his position on the hill:

> Colonel Miles came up there, I think, the day before [the Saturday battle] and called me aside. He said, "Damn 'em, fight 'em." I said "I will stay here, Colonel, until they say 'go,' and I hope you will not say that." Said he, "No, sir; I will not say 'go' "; and then he said, "Captain, if we are compelled to leave, if they come in force, we will have to spike these guns; damn 'em, they shan't have 'em."[44]

It was, of course, Miles's duty to make sure the Rebels did not get the big naval guns that were the major goal of McLaws's expedition. On the other hand the spiking of those guns would make it forever impossible for such guns to be turned on any Rebel force, as Saxton had done in May when Jackson attempted to advance from Bolivar Heights to Camp Hill.[45] We may not know with what sincerity Miles's "fight 'em, damn 'em" was uttered, but it cannot be denied that his practical concern—the spiking of the big guns—would be a precious gift, whether or not so intended, to Stonewall Jackson.

While the Rebels maintained their steady advance along Elk Ridge all day Friday, significant events had also been occurring in Harper's Ferry. About noon, General White marched his

2,500 troops from Martinsburg (including Downey's regiment from Kearneysville)[46] into the Harper's Ferry complex and into bivouac on the plateau back of Bolivar Heights.[47] The question in many minds was whether White would now assume command of Harper's Ferry.

When Trimble asked White that question, the latter replied that he couldn't say until he had talked with Miles.[48] White and Miles met that (Friday) night but Miles made no offer to step down.[49] White decided to probe Miles's defense strategy before making his own decision. He and D'Utassy, who was also present, spoke of what their facilities would be if they had to withdraw.[50] Both of them favored a plan to withdraw the whole garrison over the pontoon bridge and hold Maryland Heights. According to D'Utassy, Miles explicitly agreed to this:

> As a matter of course, it is the only choice we have.[51]

Neither Miles nor White, however, apparently made any move to renounce command and both proceeded to go their own ways, which, at least in Miles's case, was to bed.

Meanwhile, Miles had sent a verbal order to Major Hewitt on the heights, to determine whether the Rebels were cutting a road up the mountainside and also to assess what amount of force they had brought against the hill.[52] Hewitt satisfied himself that there was, indeed, a large enemy force in front of him,[53] then conferred with Colonel Sherrill of the 126th New York sometime between 9:00 and 10:00 P.M. The two of them agreed that if they were to hold the hill it was essential to have three more regiments and two mountain howitzers by dawn.[54] Hewitt immediately rode back to make this proposal to Ford, who had independently concluded that:

> Tomorrow one of two things has got to be done; we have either got to drive them from the hill or they are going to drive us from it.[55]

Ford then sent Hewitt on to Harper's Ferry to lay the case before Miles,[56] who, being awakened, hastened to his headquarters to meet Hewitt.[57] Hewitt later described this meeting with Miles as follows:

> I informed him of the probable amount of force there and that a general engagement might be expected at that point.

"And," says I, "nothing short of a force sufficient to just shove them right off the mountain will save that place, and we want reenforcements"; that was my language to him, as near as I can recollect.

. . . He asked some few questions in regard to the position of the enemy, the amount of the forces, and then assured me that there should be two regiments on the mountain by break of day, and two pieces of artillery, and also that he would send another regiment up the west side of the mountain so as to come in on their right flank. He said they should all be there by the break of day. I then returned to the mountain and went on to the front of our lines. . . . They all lay down there in line during the night until morning.[58]

Hewitt's testimony mentions no expression of skepticism on Miles's part concerning Ford's need for reinforcements, but Miles's West Point–trained Engineer, young Captain Powell, testified to having been present at this or possibly a similar Friday night discussion between Miles and a Ford emissary seeking reinforcements.[59]

I think it was on Friday evening that he said that Colonel Ford had made the remark to him that he could hold that place against all hell. Then, he continued his remark by saying, "Then what in hell does he want of more men? . . . I cannot jeopardize my force in front." At that time I do not think there was an attack . . . on Bolivar Heights.[60]

Looking at Miles's statements on the night of Friday the twelfth, it seems clear that he gave the right answers to White and D'Utassy (that is, that Maryland Heights would always be the key to his strategy and the last refuge of the Harper's Ferry garrison) and to Ford's emissary, Hewitt (i.e., that there would be three more regiments on Maryland Heights by dawn), However, his flagrant breach of both these key assurances within the next twenty-four hours must raise an inevitable question: Could Miles really have intended to keep either promise when made?

*　*　*

Friday, September 12, is notable also for a further occurrence far from Harper's Ferry except for which the outcome of the siege of Harper's Ferry seems likely to have turned out quite differently. In order to understand what happened it is necessary to recall that sometime that (Friday) morning Harper's Ferry's only remaining rail transportation and telegraphic communication with the rest of the world (westward through Cumberland, Maryland) was cut off—as Miles had correctly anticipated the previous night—by the advance of Jackson's troops in the Martinsburg area.[62] (Direct rail transportation and telegraphic communication between Harper's Ferry and Baltimore/Washington had already been cut a week earlier, it will be recalled, during Lee's advance from the Potomac River to Frederick.)[63]

All day Friday the twelfth strenuous efforts were made by McClellan's cavalry, advancing northward to Frederick and westward to Point of Rocks, to open communications with Miles, but without success.[64] In Washington, Halleck, who only the preceding (Thursday) afternoon had again turned down another McClellan plea for command of Miles's troops,* decided on Friday the twelfth that the time had come to release the Harper's Ferry garrison. The trap so expertly set by Halleck to hold Lee in Maryland until McClellan could catch up with him had obviously accomplished its purpose and Halleck could reasonably have concluded that with McClellan now within striking distance of Lee, Miles could be sprung. Be that as it may, at 1:45 P.M. on Friday the twelfth, Halleck wired McClellan "Is it not possible to open communications with Harper's Ferry so that Col. Miles's force can cooperate with yours?"[65] and shortly before 6:00 P.M. Halleck sent both McClellan[66] and Wool[67] copies of a message to Miles reading as follows:

> You will obey such orders as General McClellen may give you. You will endeavor to open communication with him and unite your forces to his at the earliest possible moment. His army is now near the line of the Monocacy.

To Halleck, McClellan immediately wired:

> . . . I this morning ordered cavalry to endeavor to open communication with Harper's Ferry and in my orders of

*37th Cong., 3rd sess., *Report of the Joint Committee on the Conduct of the War* (1863), 3: 478. "There is no way for Colonel Miles to join you at present. The only chance is to defend his works until you can open communication with him. When you do so, he will be subject to your orders."

[general] movement for tomorrow, have arranged so that I can go or send to his [Miles's] relief if necessary. I have heard no firing in that direction and if he resists at all I think [I]cannot only relieve him, but place the rebels who attack him in great danger of being cut off. Everything moves at daylight tomorrow. Your message to him [Miles] this moment received. Will forward by first opportunity.[68]

And to President Lincoln at 9:00 P.M. McClellan wired *(inter alia):*

... I have taken all possible means to communicate with Harper's Ferry, so that I may send to its relief if necessary. . . . If Harper's Ferry is still in our possession, I think I can save the garrison if they fight at all. . . .[69]

With rail and telegraphic communication no longer a possibility, McClellan's only hope for getting a message through to Miles relaying Halleck's order (to break out of Harper's Ferry and join McClellan) was a more primitive method of communication: visual signals. For this purpose a chain of signal stations had earlier been established linking the "lookout" atop Maryland Heights with similar signal stations at Point of Rocks, Sugar Loaf Mountain, Poolesville, Darnestown, Great Falls, and finally the Capitol in Washington.[70] An officer and two flagmen were continuously on duty day and night, torches being used at night for transmitting messages, as flags were used by day.[71]

When the likelihood of a Rebel invasion of Maryland had become apparent in the early days of September 1862, a party of Signal Corps officers had been sent to man these stations. Captain Louis Fortescue, a thirty-two-year-old Philadelphia bookkeeper,[72] was ordered to Maryland Heights, from which there is an extensive view of both the Shenandoah and Pleasant Valleys. When, however, the Rebels crossed the Potomac River and occupied Point of Rocks, Maryland, on September 5 and 6, the disappearance of the Point of Rocks signal station naturally followed, leaving no one with whom Captain Fortescue on Maryland Heights could communicate. Accordingly, at some time before the envelopment of Harper's Ferry, Fortescue left to join the Army of the Potomac in a round about way through Gettysburg, Baltimore, and Washington.[73]

Since it was to Fortescue's signal station on Maryland Heights that McClellan's signal officers hoped to transmit the key Halleck directive of Friday the twelfth ordering Miles to join McClellan, the effort was inevitably doomed to failure.

> On the night of the 12th [of September] Lieut. J. H. Fralick, who had gone forward with General Hancock, reached Point of Rocks, then not yet possessed by our [Union] troops. Lieut. Fralick attempted to attract thence, by means of signals, the attention of the signal officer supposed to be at Maryland Heights. Rockets were fired and the usual signals made by torch from Sugar Loaf for the same purpose. Point of Rocks is an easy signal distance from Maryland Heights, but no response was obtained from the latter post. It was afterward ascertained that Captain Fortescue had insofar misapprehended the position in which he could be of most service as to leave the Heights prior to their investment. It had not been indicated to Captain Fortescue in orders that he was to remain at that place.[74]

We find no other record of the circumstances under which Captain Fortescue abandoned the "lookout" atop Maryland Heights only a short time before its surrender and we can only speculate on what, if any, role the post commander (Miles) may have played—normally it would be an important one—in Fortescue's decision to leave what was by Friday the twelfth Harper's Ferry's last hope to communicate with the outside world in general and McClellan's relieving army in particular. Whatever Miles's role in sending Fortescue on his way, the premature abandonment of the Union signal station atop Maryland Heights well before its capture by Kershaw's Rebel troops on Saturday the thirteenth turned out to be the next-to-last step in making Dixon Miles a completely free agent. It ensured that no Lincoln, no Halleck, no McClellan would be able to interfere with Miles's plans for the "defense" of Harper's Ferry, whatever they might be.

All Friday evening and into the night, McClellan, although lacking any telecommunications, made other efforts to get through to Miles. At 11:00 P.M., when directing Burnside to pursue the Rebels westward through the Catoctin Passes at daylight, McClellan's chief of staff added: "The general desires you to learn, if possible, the condition of affairs in the direction of Harper's Ferry and to communicate the same to him."[75] A half-hour later he included in his instructions to cavalry chief Pleasanton a similar directive to "ascertain, if possible, the state of affairs at Harper's Ferry and communicate the result of your investigations to these headquarters at Frederick."[76] None of these efforts succeeded.

Incredibly, however, while neither McClellan's men nor messages could get through the encircling Rebel army into Harper's Ferry, there was no such problem with sending men or messages *out* of Harper's Ferry—*at least to the Rebels*. This was because of Miles's indefensible policy of promptly sending Rebel POWs back to their army through his own front lines. On this first day of the siege (Friday the twelfth) eighteen Rebel soldiers—including five from Lt. Rouse's Company B of the 12th Virginia Cavalry—were granted paroles to return to their own lines on condition that they bear no arms against the United States and give no aid or assistance to the Confederate government until regularly exchanged.[77] Moreover, each piously promised in writing:

> And I hereby pledge my word of honor that I will not reveal to any person or persons whomsoever what I may have heard or seen in relationship to the troops or defenses at Harper's Ferry or vicinity.[78]

But what they promised and what they in fact revealed about the defenses of Harper's Ferry after they reached the safety of their own lines could have been very different things. Most important, here was a perfect vehicle for the conveyance of any message Dixon Miles may have needed to send to Stonewall Jackson as the battle for Maryland Heights now reached a climax.

16
Maryland Heights: Saturday Morning

The advance of McLaw's troops westward up Solomon's Gap and then southward along the spine of Elk Ridge all day Friday had involved frequent skirmishing but no real battle. Saturday, however, was a horse of a different color. Now there would be real fighting, culminating in an astounding decision by the Union command to evacuate Maryland Heights voluntarily. It was a decision with which the Harper's Ferry Commission would have to be deeply concerned—almost more so than with the eventual surrender of Bolivar Heights and Harper's Ferry, which many, including Horace Greeley, simplistically believed followed directly from the loss of Maryland Heights.[1]

Because Colonel Ford was in command of Maryland Heights and was the man who actually issued the abandonment order—and to some extent simply because he was alive and Miles was dead—it was natural for Ford to take the brunt of public criticism after the event. Certainly the Know-Nothing politician proved an inept military leader, as the Commission expressly found. (See appendix.) Our task here, however, is to see through Ford's nominal responsibility and determine the extent to which Miles really predetermined the Saturday result. This he did both by stressing the likelihood of defeat to Ford and his executive, Hewitt, and by refusing to provide Ford with the additional troops necessary to "throw the rebels right off the mountain," as Hewitt had sought. In this way Miles predetermined Saturday's results just as effectively as he had predetermined Friday's results by seeing that there was no

114

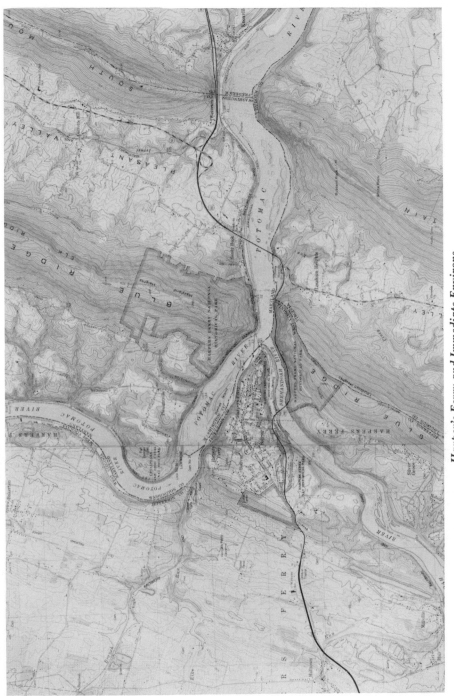

Harper's Ferry and Immediate Environs

Sections of U.S. Geological Survey maps of Charles Town and Harper's Ferry, West Virginia, quadrangles. Scale 1:24,000. Revised to 1971.

battery to greet the rebels at Solomon's Gap and no effective
body of troops, let alone fortifications, anywhere along the
spine of Elk Ridge. To understand this, painstaking attention to
detail is called for.

The two opposing forces on Maryland Heights, we have seen,
had finally joined issue just before sunset on Friday at a small
abatis about a quarter-mile north (along the ridge) from a
larger abatis,[2] immediately behind which an elementary earthwork (called by most participants "the breastworks") had
been thrown up hastily by Captain Whittier of the Potomac
Home Brigade as trouble approached on Thursday and Friday.[3] (This "breastwork," as noted above, was located about a
quarter-mile north of the log signal station known as "the
lookout"[4] at the crest of Maryland Heights, which was about
two miles up-slope from McGrath's battery[5] and Ford's nearby
headquarters,[6] both located halfway down hill toward Harper's
Ferry.)[7]

The sun was barely up—no later than seven o'clock—when
Kershaw's men, who had lain on their arms all night, moved
into the attack across the smaller (northernmost) abatis.[8] Defending the abatis were the same Union units that had been on
the ridge at the close of fighting Friday (the 126th New York
and a substantial part of the 32nd Ohio), joined now by three
companies of the 39th New York Infantry and by Russell's 1st
Maryland cavalry, dismounted and deployed as skirmishers.[9]
Kershaw's battle report estimates that it took his 1,041 men[10]
(with Barksdale's 960 just behind, in reserve)[11] only about
twenty minutes to drive the Union defenders back from the
smaller abatis to the larger abatis and "breastworks," a
quarter-mile to the south.[12] The 126th New York's regimental
history asserts that these New York recruits, who constituted
the largest part (about 950)[13] of the Union defenders,

> stood firm and contested the ground stubbornly, until their
> left being flanked and they pressed by superior numbers,
> were ordered to fall back behind the abatis and breastworks,
> [which] they did rapidly but in good order, facing about and
> firing as they went; and finally climbing over the slashing of
> timber, they formed behind the breastworks.[14]

Other accounts were less complimentary to the new recruits
from the Finger Lakes. The regiment's adjutant described this

preliminary engagement to the Harper's Ferry Commission as follows:

> We heard them [the Rebels] beat the long roll and maneuver in battalion maneuver and then they marched on us and drove in our pickets. . . . Someone gave the order to fall back after we were attacked. The center of the line was opened and the skirmishers let through. Colonel Sherrill stood in the road with his revolver drawn. The men gave way and fell back to the breastwork and, with the assistance of Colonel Sherrill and myself we stopped them at the breastwork and held them.[15]

Major Hildebrandt of the 39th New York testified:

> The line of the 126th [New York] Regiment was broken by the first fire and Major Hewitt, with the 32nd Ohio, and I with my few companies had to go out in front so as to keep the enemy back. We held them with only a small force for a very long time; after that we had to go behind a breastwork made of logs.[16]

Most uncomplimentary was the testimony of Captain Russell, "the fighting parson" from nearby Williamsport. He had just arrived at the front and was about to throw his dismounted cavalrymen out as skirmishers when a sergeant at the head of his column was shot in the thigh:

> He fell and the skirmishers of the 126th New York broke and ran. I threw my own men behind trees and rocks that were about there. I went back to where the 126th New York had retreated and begged their officers to bring their men forward. They were thrown out again as skirmishers. We skirmished there a while, until the enemy had formed its line of battle and we heard the commander of the enemy's forces give the command to "forward." We could hear them tramp through the alders and undergrowth. Then [before any enemy volley] the 126th New York broke again and fled through the line of battle that had been formed. . . . They ran right through them and some of them passed entirely back over the breastworks. Some were rallied again behind that line of battle and fought there awhile. The enemy came up and were "in line." They came pretty close to us but one of my lieutenants was shot and then the 126th broke again and

fell behind the breastworks and a goodly number of them
fled out of sight. I do not know where they stopped.[17]

It is not impossible that the "fighting parson" mistakenly
included in his testimony some of the 126th's running that
actually occurred later in the day. Nevertheless it must have
been reasonably clear by the end of this preliminary engagement on Saturday morning, if not earlier, that the principal
unit which Miles had sent across the river to reinforce Ford was
worth only about what might fairly be expected of utterly
untrained and inexperienced recruits[18]—officers as well as
men[19]—not even mustered into service until August 22[20] and
arrived at Harper's Ferry by train direct from home in New
York's Finger Lakes country on August 28.[21] Since the decision
to send such raw recruits to defend the critical position on the
Heights had to be a deliberate one on Miles's part—and, indeed,
made in the face of Ford's strenuous objection to taking raw
recruits—there is no question who bears the ultimate responsibility for what was about to happen on Maryland Heights.

As of 8:00 A.M. more than an hour after the three regiments
promised by Miles should have made their appearance on the
Heights, not one of the three regiments had arrived. Down to
Harper's Ferry with news of the enemy attack and the crying
need for Miles's promised reinforcements rode one of Ford's
officers, Lt. John Pearce. Miles's reaction was astounding: he
professed not to believe Pearce's news:

> That was the morning of the fight. I went down. He [Miles]
> said there was nobody on Maryland Heights but skirmishers
> but that we should expect an attack on the plateau on the
> Rohrersville road. I told him there was nobody there but that
> there were two brigades on the mountain. He said there was
> not. I told him he would soon find there was. He ordered me
> back and told me to tell Colonel Ford to watch the
> Rohrersville road. We had been scouting that road but had
> never found any force out there. I was out there myself 4
> miles and forced in their pickets.[22]

As for reinforcements, Pearce testified:

> The evening before Colonel Miles said we should have re-
> inforcements at daylight; but they never came. I went down
> at 8 o'clock in the morning. There was no sign of reinforce-
> ment yet. But he [Miles] immediately ordered Colonel Dow-

ney's Maryland regiment, I believe, and said if he did not get out in five minutes he would put Colonel Downey under arrest. Colonel Downey said afterward he never ordered him [previously]. We did not get reinforcements until 9 o'clock[23] [when Downey's 3rd Potomac Home Brigade regiment arrived at Ford's headquarters on the hill].[24]

Miles's profession of disbelief in Pearce's report that there were two brigades of Rebels atop Maryland Heights and his erroneous insistence that he had ordered Downey up the Heights the night before are so bizarre that one is tempted to explain them away by reference to the alcohol or drugs that had gotten Miles into such trouble at Bull Run I.[25] Additionally, certain testimony by Downey about Miles's behavior when Downey reported in before going up on the Heights tends to confirm the hypothesis that on Friday night, at least, Miles may have broken his vow—apparently generally kept at Harper's Ferry—to drink no more liquor.[26] Downey testified before the Harper's Ferry Commission:

> On the morning that I marched with my regiment on Maryland Heights Colonel Miles' verbal orders were, "I desire you to report to Colonel Hall, on Maryland Heights." He named over three or four names. At last I said, "You mean Colonel Ford." "Yes, sir," said he, and from that conversation I came to the conclusion that Colonel was not in a condition to command. That is my candid opinion.[27]

Whatever Miles's mental condition on Saturday morning, he did get Downey's 600-man 3rd Maryland (Potomac Home Brigade), a relatively experienced regiment,[28] up on the Heights as we shall see, just in time for the main rebel attack about ten o'clock Saturday morning. Not so, however, with the other two of the three regiments Miles had promised Ford on Friday night. Sammon's 900-man 115th New York Infantry[29] was apparently not ordered up (or at least did not arrive) at Ford's headquarters until about noon,[30] while Cameron's 800-man 65th Illinois Infantry,[31] although alerted sometime Saturday morning, was never actually ordered to leave Bolivar Heights, and even its alert was canceled about 1:00 P.M.[32]

Despite Miles's gross breach of his assurance to Ford that he would have three or more regiments on the Heights by dawn on Saturday, the one man who could lawfully have replaced

Miles now finally made up his mind—probably without knowledge or at least without adequate understanding of what was
going on across the river—*not* to do so. Early Saturday morning
General White stopped in to tell Colonel Trimble that with
General Wool so clearly indicating by his manifestations of
preference for Miles that Wool desired Miles to be in command, he (White) did not feel at liberty to assume command
himself.[33] Trimble said that much as he might desire White to
take the command, under the circumstances he would not ask
him to do so.[34] White then rode on down to Miles's headquarters
where he found no Miles but encountered Colonel Willard of
the 125th New York.[35] Willard later testified before the
Harper's Ferry Commission:

> He [White] said that on his return from Winchester he had
> been ordered to Martinsburg by General Wool, with a com-
> mand less in number than that left with Colonel Miles and that
> would seem to indicate a disposition or intention on the part
> of General Wool to leave Colonel Miles, a permanent officer,
> at Harper's Ferry. Under these circumstances he felt—I
> think he feared some difficulty or that there might be some.
> At any rate he wanted to know what my opinion was in
> regard the matter. . . .
> General White said that he did not know the topography of
> the country, the number of troops, the means of defense, etc.
> I told him that I should certainly deem it exceedingly
> hazardous to assume the command of Harper's Ferry. Said I,
> "General, the enemy are already attacking now; you can hear
> their guns as we sit here; you do not know the number of
> cannon; you do not know the troops; you do not know where
> they are located; and, if you should ask me, I should frankly
> say that in your place I should offer my services and those of
> my whole command to Colonel Miles at once, and, when you
> have become acquainted with the place, you can assume the
> command if you find it necessary to do so."[36]

White did not, however, consummate his tentative decision
without once again reassuring himself as to the soundness of
Miles's basic strategy, as laid down to him and D'Utassy the
previous (Friday) night. When Miles came into his office with
the news that "Ford is stampeded; he wants reinforcements and
I am afraid we will lose Maryland Heights,"[37] White took the
occasion to again seek such an assurance. His later summation

to the Harper's Ferry Commission described the very important discussion which ensued.

> Prior to notifying Miles that I should not assume the command, I consulted with him as to his plan of defense, and suggested that Maryland Heights, from its commanding elevation and the heavy battery established there, was the key to the whole position; that it afforded the only feasible route for the escape of the command, should evacuation become necessary, and *ought to be held at all hazards, even if the entire force at his disposal should be required for its defense;* that *Colonel Miles concurred in these views and gave me to understand they would be executed by him.* (Emphasis added.)[38]*

With this assurance that Maryland Heights would be reinforced to whatever extent was necessary to hold it, White now sat down and wrote Miles a letter renouncing his right of command. Miles, understandably delighted, issued a general order accepting "this act of high-toned chivalric generosity,"[39] and promptly departed with his aides, Binney and Willmon, to look into the deteriorating situation on Maryland Heights.

Meanwhile, on Maryland Heights between 10:00 and 10:30 A.M. the decisive action of the day was already occurring. The subsequent Rebel and Union battle reports differ in significant respects. We start with what the Rebels saw, but with a warning that this is an overly simplistic view of what really happened.

Kershaw's basic strategy was to push his own brigade (which had already taken the first [smaller] abatis), south along the crest of Elk Ridge to capture the second (larger) abatis and breastworks behind it, meanwhile sending Barksdale's brigade forward on a parallel course along the steep eastern slope of the

---

*General White's aide, Captain Curtis, testified before the Harper's Ferry Commission that he heard White take such a position with Miles "more than once." WR/OR, series I, vol. XIX, pt. I, p. 687. However, he did not recall Miles's concurrence but thought Miles "appeared to doubt whether holding Maryland Heights would be holding Harper's Ferry" (as ordered). Ibid. Curtis could not recollect when this alleged statement by Miles was made (ibid.), but we are inclined to believe it was made after Maryland Heights was evacuated and the question was whether they should be reoccupied. Whenever it was made, it had to be utterly false, in light of Miles's knowledge of General Cullum's earlier warning "to mainly confine his defense, in case he [Miles] was attacked by superior forces, to the position of Maryland Heights." Frank Moore, *Rebellion Record,* 12 vols. Volumes 1–6, New York: Putnam, 1861–63, Volumes 7–12, New York: Van Nostrand, 1864–68; Volumes 1–12, New York: Arno Press, 1977, 6: 220.

mountain in order to flank the Union defenders and eventually take them in the rear.[40]

About ten o'clock, two of Kershaw's regiments began their advance along the ridge, but they encountered "obstinate resistance."[41] A "fierce fire" at some hundred yards distance resulted in "heavy loss" to the Rebels.[42] Kershaw thereupon ordered another of his regiments (Nance's 3rd North Carolina) to pass through his front line troops and try to carry the breastworks.[43] However, they too were "stoutly resisted," receiving a "deadly volley" from the Union defenders as they (the Rebels) entered forty yards of abatised area.[44] Nance dropped his plan for an immediate bayonet charge and decided, instead, to let the firing continue a while so that he might better fix the enemy's position and force.[45]

By this time Barksdale's troops, laboriously moving south along the east side of the mountain, had reached their desired position in the Union rear but Barksdale could not mount them to the crest of the ridge behind the Union troops without encountering the fire of their own troops on the ridge.[46] Notified of this situation, Kershaw sent an order to Nance to cease fire so that Barksdale could make a demonstration on the east slope.[47] Before this order could be carried out, however, about 10:30 A.M. the union defense line suddenly broke and most of the defenders fled precipitately down the south slope toward McGrath's battery.[48] When Nance ordered a cease-fire it was immediately discovered that the Union works were entirely deserted.[49] Nance promptly moved forward and seized them.[50] Barksdale then proceeded to occupy the signal station ("lookout") south of the breastworks.[51]

Why some seventeen hundred boys in blue fled so precipitately from no more than two thousand boys in gray is the critical question.* Rebel General Kershaw's explanation was simple:

Before this [cease-fire] order was extended, the right company of Colonel Fizer's regiment, Barksdale's brigade, fired

---

*Between them, Kershaw's and Barksdale's brigades had 1041 and 960 men respectively engaged on the Heights. WR/OR, series I, vol. XIX, pt. I, pp. 860–61. The Union units actually on the Heights at the critical moment included 350 men of Ford's own 32nd Ohio (ibid., p. 572); 950 men of Sherrill's 126th New York (ibid., p. 583); and 400 men of Downey's 3rd Maryland (PHB) (ibid., p. 620). Russell's dismounted 1st Maryland Cavalry added a relatively small number to the Union force. (Ibid., p. 727.) The Union strength was thus over seventeen hundred men at its peak.

into a body of the enemy's sharpshooters lodged in the rocks above them, and their whole line broke into a perfect rout, escaping down the mountain sides to their rear.[52]

That most of the Union line broke at about this time is clear, and this no doubt added to the general confusion. However, it is equally clear that the Union defenders of "the breastwork" did *not* give way at this time until they were ordered to retreat[53] (in order to avoid being caught in the projected Kershaw/Barksdale pincer movement.[54] Kershaw's attack along the ridge had already been brought to a standstill and the merest inspection of the steep—almost perpendicular—east slope of the ridge suggests grave doubt that Barksdale's troops, if fairly opposed, could ever have reached the crest of the ridge. We must, therefore, ask why such a disastrous order was even given and who was responsible for it. This requires reference to the Union sources.

As we have already seen from the Rebel battle reports, the Union defense of the "breastworks" undoubtedly went quite well for some time. Captain Russell, the "fighting parson" whose dismounted cavalry were a small but important part of the defense, later testified before the Harper's Ferry Commission:

> The men were holding their ground well then; they were not going at all. The enemy had tried to come up in front three times and we had driven them back.[55]

Nor is there any question that at some point Colonel Sherrill of the 126th New York, who had been courageously but recklessly striding back and forth along the "breastworks" exhorting his troops to withstand the enemy attack, was struck by a Rebel ball that tore off his tongue, so that he was unable to speak.[56] As he was carried, bleeding profusely, from the field of battle, it might not have been surprising for his green troops to have panicked and fled. This was the impression that Major Hewitt, Ford's executive on the hill, later tried to create in his testimony before the Harper's Ferry Commission:

> The most critical moment seemed to be at the time when the Colonel of the 126th was wounded and his men fell back en masse; and it left but very few men at the breastwork; and I sent these instructions forward to have them hold up as long

as possible and if compelled to fall back, why do it in good order. At that same time I was endeavoring to stop these men [of the 126th] and prevent them from leaving.[57]

Hewitt also testified that:

this [order] was [given] at the time the 126th fell back after Colonel Sherrill was wounded. I was back trying to rally those men and I sent forward a Lt. Carnes of our regiment to tell them to hold out as long as possible; but if they were compelled to fall back, if they were overpowered, to fall back in good order. . . .[58]

Careful analysis of the testimony of others, however, makes it clear that it was *not* the wounding of Colonel Sherrill which caused the flight of the 126th from the "breastworks" but that that flight was caused by Hewitt's order—sometime *after* Sherrill's wounding—to abandon the breastworks. Thus Russell's testimony, after describing how the Rebels were driven back three times, continues:

Then, while they were turning our left,[59] our men standing their ground well, there was a cavalier [Lt. Carnes] riding down from the lookout upon his horse, waving his hat and motioning us back. I went to him and asked him what he wanted. He said the order was for us to fall back. I communicated the order to the captains [of the 126th] there. The Colonel of the One hundred and twenty-sixth had been wounded. The major I did not see. . . . I communicated that order and the men fell back. The order was to fall back to the heights [i.e., the lookout] further back on the hill.[60]

The "fighting parson's" version of why the 126th fled the "breastworks" is confirmed by the testimony of Colonel Downey, whose 3rd Maryland (PHB), it will be recalled, had arrived at the lookout just as the second engagement started, and became the second largest unit of the defense. Downey makes it quite clear that it was Hewitt's order which precipitated the flight of the 126th:

I immediately headed my men and took the seven companies in behind this log work. The firing was very brisk and heavy. With the forces I brought we held the enemy. I had no straps on; I was dressed as I am now. I reported to Colonel Sherrill

who I was and said that I had command of the regiment that
had just re-enforced him. He started over toward the left and
I kept my position to the right, perhaps toward the center it
was, and kept walking backward and forward, rallying the
men, getting them up to the breastworks, when an orderly
rode up to the line—the fight had continued some time; I do
not know how long, perhaps a half hour, perhaps three-
quarters—an orderly rode up to the line on a horse; said he,
"The order is to retreat." I turned to him and said, "Who
gives that order?" I understood him to say it was the order of
Colonel Ford. Said I, "Sir, there can be no order to retreat." I
turned to the officers and men, and said, "There certainly
cannot be an order to retreat from this position." Although I
had never been there before, I had looked around and seen
the position of things. I said, "If we lose this position, we lose
everything; we can hold this position unless the enemy press
heavier than they do now." Someone else rode up to the line,
and said, "The order is to retreat." The men commenced
falling back. I turned to the men and said, "For God's sake,
don't fall back; we must hold this position." But they commenced retreating.[61]

The best detail comes—as might be expected—from the
regimental history of the 126th New York, written a half-dozen
years later. Since that book was inevitably an apology for the
126th's often indefensible conduct, it would no doubt be a
mistake to base our understanding of the disaster of Maryland
Heights solely on such a source. Confirmed in its essentials,
however, by the Downey and Russell testimony, just reviewed,
there seems no objection to its use to fill in the details. This
is particularly true since the principal authority to the contrary—Major Hewitt—was the architect of the retreat order
and had every interest in foisting the blame for the disaster off
on the 126th. Here is the way the historian of the 126th
described it:

For sometime [after the start of the second attack] the fire
was very heavy on both sides, and the enemy still kept beyond
the abatis but at length a movement to the left was observed
among them and their fire slackened a little. Colonel Sherrill,
who, from his exposed post on the breastworks observed this,
instantly ordered Captain Phillips, who acted for the time as
Major, to take two companies and deploy them to the left and
rear and meet the enemy's flanking party. . . . Fighting im-

mediately commenced but Companies C and D succeeded in holding their position and completely foiling the enemy in their effort to turn the left flank.[62]

. . . .

The fire, which had slackened at the breastworks, raged again with great fury. Colonel Sherrill, standing on the logs, encouraged his men and directed their fire, regardless of the expostulations of his officers. He was just indignantly replying to their suggestions of his personal danger, when a shot struck him in the face, tearing through both cheeks and wounding the tongue so as to render him speechless. He was borne to the rear but his Regiment only fought more desperately, as if to avenge his loss, and not a thought of retreat entered their minds.

. . . .

The soldiers, . . . inspirited by success, needed no command to maintain their ground; they felt that their position was strong; the enemy had only once attempted to advance beyond the abatis and then had been repulsed; the men, although they had been fighting since daylight, were still vigorous and gaining every moment in steadiness and self possession. . .[63]

It was at this point, however, that the bottom fell out of the defense of Maryland Heights. The regimental history continues:

[A] lieutenant, who gave himself out as acting Aide to Colonel Ford, brought a verbal order to Phillips to withdraw the troops in good order from the breastworks. Phillips declined to give the order. It was not in writing; he did not know the bearer; and it seemed utterly unreasonable. The Lieutenant again gave the order to withdraw the men to the rear of the lookout, as McGrath's battery was about to shell the woods where they were. Captain Phillips, being in command of the left, referred the order to Major Baird who he supposed to be on the right. The bearer in the meantime carried the order to the other troops, who immediately retired from their position, so that the 126th found themselves alone. They then reluctantly fell back to the rear of the lookout.[64]

As to whether the men of the 126th were the first or the last to leave the "breastworks," we express no opinion, because the sources are in conflict, the representative of each unit there generally claiming that the others left first. *But the sequence of leaving would seem to be of little importance, if the defenders left not because of fear of the enemy but because of an order to do so.* The order seemed incomprehensible to most of the defenders: "As we were holding them in check at all points, it was a mystery to all why we should be ordered to fall back, which we did not do until the third order came."[65] *Nonetheless, an order is an order and the important question is not why it was generally obeyed but why it was ever given.* To that we now turn.

Major Hewitt testified twice before the Harper's Ferry Commission. The first time (early in the hearings) he admitted frankly having sent Lieutenant Carnes, of his regiment, forward to order a retreat from the breastworks:

> I sent forward a lieutenant and instructed him to tell the men to fall back gradually and in order.[66]

By the time he testified again (near the end of the hearing), Hewitt was under considerable pressure to clean up his testimony to meet the intervening challenges of Coloney Downey and Captain Russell, both of whom, as we have just seen, had strongly attacked the necessity for Hewitt's retreat order. During his second appearance, therefore, Hewitt backed water. He denied that he had sent Carnes forward to order a retreat, trying to make the order out as conditional and applicable only if there was no alternative:

> There was no positive order in reference to it. . . . [After] Colonel Sherrill was wounded, I was back trying to rally those men [of the 126th] and I sent forward a Lieutenant Carnes of our regiment to tell them to hold out as long as possible; but if they were compelled to fall back, if they were overpowered, to fall back in good order. That was by way of instruction. . . .[67]

That Hewitt's original testimony was the truth is confirmed by those who received the order, all of whom testified to an unconditional order to retreat.[68] (Strangely, Lieutenant Carnes, the man who actually carried the order, although a witness at the behest of Colonel Ford, was never asked about the order.)[69] In any event the very reason for giving the order (i.e., to clear the area for artillery fire) would seem to require an absolute rather than a conditional order. Hewitt's own theory suggests this.

The order to retreat from the breastworks, according to Hewitt, merely carried out a written order which he had received from Miles late the previous afternoon. That order, as we have seen,[70] was to leave a bundle of combustibles on the exposed southeastern point of the mountain (near recently abandoned Sandy Hook) and to ignite it as a signal for Union artillery on both sides of the river to play upon Maryland Heights, in case the defenders thereof should be forced to fall back—but only "after the men were drawn out of the way under cover of these guns."[71] This "beacon" was never ignited; Hewitt testified that he did not know why it was not lighted and noted with puzzlement that even the last order he received (i.e., to evacuate Maryland Heights) contained no order to ignite the beacon.[72] This testimony would seem to imply that Hewitt thought someone else was to give the ignition order, although his own testimony is that Miles's order was directed to him (Hewitt).[73] Be that as it may, neither he nor anyone else apparently ever lighted the beacon.

Nevertheless Hewitt clearly viewed his own Saturday order to fall back and let the artillery shell the breastworks as a mere implementation of Miles's Friday order to fall back and signal for artillery if pressed too hard:

> My reason for it [the order] was that it was in compliance with the order I received [from Colonel Miles] when I went on the mountain.[74] . . . It [the order] was simply instructions in obedience to the orders that I received from Colonel Miles on Friday.[75]

When questioned about Downey's testimony that Hewitt had conceded giving the retreat order, the latter again tied his action to Miles's "combustible" order:

> I referred to those instructions I sent forward in obedience to the orders from Colonel Miles.[76]

All this inference from the record of the Harper's Ferry Commission as to why Hewitt gave such an order is further confirmed by a carefully prepared letter from the officers of the 126th New York to the editors of leading Northern newspapers dated November 11, 1862 (immediately after release of the Commission's report), which stated in part:

> That an order, unnecessary even if not criminal, to abandon the breastworks was given by a member of Colonel Ford's staff to Captain Phillips, who was appointed by our Colonel to the command of our left wing; that the breastworks could have been held, and, in our opinion should have been held, for a long time, if not altogether, by the force there present, and *that the order to abandon them was based upon the ground that the woods were to be shelled by our guns.* (Emphasis added.)[77]

Hewitt's intent to substitute an artillery barrage for an infantry defense of Maryland Heights being thus established, it remains only to ask what emergency seemed to justify such a strategy in Hewitt's mind. Since we have already established that the defenders of the breastworks did not flee until *after* receiving the Carnes retreat order, it was obviously not the flight of the 126th or any other Northern troops which led Hewitt to order the retreat. The reason for the retreat order seems rather to have been that Hewitt, from his vantage point at the lookout (with an assist from Carnes, until just recently a professional scout),[78] panicked when he realized Barksdale's men had made their way south along the steep eastern slope to where they were now in the rear of the Union defense line. Indeed, it may have been the upward Rebel volley credited by McLaws with panicking the Union defenders which, in fact, panicked Hewitt and led him to send Carnes forward with the order to retreat.

Hewitt's voluntary relinquishment of "the breastworks" was obviously a mistake of the first magnitude. *In the first place it was the last easily defensible position on the Heights.* The Rebels had fought their way almost to the lookout—the peak of Maryland Heights—and from there on south it would be literally all downhill for them.[79] Downey had to be right when he pleaded with the troops that if this position was lost, all was lost.[80] *Secondly, the Union defensive position was not that bad.* Even without the blockhouse that Wool had wanted in order to make the position impregnable, "the breastworks" inspired the respect of attacking Rebel Colonel Nance:

> The enemy had made the approach to their well and heavily

constructed breastworks (made of chestnut logs) very
difficult by the felling of timber for the distance of about 40
yards to their front.[81]

*Thirdly and most important, Hewitt's panic reaction to the Rebel
flanking threat was probably unjustified.* It must be remembered
that Barksdale's troops, although now south of the Union
defenders, had yet to climb up to the crest of Elk Ridge; they
were not really in Hewitt's "rear." All Hewitt had to do was to
move some of his sharpshooters south along Elk Ridge and let
them pick off Barksdale's troops below them as the latter
attempted to reach the crest of the mountain. "The east or
Pleasant Valley side," wrote one of the 7th Rhode Island
Cavalry, "was so steep that no works were necessary."[82] Inspection of the steep eastern slope today makes it clear that dispos-
ing of the Rebels as they tried to pull themselves to the top
would have been like shooting fish in a barrel. It is not every
flanking movement which calls for a withdrawal, and this, at
least, was not one.

Such a devastating order might suggest some question about
the loyalty of Major Hewitt and/or Lieutenant Carnes but—
unlike the circumstantial case against Miles—we have been
unable to find any *other* evidence even remotely suggesting that
either of these two Ohioans was disloyal to the Union. The
retreat order must thus be viewed as merely the product of
Hewitt's inexperience and/or incompetence. The question
arises, however, how Hewitt was ever led to make such a
mistake? The answer to that question leads directly back to
Dixon Miles.

As we have seen, it was an order from Miles that first
suggested to Hewitt the probable need to withdraw the Union
defenders on Maryland Heights and the strategy of letting
McGrath's guns play on the evacuated area, if the defenders
should be too hard pressed. The "beacon" ordered by Miles
had made this a very concrete idea, and the evidence shows that
Hewitt took it very seriously. In the interval between the two
engagements atop Maryland Heights on Saturday morning,
Hewitt went to Colonel Sherrill of the 126th New York and
expressly warned him that while he (Sherrill) should hold the
works as long as possible, if necessary he should retreat down
the path on the northwest slope to McGrath's battery and try to
hold that position.[83] Similarly, when Downey's reinforcements

arrived at the lookout, just as the second engagement was starting, Hewitt testified, he ordered Downey to hold a front position "as long as possible" but "if compelled to fall back, to fall back gradually and in order . . . from the west side of the mountain. . . . They could fall back that way with less confusion and with more safety, I judged."[84]

Plainly, Hewitt was mentally committed to retreat from the key position on Maryland Heights even before there was a crucial frontal attack, let alone flank attack. And just as plainly it was Miles's "beacon order" of the previous afternoon which established the pattern of Hewitt's thinking. By telling Hewitt that retreat was virtually inevitable, Miles made it, in fact, inevitable.

17
Maryland Heights: Saturday Afternoon

Once the breastworks and the lookout had fallen to the Rebels, it is fair to say, the bulk of the 126th New York and many others of Ford's troops seem to have lost all organization and discipline. Most of them fled down the wooded south slope of Maryland Heights to the general area of McGrath's artillery. ("I looked on it as a general stampede," the latter later testified.)[1] Some fled on down to the C & O Canal at river level. ("Some of them went clean down below my works, down the side of the hill toward the Canal. They broke in every direction.")[2] Accounts of their wandering aimlessly through the woods in knots of a dozen or more are repeated constantly in the testimony of most of the witnesses before the Harper's Ferry Commission. The testimony of Lieutenant Pearce of the 32nd Ohio was particularly graphic:

> They were running in every direction on Saturday. I was carrying orders to the top of the heights and I met them running and saw them in the bushes and behind trees and rocks and every place else. They appeared to be coming from every direction, most. . . . They were in wild confusion and dismay [disarray?].
>
> . . . .
>
> It continued all the time until we left the heights. We tried to rally them. I took a squad of them up to the top of the heights but we could never get them up to the top of the heights. They scattered in every direction. There were so many paths

132

and by-roads there that there was every opportunity to escape. Nobody could possibly hold them.[3]

Young Colonel Downey told the Commission how those officers of the 126th remaining on the Heights held a council of war and informed him of their conclusion that "the men will not fight."[4] Downey then jumped up on a stump and pleaded with the sullen troops milling about to join him in an effort to retake the lost fortification.[5] The result of his "stump speech" was almost nil, however; only five men stepped forward to volunteer their services and no counterattack materialized.[6]

Most of the Union officers' efforts during the rest of the day were devoted to trying to get the panicked troops back up the hill, where, oddly enough, the Rebels had halted their advance, once the breastwork and lookout were in their hands. When the fleeing Union troops first began showing up in the area of McGrath's battery and Ford's nearby headquarters, Ford ordered Major Hildebrandt's Garibaldians (39th New York), who had been positioned to defend McGrath's guns,[7] to fix bayonets and stop the fleeing troops at any cost.[8] Such measures resulted in sending large numbers of fugitives back up the hill but somehow these groups never managed to reach the "front line" before dissolving again: "We brought them back but in a few moments they came down again; they skedaddled again," Hildebrandt testified.[9] Captain Whittier, on Ford's staff, described similar efforts:

> I discovered the 126th Regiment, New York Volunteers, very visible, in the woods coming down. I heard Colonel Ford order them back and order a guard to be stationed there to send them back. I saw them sent back and saw them crawl in the woods. I afterwards notified a sergeant-major who was there that they were all lying in the woods; that the woods were all full of them; that they did not go up. He went up and tried to get them out but could not get them.
> . . . .
> I tried all I could to get the men back. I told them they must go back; that as we had but few men there, what men we had there must go back. They would not pay any attention to anyone. They were worthless; not worth anything.[10]

It will be recalled that Colonel Miles had just concluded a conference with General White in which the latter renounced command of Harper's Ferry—after impressing Miles with the critical importance of holding Maryland Heights—when a message was received from Ford that he was stampeded.* Miles and his staff quickly got their horses and rode across the pontoon bridge to see what the trouble was.[11] They had little more than reached the canal on the Maryland side of the Potomac when they began to encounter fugitives from the hill. Said Miles:

> "Boys, what are you doing here?" Said they, "We have been ordered to fall back." Said he "By whom?" "By some major," says one. Said Colonel Miles, "There has been no order to give orders to fall back. I have given no order to fall back and no major could get one unless he got it from me."[12]

Miles thereupon detailed an aide, Lieutenant Binney, to fall back and bring up these fugitives to the "front" (if such a term can be thought appropriate). Reaching the area of McGrath's battery and Ford's headquarters, Miles found a great many stragglers there.[13] Again he questioned the men and was told: "We have been ordered to fall back."[14] Again he expressly denied this ("There has been no order to fall back")[15] and this time sent his other aide, Lieutenant Willmon, to

> go up on the hill and reform the 126th and try to get it to the front; and tell every officer and man you see that there is no order given to fall back, but the order is to go to the front immediately and do his duty there to the last.[16]

Willmon spent over an hour trying to bring some kind of order out of the chaos of an estimated five-hundred members of the 126th and some from other units that he found there, largely officerless.[17] After getting them into "some kind of ship-shape" and turning them over to their adjutant Barras to march them to the front, Willmon returned to the Battery area and reported to Miles that he had done all he could but that it was almost an impossible matter to get the men together."[18] To this Miles replied:"Well, damn them, they will run; just what I thought they would do."[19]

*The text reads: "The 126th New York has given way and [is] struggling through the woods—All of our forces are falling back." Although not time-marked, Binney "thought" this was written "early in the forenoon of Saturday before Colonel Miles went on the heights." He recalled that "there was some such note came, but I did not see it." See WR/OR, series I, vol. XIX, pt. I, pp. 546, 760–61.

During the intervening hour Miles, Ford, and Binney had been busying themselves with reprimanding each new group of fugitives (Miles called them "damned scoundrels" whenever he met them)[20] and trying, with sword and pistol, to get them back up the hill.[21] Neither Miles nor Ford, however, made even a gesture to inspect the "front" himself and—most significantly—they jointly concluded *not* to send up to the "front" a new 900-man reinforcing regiment (Colonel Sammon's 115th New York),[22] which had arrived in the battery area sometime after Miles did (probably about noon).[23] The record is clear that the two men consulted about what to do with Sammon's reinforcements,[24] and we must therefore presume that the final responsibility was Miles's. Most of Sammon's regiment was then positioned nearby, just to the left of McGrath's guns, "to protect them and not allow the enemy to outflank us."[25] As it turned out, Sammon later testified, his men hardly heard a shot fired in anger the rest of the day:

I came there near 12 o'clock on Saturday, the day of the evacuation, and was assigned a position in front of McGrath's battery. I saw none of the Federal forces, where they were stationed, and but few of the enemy, very few, indeed. Between 3 and 4 o'clock of the same afternoon I was ordered to retire in good order to Harper's Ferry and did so.[26]

Miles's directive to hold Sammon's relieving regiment at or near McGrath's battery is most significant. Even if it was reasonable to assume that the Rebel capture of the peak of Maryland Heights would soon be followed by a down hill attack on McGrath's battery (which was, of course, the chief prize on the Heights), no such attack had yet developed and a substantial number of the Union defenders (at least 350-400)[27] were still in position on the ridge, about four hundred yards south of the lookout.[28] Since Kershaw and Barksdale together had no more than two-thousand Rebel troops on the mountain at any time,[29] it seems apparent that throwing almost one thousand fresh Union troops up on the ridge at this moment could have changed the situation favorably for the Union—particularly if another eight hundred men in Cameron's 65th Illinois[30] had been brought across the river and thrown into the battle as originally planned.

Note well that we are not conjuring up a purely theoretical

situation. Both Downey and Russell testified that they were urging Miles and Ford to counterattack, although also explaining that they must have reinforcements to do so.[31] Here were the reinforcements, and Miles's directive to *withhold* them from the front is hard to explain in terms of a mere mistake in judgment.

Moreover, it appears from other evidence that the decision not to send the 115th New York on up the hill was merely one facet of a consistent policy by Miles *not* to reinforce the Union defenders of Maryland Heights, contrary both to the instructions received from Halleck's emissary, General Cullum, and also to the urgings of General White (only an hour or two earlier) to make Maryland Heights the principal defense position of the Harper's Ferry complex. This evidence deserves careful attention.

During his hour on Maryland Heights on Saturday, September 13, Miles had a private meeting with Ford in an old house (the Unsell farmhouse)[32] used by the latter as his headquarters. Significantly, Miles ordered everybody else except his aide Binney out of the House;[33] this was obviously a matter of great delicacy. By the time of the Harper's Ferry Commission hearings Miles was dead and Ford, under the evidentiary rules of those days, was refused permission to testify in his own behalf.[34] Binney, possibly believing himself the only one who could testify to this private conversation, testified early during the inquiry that Miles had told Ford how "one regiment skedaddling that way would cause a panic through the whole, unless some stringent means were used to prevent it" and that "it would eventually cause the evacuation of the heights."[35] According to Binney, Miles went on to tell Ford (as he had told McGrath the previous day)[36] that

> if you [Ford]were forced by overwhelming numbers to leave the position, not to do so without spiking the siege guns and rolling them down the hill as far as you could, that the position was not to be abandoned without spiking the guns.[37]

Finally, Binney testified:

> While he[Miles] was there you [Ford] wanted reinforcements and he said he would send them to you if he could spare them from the front.[38]

Note well how the language used by Miles's constant apologist, Binney, accentuates the positive: Binney has Miles directing Ford to spike the big guns only as a remote contingency and Miles will make a real effort to send Ford reinforcements.

Rather different is the subsequent testimony of a surprise witness—an eavesdropper on this conference. Elizabeth Brown was the illiterate but smart and spunky wife of a Winchester, Virginia, carpenter who wanted no part of the Confederacy and, instead, had joined western Maryland's Potomac Home Brigade, where he was now a captain (and would eventually become a lieutenant colonel).[39] The Browns could not have been welcome in secessionist Winchester and an 1883 deposition in her pension file confirms that she stayed with her husband a great deal during his service in the 1st Maryland (PHB) at various places on the B & O Railroad.[40] On the morning of Saturday, September 13, her husband was in command of one of the two companies of the 1st Maryland (PHB) defending Maryland Heights and she was not unreasonably worried about his fate.[41] About noon, from a bedroom on the second floor of the old Unsell house, she peered down through an empty stove hole and listened to Miles's and Ford's secret—or what they no doubt thought were secret—discussions.* Before the Harper's Ferry Commission she later testified:

> I heard Colonel Miles tell you [Ford] that your men would have to fall back to the Ferry; they could not hold the heights; the thing was impossible; the rebel force was too strong. You rose to your feet and swore you would be damned if you could not hold it, provided he would send reinforcements. He said he had sent all he could spare. You were swearing and said that it was a shame that the men should have to give up.
>
> . . . .
>
> That was all I heard. I slipped my gaiters on again and went down stairs after that and picked up what I could carry away with me, when I found I had to leave.

. . . .

*This was "up in Mrs. Buckle's room, where Colonel Ford stayed. I was listening down the stove-hole. There was nothing but a board floor and a tin over the hole, which I lifted up." Asked expressly whether there was anyone else in the room besides Colonel Miles and Colonel Ford, she testified: "No one but their two selves. . . . I could look them right in the face but they did not see me, they were busily engaged." WR/OR, series I, vol. XIX, pt. I, pp. 719–20.

> When I left they were both standing on their feet together. When I got downstairs Colonel Miles was at the door.[42]

Recalled, Binney continued to maintain to the commission that he was present at the Miles-Ford confidential discussions but tried unsuccessfully to smooth over the obvious differences in the tenor of his and Mrs. Brown's testimony: "My evidence is the same as hers exactly; the wording may be a little different but it is the same in substance."[43]

Mrs. Brown's testimony, which has great credibility, clarifies a confused subject remarkably well. Despite a welter of conflicting allegations in the public prints and in other testimony before the commission as to who took the initiative and who took the ultimate responsibility for ordering the Union evacuation of Maryland Heights on Saturday afternoon, Elizabeth Brown's testimony makes it clear that when Miles left Ford's headquarters shortly after noon, both Miles and Ford were in substantial agreement that their troops would be driven from the east side of the Potomac unless they were to be reinforced as Ford demanded, and Miles had told Ford flatly that he (Ford) might as well evacuate because he (Miles) had "sent all he could spare."[44]

Now Miles was telling Ford what before he had constantly implied but had never stated so frankly. Until now he had frequently suggested the thought of ultimate defeat, but always in carefully guarded contingent terms. Hewitt was to light a beacon and fall back—if and when pressed too hard.[45] McGrath was to spike his big guns—if and when he might feel about to be overrun.[46] Binney's testimony would have continued this euphemism: he had Miles telling Ford to leave his position—but still only if and when forced to do so by overwhelming numbers.[47] Now a chance auditor of a confidential talk could strip away the forensic euphemism and the contingency talk, repeating what was actually said:

> I heard Colonel Miles tell you [Ford] that your men would have to fall back to the Ferry; they could not hold the heights; the thing was impossible; the rebel force was too strong. . . .[48]

Now the chips were down and Miles was not leaving evacuation to innuendo. In "consultation" with Ford he had assigned the 115th New York a useless position. He had made it crystal clear to Ford that there would be no further reinforcements. And he had expressly told Ford that he expected him to evacuate Maryland Heights—all without publicly exposing his own dominant role in these critical decisions.

There remained only one more decision necessary to seal the doom of the Union defenders of Maryland Heights. Of the three regiments alerted to go across the river only one, Downey's small 3rd Maryland (PHB), had gotten up the hill in time for any of the fighting. The second (Sammon's 115th New York) had reached the battery area about noon but had been held there by Miles, where it could do no good. The third regiment alerted by Miles for duty on Maryland Heights early Saturday morning but still in bivouac on the Bolivar plateau was Colonel Cameron's 800-man 65th Illinois Infantry.[49] Although the 65th had arrived with White by forced march from Martinsburg only the previous evening, Cameron [50] had had his regiment in readiness all morning waiting for the call to Maryland Heights.[51]

Much to Cameron's surprise, about one o'clock Miles's order was countermanded, Cameron later testified, because Miles "thought we would not be wanted there."[52] Cameron was ordered to report instead to Colonel D'Utassy on the Bolivar Heights front,[53] where Stonewall Jackson's troops were now coming into sight.[54] At the Commission's hearing Cameron was questioned closely about the rationale of the countermand:

Q. When Colonel Miles informed you that obedience to the order to go to Maryland Heights was not necessary, what did you infer from it—that the order had been given to have the heights abandoned?
A. Quite the opposite.
Q. What reason was given that it was not necessary for you to go?
A. He assigned no reason; simply said we would not be wanted there; that it was not necessary I should go.
Q. That was an hour before evacuation?
A. It might be an hour and a half even two hours. . . .[55]

Cameron testified that his men were "disappointed" at not going to Maryland Heights, as had been announced in the morning.[56] They were not the only ones disappointed. About a half-hour after Miles called on Cameron the latter was visited by two much concerned men: General White and Colonel Trimble.[57] Cameron later testified:

> The General asked me if I had got any orders. I said that I had; that I was not going to the heights but was under orders to report to Colonel D'Utassy for service in the First Brigade. General White said that he was very much disappointed; that he thought the regiment could have been used to better purpose elsewhere and he added that it was his intention to have gone with us. I told him that I was anxious to go and asked him to countermand the order. He turned to Colonel Trimble and said that he believed it would be best for him not to do it; that he did not wish to countermand the order. He said he was sorry; that it was not the service that he wished to see the regiment engaged in.[58]

White's reluctance to overrule Miles so soon after publicly relinquishing command of Harper's Ferry is no doubt understandable, but White's weakness at this critical moment in fact put an end to whatever chance there might still have been of holding Maryland Heights.[59] The end was not long in coming.

We have already seen how, during the two to three hours that followed Miles's departure from Maryland Heights, an estimated three hundred fifty to four hundred men held a Union "front line" on the ridge about three hundred fifty to four hundred yards south of the lookout.[60] Both Colonel Downey and Captain Russell, who seem to have carried the burden of leadership of the remaining Union forces, repeatedly sought reinforcements from Ford, but without success. Downey personally rode down the hill to make an appeal to Ford for reinforcements not long after the debacle that resulted from Hewitt's retreat order.[61] Again, after his troops had reached within about four hundred yards of the lookout and driven in the enemy skirmishers, Downey and his major concluded they could advance no farther without reinforcements.[62] Accordingly they sent the adjutant down the hill to tell Ford they must have reinforcements if they were even to hold their existing position and still more reinforcements if they were to retake the lookout.[63]

The action continued in a desultory, seesaw pattern for some time until shortly before the final order to evacuate Maryland Heights, when the Union advance reported that the enemy was massing his troops for an attack.[64] Downey promptly sent that information on to Ford because he "wanted to be prepared for them; they could easily flank us."[65] At the same time his adjutant again reported to Ford that they must have reinforcements to hold their position.[66]

Captain Russell, "the fighting parson," testified to much the same effect. At the commission's hearing Ford questioned him:

> Q. Did you come back off the heights and report to me that with my force it was impossible for me to hold those heights; that they were driving us as they pleased there? During the day, 12 o'clock or 1, when you were wounded and came down, you spoke of the condition of the troops, their running and our small force. Did you speak of the necessity of new re-enforcements?
> A. Yes, sir. I think I asked you the question why Colonel Miles did not send us re-enforcements; that it was impossible for us to hold the heights with the men we had there.[67]

In the end what seems to have triggered Ford's decision to call it quits was a threat—whether real or not is hard to judge—that the whole Union defense would be caught in a pincers movement by Rebels advancing south along both the east and west sides of Elk Ridge. Ford's scout, Carnes, testified: "We were flanked, right and left both; on each side of the mountain."[68] About two o'clock Captain Crumbecker, who commanded Ford's outpost on the southeast point of the mountain, reported to Ford that the Union forces were being flanked by a brigade on the eastern slope of the mountain.[69] It was probably about this time that Ford messaged Miles:

> The enemy are extending their lines from the top of the mountain down to the river.[70]

Shortly thereafter Ford found himself running out of ammunition and sent three times to Harper's Ferry for a supply which Miles eventually sent over, but whether it reached Ford before the evacuation Miles's aide, Binney, could not say.[71] A note from Ford to Miles which apparently accompanied one of his requests for ammunition reveals the extent to which Ford, deprived of all hope by Miles's refusal to reinforce him, was now ready to flee from what must have seemed an impossible situation:

I cannot hold my men. The 126th all run and the 32nd Ohio (are) out of ammunition. *I must leave the Hill unless you direct otherwise.*[72] (Emphasis added.)

Whether Miles ever responded to this and, if so, what the tenor of his response was became the subject of much dispute after the event. There has never been a satisfactory resolution of this issue. For what they are worth, here are the claims.

Colonel Ford claimed that he did receive such a response, in writing, and that it was *a peremptory order from Miles to leave the Heights.*[73] Unfortunately for Ford, he had allegedly lost his copy of this crucial order.[74] Before the commission he tried in vain to get his artillerist, Captain McGrath, to recall the wording of the message from Miles. McGrath, however, had not himself read the alleged order and could remember only that Ford had purported to read him some order said to have come from Miles, to abandon the place and spike the guns, if necessary. The important details McGrath could no longer remember.[75] While we hesitate to attribute much weight to such evidence, its tenor is not inconsistent with the rest of the evidence—except that of Miles's aide, Binney.

Lieutenant Binney claimed that Miles not only sent Ford no such message but, on the contrary, sent Ford *a peremptory order not to leave the Heights.* Although unable to substantiate his claim because he had allegedly sent the post order-book by Adams Express to Camp Parole at Annapolis and never recovered it,[76] Binney purported to recite verbatim the following alleged Saturday afternoon message from Miles to Ford:

"Since I returned to this side, on close inspection I find your position more defensible than it appears when at your station. Covered as it is at all points by the cannon of Camp Hill, you will hold on and can hold on, until the cows' tails drop off."[77]

We have, of course, given careful consideration to Binney's alleged "cows' tails" message but we have concluded that it is almost certainly an unreliable concoction after the event. Consider first the source. We have had occasion here more than once to note the blatant inaccuracy of Binney's retrospective "journal". Moreover, some, at least, of his inaccuracies were clearly not innocent. Thus in a letter to the editor of the Boston

Journal asserting that "the last order he (Ford) had from Col. Miles was a peremptory one to hold the heights," Lieutenant Binney unabashedly promoted himself to "Captain and Aide-de-Camp to Col. D. S. Miles, commanding Division."[78] Significantly, President Lincoln would shortly order dismissal of Binney from the service for "attempting to practice a gross deception on the War Department" (in yet another matter).[79] Anything Binney said is suspect.

Moreover, Binney's claim is quite inconsistent with other, more credible testimony. When General White on Saturday afternoon asked Miles why Maryland Heights had been evacuated, the latter denied giving the evacuation order but conceded that he had given Ford discretionary authority to spike his guns and leave.[80] *In this conversation Miles never even mentioned the alleged "cows' tails" message or any other order not to leave the Heights.*[81] Consequently, we put no more confidence in Binney's "cows' tails" story than in his similar testimony that at the Unsell House Miles had earlier ordered Ford to "hold the heights at all hazards"[82]—a version of the conversation which Mrs. Brown, looking down through her stove-hole in the ceiling, was fortunately able to contradict flatly. It is our considered opinion that no greater reliance should be placed on Binney's "cows' tails" story, which is not supported by any documentary evidence and is inconsistent with the explanation Miles gave White immediately after the evacuation of Maryland Heights.[83]

Whatever the authority on which he acted, about three o'clock in the afternoon of Saturday the thirteenth Colonel Ford issued the following order to his troops:

> You are hereby ordered to fall back to Harper's Ferry in good order. Be careful to do so in good order.[84]

Slowly but "in good order" the Union defenders of Maryland Heights began their march down a road on the west side of the mountain which was invisible to the Rebel forces but extremely visible from Bolivar Heights on the other side of the Potomac River, where Miles happened to be riding at that moment. Standing near him was the Reverend Sylvester Clemens, chaplain of the 115th New York, who later described as follows Miles's dramatic reaction to his first sight of the Union column winding its way down the mountain:

I was standing on Bolivar Heights. Colonel Miles rode up there and halted his horse, perhaps 30 feet from me, and with his glass took a survey of the heights. In his apparent astonishment, as he saw the first movement of the retreat from Maryland Heights, I could give his own language, if necessary. [The judge advocate thereupon instructed the chaplain to "give it."] He exlaimed "God Almighty; what does that mean? They are coming down. Hell and damnation!" He wheeled his horse and rode toward Camp Hill.[85]

Had these exclamations been made by almost anyone else at Harper's Ferry they might well have tended to prove an absence of complicity in the evacuation of Maryland Heights. In the mouth of Dixon Miles, however, they tended strongly to prove exactly the opposite. One who, only three hours ago had warned Ford that he would "have to fall back to the Ferry" could hardly have felt such surprise to see it happen. The proper inference to be drawn from such a performance is thus that Miles could only have been seeking to disguise his own responsibility for the loss of this key position.

The garrison as a whole was visibly shaken, wrote the *Tribune* correspondent:

Officers and men were thunderstruck at the performance and Col. D'Utassy, commanding the first brigade, offered to re-take and hold the position but Col. Miles refused. The evacuation received the merited condemnation of officers and men.[86] Everyone saw that the way for the Rebels was now open: the door locked, it is true, but the key hung outside. . . . While officers and men continued in good spirits and anxious for the fight, it was apparent that the evacuation of the position across the Potomac had made an impression upon them and Saturday night closed upon them, each full of speculation as to what the morrow might bring forth.[87]

At his 1st Brigade headquarters on Saturday night D'Utassy issued a typically flamboyant general order:

Commanders of regiments and batteries will prepare cooked rations for their men and fill all canteens with water tonight. We are entirely surrounded. The only hope we have is in conquering the enemy. Let our watchword and rallying cry then be "victory or death." Regiments will be ready to fall in promptly at 4 A.M. tomorrow, as we shall, in all probability, be attacked at daybreak.[88]

But—surprisingly—the Union garrison at Harper's Ferry would *not* be attacked at daybreak.

18
Strange Interlude

Although Ford's evacuation of Maryland Heights occurred between three and four o'clock in the afternoon of Saturday the thirteenth, it was not until about two o'clock in the afternoon on Sunday the fourteenth—nearly twenty-four hours later—that the Rebels began their bombardment and attack on Bolivar Heights, the western front of the Harper's Ferry complex. This strange delay occurred despite the fact that all three elements of Jackson's task force were in position by Saturday afternoon, and were already more than a day behind Lee's schedule. Moreover, it occurred despite the emergence during this very period of a very serious, originally unanticipated threat from McClellan to the now widely separated elements of Lee's invading army. The threat from McClellan, and particularly from his left wing under Franklin, must be explained.

During the first days of the preceding week McClellan had marched his Army of the Potomac north from Rockville but only very slowly and on a broad front, in order to retain maximum flexibility, so that if necessary he could parry any thrust by Lee toward Washington, Baltimore, or Harrisburg.[1] However, by the time Lee had evacuated Frederick (Wednesday the tenth) McClellan was correctly convinced that neither Washington nor Baltimore was in danger.[2] Accordingly he began stepping up his northward pursuit of the Rebel invaders, most of whom he believed were now heading for Pennsylvania[3] via Hagerstown.[4]

McClellan's main body of troops, under Burnside, occupied Frederick on the evening of Friday the twelfth and turned west over the Catoctin mountains, following the route of the Rebels along the National Road two days earlier. McClellan's left flank under Franklin (positioned closer to the Potomac River) also moved west but from a point farther south than Burnside.[5] A major mission of the left flank was to open communications with Miles's garrison at Harper's Ferry,[6] which, it will be re-called, had just been placed under McClellan's command by Halleck during the afternnon of Friday the twelfth.[7] Ironically, Franklin, the man in immediate charge of relieving Harper's Ferry, had been president of the Court of Inquiry which less than a year earlier had found Miles drunk on duty at Bull Run I.[8] (How, if at all, this may have affected Franklin's tactical decisions in carrying out his mission to relieve Miles we do not know.) Franklin himself was now awaiting a court-martial (along with FitzJohn Porter) on charges by General Pope that McClellan's generals, including Franklin and Porter, had delib-erately failed to come to Pope's rescue at Bull Run II.[9] McClel-lan had convinced Washington, however, that it was essential for him to have Franklin with him during the Maryland Cam-paign, and Franklin was still very much in command of the Army of the Potomac's VI Army Corps.[10]

This was how things stood when, about noon on Saturday the thirteenth, an incredible thing happened. A Union Soldier, bivouacking on a recent Rebel campground outside Frederick, found on the earth, wrapped around three cigars, a copy of Lee's Special Order #191 with a detailed description of exactly how his invading army was to be dispersed in order to effect the capture of Harper's Ferry before proceeding north.[11] The signature of Lee's adjutant general, Chilton, was promptly and positively verified by McClellan's staff,[12] and about three o'clock McClellan's cavalry was ordered to verify that the Rebels had, in fact, followed the routes laid out in Order #191.[13]

McClellan was properly jubilant. Not only was his general idea[14] of Lee's movements confirmed and expanded with the greatest specificity but he was now sure that he had caught Lee in a terrible tactical error and could probably destroy him in detail before Lee could reunite the separate elements of his army.* That McClellan, through his native slowness, ultimately

---

*About midnight McClellan sent Lincoln one of his rare reports: "I think Lee has made a gross mistake and that he will be severely punished for it. The army is in motion as rapidly as possible. I hope for great success if the plans of the rebels remain unchanged ... [and] if my men are equal to the emergency." 37th Cong., 3rd sess., House of Representatives, *Report of the Joint Committee on the Conduct of the War* (1863), p. 485.

failed in the execution of this plan is irrelevant. It was a fabulous opportunity and McClellan did, in fact, make a real effort to capitalize on it.*

About 6:00 P.M. on Saturday, McClellan messaged Franklin the fact of his great find and explained the Rebel's three-pronged pincer movement against Harper's Ferry.[15] He directed Franklin to move as swiftly as possible across the Catoctin Valley and South Mountain in order to come between Lee's forces in the Boonsboro area and McLaws's in Pleasant Valley, destroy McLaws's and relieve Miles, who "the firing shows . . . still holds out."[16] McClellan's message closed by urging upon Franklin "at this important moment, all your intellect and the utmost activity that a general can exercise."[17] At 9:00 P.M. McClellan wisely thought to order his advance cavalry units to "fire occasionally a few artillery shots (even though no enemy be in your front to fire at), so as to let Colonel Miles at Harper's Ferry know that our troops are near him."[18] At 11:00 P.M. McClellan finally got around to letting Halleck in on the action. After explaining that Lee's order to capture the Martinsburg and Harper's Ferry garrisons had accidentally come into his hands "this evening" and that the Union advance had now caught up with the enemy on the Middletown and Harper's Ferry roads, McClellan sent this word:

> The army marches forward early[19] tomorrow morning and will make forced marches to endeavor to relieve Colonel Miles but I fear, unless he makes a stout resistance, we may[20] be too late. A report came in just this moment that Miles was attacked today and repulsed the enemy but I do not know what credit to attach to the statement. I shall do everything in my power to save Miles if he still holds out.[21]

Unless Lee had changed his plans, McClellan concluded, a "severe general engagement" was to be expected on the morrow.**

*Stonewall Jackson's aide, Kyd Douglas, later wrote: "The plans of the Federal Commander were quickly and skillfully made: they threatened the destruction of the Confederate army. Tardy execution and most culpable slowness or incapacity somewhere, prevented General McClellan from reaping the results his fortunate find put in his power. He ought to have driven Lee out of Maryland in pieces. This he did not do." H. Kyd Douglas, *I Rode with Stonewall* (Chapel Hill, N.C.: University of North Carolina Press, 1940; Greenwich, Conn.: Fawcett Publications, Inc., 1966), p. 158.

**Interestingly, this warning was apparently passed on to Clara Barton, who left Washington Sunday morning with a quartermaster's wagon for Harper's Ferry but

Little Mac has been widely criticized for his delay of six hours after finding Lee's Order #191 before sending off the above message to Franklin. However, his Saturday afternoon efforts to make sure that the paper so surprisingly left by one of Lee's commanders in Frederick was not a trap can hardly be called unreasonable. Be that as it may, by the evening of Saturday the thirteenth the responsibility for relieving Harper's Ferry had shifted primarily to the shoulders of Franklin, who promised to start his troops off at 5:30 next morning on a six-mile march across the Catoctin Valley to Crampton's Gap, the key to Pleasant Valley.[22]

It was apparently on the night of Saturday the thirteenth that Lee first realized that the basic assumption on which he had dared to disperse his army (i.e., McClellan's inveterate slowness) had unexpectedly failed.[23] By then Stuart's cavalry were reporting that Burnside's troops were unexpectedly approaching the base of South Mountain and threatening Turner's Gap and Fox's Gap, the keys to the Boonsboro area.[24] It is unclear whether it was on Saturday night or on Sunday morning that Lee received the devastating news from Stuart (reported by a Southern-sympathizing Frederick merchant who happened to be present when the copy of Order #191 was brought to McClellan) that McClellan was now in full possession of Lee's plans.[25] The record is clear, however, that by 10:00 P.M. on the night of Saturday the thirteenth Lee had an intimation of some kind that McClellan was moving faster than expected. An aide messaged McLaws at that hour as follows:

> General Lee directs me to say that, from reports reaching him, he believes the enemy is moving toward Harper's Ferry to relieve the force they have there. You will see, therefore, the necessity of expediting your operations as much as possible. As soon as they are completed, he desires you, unless you receive orders from General Jackson, to move your force as rapidly as possible to Sharpsburg. . . .[26]

This message seems to confirm that while Jackson was in overall charge of the Harper's Ferry task force,[27] nevertheless,

---

failed to reach it in time and was shunted on to Antietam. In her memoirs, she later wrote: "Who it was that whispered hastily on Saturday night, September 13—'Harper's Ferry, not a moment to be lost'—I have never dared to name." W. E. Barton, *The Life of Clara Barton* (Boston/New York: Houghton Mifflin Co., 1922), p. 194.

as late as ten o'clock Saturday night, seven hours after the Union evacuation of Maryland Heights, Lee still viewed McLaws's operation as the principal thrust of the Harper's Ferry expedition. Did Lee still have reason to believe—as he apparently did when he dictated Order #191—that once Maryland Heights was in Rebel hands Miles would now surrender Harper's Ferry?

Be that as it may, McLaws certainly seemed to think he had done all he was supposed to do, once his men had seized the top of the mountain. Once the "lookout" was in Rebel hands, McLaws made no effort at all—and it must have been a *deliberate* neglect—to pursue the defeated and disorganized Yankees downhill or to occupy the forward slope of Maryland Heights, with its great prize, the battery of big naval guns that could command the country for miles around.[28] Indeed, the forward slope *never* was occupied by McLaws, as some of D'Utassy's troops learned late Sunday morning when they returned to Maryland Heights looking to recover some of the guns and ammunition left there during the Saturday afternoon evacuation[29]—and this although something led Jackson early Sunday morning to message McLaws to "move forward until you get complete possession of the Maryland Heights."[30]

We turn then to an intriguing question to which there is no good answer: Was the long delay in the Rebel attack on Harper's Ferry due in some way to the pendency of negotiations between Jackson and Miles? There *is* some circumstantial evidence to that effect but it is ambiguous, as we shall now see.

Two of Miles's fellow Marylanders on Lee's staff (Colonel Bradley T. Johnson of Frederick and Captain H. Kyd Douglas of Shepherdstown) after the war insisted vehemently that there *never* were any surrender talks between Jackson and Miles. Douglas, Jackson's aide, wrote many years later:

> I am not aware that General Jackson made any demand for the surrender of the [Harper's Ferry] garrison and do not believe he did. Nor did he to my knowledge have any communications with the enemy in regard to non-combatants. He knew that at that time all delay was dangerous.[31]

The postwar memoirs of Rebel General Walker, however, raised a serious question about this:

"I never knew whether or not Jackson actually made a formal demand for the surrender of the Federal garrison but *I had his word for it that he intended to do so.* Besides, such a course was in harmony with the humanity of his generous nature and with his constant practice of doing as little harm as possible to non-combatants. (Emphasis added.)[32]

Walker recalled that between 10:30 A.M. and noon on Sunday the fourteenth Jackson had signaled him "substantially the following dispatch":

Harper's Ferry is now completely invested. *I shall summon its commander to surrender. Should he refuse, I shall give him 24 hours to remove the non-combatants and then carry the place by assault.* Do not fire unless forced to. (Emphasis added.)[33]

Shortly after this controversy was aired in the public prints, the War Department turned up a Sunday morning message from Jackson to McLaws time-stamped "7:20 A.M." (a copy of which would logically have gone to Walker, too).[34] This 7:20 A.M. message confirmed Walker's memory that Jackson intended to send in a flag of truce to get out the noncombatants as soon as all Rebel batteries were ready to fire, *if Miles refused to surrender.* The precise wording of this part of the message is as follows:

So soon as you[McLaws] get your batteries all planted, let me know, as I desire, after yourself, Walker and myself have our batteries ready to open, *to send in a flag of truce,* for the purpose of getting out the non-combatants, *should the commanding officer refuse to surrender.* Should we have to attack, let the work be done thoroughly; fire on the houses when necessary. The citizens can keep out of harm's way from your artillery. Demolish the place *if it is occupied by the enemy and does not surrender.* (Emphasis added.)[35]

It will be observed that this message, while confirming Jackson's intent to try to negotiate surrender, is ambiguous as to whether such negotiations, like the proposed evacuation of civilians, would wait until all batteries were ready to fire. It should also be noted that this message does not confirm Walker's memory that the truce of which Jackson was thinking was a 24-hour one. However, the "24 hour" figure might have reached Walker otherwise and it is a little hard to see why Walker had that particular figure in mind unless he had received some communication to such effect from Jackson.*

Further evidence of Jackson's intent to set up surrender negotiations (although not necessarily to give Miles 24 hours) is found in the recently published diary of Jackson's map-maker and confidante, Jed Hotchkiss.[36] Atop Loudon Heights, where he had been sent to help establish Walker's communications with Jackson, on the night of Saturday the thirteenth Hotchkiss wrote: "We slept on the top of the Mt. We have the enemy surrounded and hope to take them tomorrow."[37] Yet on Sunday night Hotchkiss had to write: "Gen. Jackson intended to advance and storm the place today, *after demanding a surrender,* but he did not advance; *why I know not. . . . .* I suppose we will attack them tomorrow, as we are fully prepared."[38] (Emphasis added.)

It can be argued that while Jackson was clearly planning surrender negotiations at 7:20 A.M. on the morning of Sunday the fourteenth, by the very terms of the same 7:20 A.M. message Jackson intended to delay surrender negotiations (as well as the evacuation of civilians) until all batteries were ready to fire, a condition which apparently did not occur until about 2 o'clock Sunday afternoon.[39] By that time, Franklin's Union relief force was audibly battling its way through Crampton's Gap into Pleasant Valley—a good reason not to delay the Rebel bombardment of Harper's Ferry any longer (assuming Jackson understood the import of the firing in Pleasant Valley).** If this was the way it happened, the intended surrender negotiations probably never happened.

However, a careful reading of Jackson's 7:20 A.M. message really leaves it unsure whether Jackson intended to delay surrender negotiations (as distinguished from delaying the pro-

*Walker's memory was later confirmed (as to Jackson's intention to negotiate a surrender and evacuate civilians if a surrender demand be refused) by Walker's adjutant, who was present when the order was received. W. A. Smith, "Stonewall Jackson's Intentions at Harper's Ferry," *Century Magazine* 38 (N.s. 16) (June 1889): 310. The adjutant, however, did not confirm the 24-hour figure and added nothing to resolve the ambiguity referred to in the text.

**Walker stated that from Loudon Heights he could see a major action developing in the Pleasant Valley area but that he could not persuade Jackson it was any more than a minor cavalry action. Walker, "Jackson's Capture of Harper's Ferry," p. 609. Bradley, however, insisted that Jackson was well aware all day Sunday that McClellan's army was suddenly and surprisingly making its appearance. Ibid., p. 616.

posed evacuation of civilians) until all batteries were ready to fire. If Jackson did *not* mean to delay his intended surrender negotiations with Miles until all batteries were ready to fire, such talks could well have occurred anytime Sunday morning or early afternoon. The intent to do an act is legally admissible and ordinarily convincing evidence that such intent was carried out and the act in fact done, absent proof to the contrary.[40] In this case a considerable length of time elapsed between the 7:20 A.M. wire and the Rebel bombardment about 2:00 P.M. It is hard to believe Jackson just sat around, so to speak, during all that time when he (or his emissaries) could have been negotiating with Miles (or his emissaries)—*as Jackson had expressly said was his intention.*

That there had, in fact, been negotiations between Jackson and Miles might also seem to be suggested by a strange remark Miles made to Colonel Cameron of the 65th Illinois, probably around Sunday noon. It must have represented either knowledge from conversations with Rebel officers or unbelievably accurate speculation by Miles that Jackson was thinking in terms of a 24-hour delay to be followed by a Union surrender. Miles's words, as later testified to by Colonel Cameron, were as follows:

> I asked him [Miles] when he supposed the assault would be made upon us. He said he did not believe there was going to be any; that the enemy were not going to throw away their men, as *they knew our condition;* it was *only a matter of a day or so.* (Emphasis added.)[41]

This remark, which was the first of several such statements apparently intended to set the stage for a Monday surrender, seems so close to Jackson's real thinking as to strongly suggest that Miles was privy to the Rebel commander's planning.

Equally important is the fact that both Jackson and Miles were talking about a *24-hour* truce before a surrender on the *morning* of Monday the fifteenth, whereas only the evening before, as we are about to see, Miles had sent McClellan two messages assuring the commanding general that he (Miles) could hold out for 48 hours, i.e., until the *evening* of Monday the fifteenth. Because of this discrepancy as well as because of its own intrinsic importance, we must now review carefully the evidence surrounding Miles's crucially important messages to McClellan.

19
Messages to McClellan

About nine o'clock on the night of Saturday the thirteenth, in the wake of Ford's evacuation of Maryland Heights, Miles called in Captain Charles Russell, the "fighting parson" of the 1st Maryland Cavalry.[1] In the presence of White, Ford, and Davis (commander of the 8th New York Cavalry) Miles gave Russell an oral message for "any general of the United States Army or any telegraph station or, if possible to get to McClellan, whom he [Miles] supposed was at Frederick,"

> to report that he [Miles] thought he could hold out forty-eight hours; that he had subsistence for forty-eight hours; but if he was not relieved in that time he would have to surrender the place.[2]

There was, in fact, no basis for Miles's statement that he could not hold out more than forty-eight hours because his rations would by then be gone. It appears that when the surrender came Monday morning Miles still had another forty-eight hours' rations left[3] and the troops could presumably have lasted a while even after those rations were gone. Since a shortage of rations could not have been the real reason why Miles selected the figure of forty-eight hours, it becomes a critical question why Miles *did* use that figure.

Miles's message to McClellan ("to report that he thought he could hold out forty-eight hours") has usually been thought of as a *warning* that relief must arrive within forty-eight hours in order to be effective. Looked at a little differently, however, it was in effect an *assurance* that relief need *not* arrive for forty-eight hours. *If, as we have just seen, Jackson and Miles were both*

154

thinking in terms of a Monday morning *surrender, an assurance to McClellan that Miles could hold out until Monday* evening *was patently a trap of the worst kind.* Such an assurance—to McClellan and Franklin of all people—must have tended inevitably to relax the sense of urgency needed to rescue the Harper's Ferry garrison. This is precisely what happened.

After getting Miles's message Russell picked nine of his cavalrymen, led them over the Federal pontoon bridge across the Potomac River to the Maryland side and disappeared into the night through enemy-held country: north toward Sharpsburg and then east across South Mountain to the main Union army.[4] By 9:00 A.M. on Sunday the fourteenth Russell was delivering his message to McClellan in person at the latter's headquarters near Frederick.[5]

The great importance attached by McClellan to this message and its assurance of two days grace appears from the dispatch that he promptly (9:00 A.M.) sent back to Washington:

> A courier from Colonel Miles, who left in the night, has just arrived, and says Colonel Miles is surrounded by a large force of the enemy but *thinks he can hold out two days.* . . . If he holds out *today,* I can probably save him. The whole army is moving as rapidly as possible. . . . (Emphasis added.)[6]

Secretary Chase, who visited the War Department on the afternoon of Sunday the fourteenth, emphasized the two days assurance in his diary that night:

> Courier from Miles [presumably Russell] says he [Miles] can hold out *two days* but enemy is in possession of Maryland Heights; McC. hopes *before two days* to relieve Miles. . . . (Emphasis added.)[7]

McClellan then asked if Russell could carry a reply back to Miles at Harper's Ferry, but Russell did not think it could be done (during daylight hours).[8] Accordingly McClellan sent Russell on to Franklin at Crampton's Gap to give that general the benefit of Russell's knowledge of the local terrain and both sides' troop dispositions.[9] Russell arrived on Sunday afternoon while Franklin was still fighting the battle of the gap.[10]

It can hardly be doubted that the knowledge brought by Russell concerning Miles's assurance to McClellan that he could hold out until Monday *evening* must have played a crucial role in Franklin's decision—once his troops had taken Crampton's Gap and debouched into Pleasant Valley by Sunday evening—to give those troops a Sunday night breather just six miles short of Harper's Ferry.* Franklin's decision—a reasonably foreseeable consequence of Miles's assurance that he could hold out until Monday evening—had to be fatal to a garrison which Miles seems to have intended to surrender and in any event *did* surrender on Monday morning.**

We might leave the matter of Miles's message to McClellan in this posture, as did the Harper's Ferry Commission and as most historians of the surrender have done.[11] It is clear, however, that Russell was *not* the only messenger dispatched by Miles to McClellan on the night of Saturday the thirteenth. About midnight Miles sent off a second messenger to McClellan: Captain Henry Cole, commander of the Potomac Home Brigade's cavalry (universally known as "Cole's Cavalry").[12]

Unfortunately we know much less about Cole's actions than we do about Russell's. Whereas Russell told his whole story in detail to the Harper's Ferry Commission, Cole, *though originally subpoenaed to testify,* [13] was for some reason dropped by the judge advocate as a government witness and never testified. Almost all that we know about this second Saturday night mission to McClellan is found in the following extract from the postwar history of Cole's Cavalry:

*"The retreating confederates had formed a defensive line of battle a little further down the valley. Franklin sent out feelers and came to the conclusion that the Confederate position was strong and that he was outnumbered two to one. . . . [He] missed the last possible opportunity to save Harper's Ferry by not following through with his attack. Instead he remained where he had stopped on the night of the 14th . . ." J. V. Murfin, *The Gleam of Bayonets* (New York & London: Thomas Yoseloff, 1965), pp. 183–84. See also E. H. Ripley, "Memories of the Ninth Vermont at the Tragedy of Harper's Ferry, Sept. 15, 1862," in M.O.L.L.U.S., in *Personal Recollections of the War of the Rebellion* (M.O.L.L.U.S., New York Commandery, 1909), 4: 140: "The enemy was driven from the Gap after a three hours fight opening at noon, and Franklin, too easily satisfied with his easy success, rested, and let the enemy make new combinations. . . . We think he should have hurried on that evening."

**Caveat: The assurance that Miles could hold out until Monday evening was certainly not the only factor in Franklin's failure to relieve Harper's Ferry. His later judgment (on Monday morning) that McLaws's smaller force (2,200 vs. Franklin's 6,500 effective strength) seemed too strong to be attacked (W. B. Franklin, "Notes on Crampton's Gap and Antietam," in R. U. Johnson and C. C. Buel, *Battles and Leaders of the Civil War* [1956], 2: 596) must have been one of the worst miscalculations of the war. But that was on Monday morning. The crucial decision (to stop and rest) was made on Sunday night.

It is just and proper that I should mention an incident that occurred during the siege of Harper's Ferry. Colonel Miles desired to communicate with General McClellan, who was then in Middletown [a few miles west of Frederick], Maryland. Miles sent for Major, then Captain Cole and communicated his wishes, as it was necessary to have someone carry this important message who possessed undoubted courage. The message was of too great importance to entrust to one of his men and Colonel Miles stated he desired Major Cole should deliver the dispatch to General McClellan in person. Major Cole left headquarters at midnight and passed through the Rebel lines and safely delivered the message.[14]

It must have been midday on Sunday the fourteenth when Cole reached McClellan, by then at Middletown. Unlike Russell, Cole was willing to try to carry back to Miles a reply from McClellan. *The message that Little Mac felt must get through to Miles was that McClellan was "approaching rapidly and felt confident [he] could relieve the place.* Not content even with this, McClellan also wrote the following letter to Miles and dispatched three copies by three different couriers on different routes:

Colonel: The army is being rapidly concentrated here. We are now attacking the pass on the Hagerstown Road over the Blue Ridge. A column is about attacking the Burkittsville [i.e., Crampton's Gap] and Boonsborough Passes. You may count on our making every effort to relieve you. You may rely upon my speedily accomplishing that object. *Hold out to the last extremity.* If it is possible, reoccupy the Maryland Heights with your whole force. If you can do that, I will certainly be able to relieve you. As the Catoctin Valley is in our possession, you can safely cross the [Potomac] river at Berlin [modern Brunswick] or its vicinity, so far as opposition

---

*WR/OR, series I, vol. XIX, pt. I, p. 45 (McClellan's Official Report, dated August 4, 1863). See also George B. McClellan, *McClellan's Own Story* (New York: C. L. Webster & Co., 1887), pp. 560–61, repeating McClellan's official report almost verbatim. In neither report did McClellan identify either Russell or Cole, and he spoke only of a single "messenger" from Miles, who not only brought Miles's message that "he could hold with certainty two days longer" (McClellan's language) but received McClellan's return message for Miles. Since Russell's testimony before the Harper's Ferry Commission leaves no doubt that he (Russell) declined to carry a return message to Miles, it is apparent that by August 1863 McClellan's memory had mistakenly fused the two messengers (Russell and Cole) into one.

on this side of the river is concerned. *Hold out to the last.*
(Emphasis added.)*

In his official report, written nearly a year later, after reciting
these efforts to get his message through to Miles, McClellan
recalled that he "did not, however, learn that any of these men
succeeded in reaching Harper's Ferry."[15] McClellan's report,
like Russell's testimony before the Harper's Ferry Commission,
thus stopped short of an assertion that Miles was ever made
aware of how near the relieving army really was. *Unlike the
Commission record, however, the later McClellan report makes it clear
that Cole and others were actually dispatched on a return mission to
Miles.* Cole—clearly the most important of these messengers—must have been on his way back to the Ferry when,
about 2:00 P.M. on Sunday the fourteenth, the Rebel bombardment of Harper's Ferry commenced.

*WR/OR, series I, vol. XIX, pt. I, p. 45. One of the three unknown couriers seems to
have been recruited by the noted illustrator, "Porte Crayon" (then on McClellan's staff),
who had local connections. He noted in his diary for Sunday the fourteenth that he was
sent for by the commander in chief, who wished him to find a man "true and reliable to
go to Harper's Ferry to carry a message to Miles." He found one such man. D. H.
Strother, *A Virginia Yankee in the Civil War: The Diaries of David Hunter Strother*, ed. C. D.
Eby (Chapel Hill (North Carolina): University of North Carolina Press, 1961), p. 106.

20
Bolivar Heights: Sunday Afternoon

Strange as it may seem, the second stage of the siege and capture of Harper's Ferry—the bombardment of Bolivar Heights—was begun *not* on orders from Stonewall Jackson but in subtle *contravention* thereof. As early as ten o'clock Sunday morning Jackson had expressly refused Walker permission to commence firing the six rifled pieces which the latter by then had in position.[1] Sometime later Walker warned Jackson: "General McLaws informs me that the enemy [i.e., Franklin's troops] are in his rear and that he can do but little more than he had done," and again pointedly declared that he was "now ready to open."[2] Jackson, however, again refused to be drawn into battle,[3] asserting blandly, in the face of McLaws's and Walker's observations, that the activity they were reporting was probably nothing but "a minor cavalry skirmish."[4] Was the great general really as sanguine about this news as he seemed to be? Or was he stubbornly prolonging Saturday's and Sunday's strange interlude despite these warnings, in the hope of reaching a satisfactory agreement with Miles concerning Harper's Ferry's surrender?

Whatever Jackson was up to, his effort to prolong the strange interlude was eventually frustrated by Walker, who decided to do something that Stonewall Jackson's subordinates almost never did: he subtly disobeyed orders—and got away with it.[5] The only loophole in Jackson's standing instruction allowed Walker to begin firing if he was "forced" to do so.[6] As Walker later told the story, he deliberately ordered some of his troops out into the open in order to draw enemy fire. As soon as he got the reaction he expected, Walker promptly ordered his own artillery into action under the pretext that he was "forced" to do so.[7] The fat was in the fire and soon Jackson's own artillery and McLaws's two guns on Maryland Heights were joining in the fray[8]—but it was none of Jackson's doings.

The Rebel bombardment of Harper's Ferry and Bolivar Heights lasted all Sunday afternoon and well into dusk. Like the Saturday afternoon evacuation of Maryland Heights, Sunday afternoon's bombardment had a tremendous psychological effect on the Harper's Ferry garrison. The regimental histories are replete with accounts of how many of the Yankees, particularly the raw recruits, were panicked by the torrent of shells coming at them from several different directions, as carefully planned by that master artilleryman, Stonewall Jackson. Like Sherrill's 126th New York on Maryland Heights the previous day, Willard's equally green 125th New York on Sunday afternoon fled wildly from their encampment on a plateau east of Bolivar Heights into deep, wooded ravines along the north shore of the Shenandoah River.[9] The New York Times correspondent described this bombardment as "furious fire" and wrote: "Shot and shell flew in every direction and the soldiers and citizens were compelled to take refuge behind rocks, in houses and elsewhere.[10] Miles's aide, Binney, in his retrospective "journal" wrote: "The cannonade is now terrific. The enemy's shot and shell fall in every direction; houses are demolished and detonation among the hills is terrible."[11]

Notwithstanding the undoubted psychological effects of this bombardment, however, the damage done was not really great, as evidenced by the negligible casualties.[12] "Shot and shell flew in every direction but, as is usually the case in such artillery duels," wrote one cavalryman, "less injury was done to life and property than would be expected."[13] Another cavalryman ascribed the fewness of the casualties to the fact that most of the "screaming shells" were of the percussion type which struck in soft mud.* Others present noted the large number of prema-

---

*W. M. Luff, "March of the Cavalry from Harper's Ferry, September 14, 1862," in Military Essays and Recollections (Chicago: M.O.L.L.U.S., Illinois, 1894), 2: 37. Artillerist Graham later testified that he watched 20–30 or more percussion shells land without exploding on Saturday and Sunday. WR/OR, series I, vol. XIX, pt. 1, p. 663. Artillerist Phillips testified to the large number of enemy shells that simply never burst: "They fell all around us, though not one in ten bursted, owing, I suppose, to the shell striking the sandy substance there, choking the fuse. They seemed to use too long a fuse in their shell. . . ." Ibid., p. 686.

ture midair explosions.[14] Finally, there was the considerable distance from Maryland Heights to Bolivar Heights, which slowed the Rebel shells down so much they could be dodged.[15] In short, the Rebel bombardment on Sunday really had little practical effect or importance—with one exception.

That exception was the extent to which Union counter-battery fire dug deeply into Harper's Ferry's ammunition supply. It appears that the Union batteries put out a tremendous volume of fire on both Saturday and Sunday,[16] much if not most of which was a "wicked waste of ammunition," as one young officer put it.[17] It was a waste because in some cases the shells were incapable of reaching the target[18] and in other cases because the target could not even be seen.[19]

Such a "waste of ammunition" is not uncommon, particularly with inexperienced, nervous gun crews, but senior officers are supposed to keep this tendency under control. In his retro-spective "journal" and again before the Harper's Ferry Commission, Miles's aide, Binney, testified that about noon on Sunday the fourteenth Miles "ordered us to save the ammunition unless we saw something to fire at."[20] However it seems probable from the testimony of other witnesses that Miles was prompted to give this order by General White, who had been watching a battery "wasting ammunition" for two hours at targets beyond reach of its guns.[21] White not only corrected the artillerists personally[22] but came to Miles's office to get *him* to stop it.[23] By Sunday night, when the Union artillery officials toted up their remaining ammunition and requisitioned replacements with little success, it was plain that the shortage of ammunition would be a serious problem next day.[24] (It would, in fact, become one of the ostensible reasons for the surrender.)[25] Did Miles's tolerance of this "wicked waste of ammunition" evidence only his gross incompetence? Or did it evidence a deliberate intent on his part to create a condition where surrender would be inevitable?

Not until midafternoon did the Rebel infantry join the artillery in their attack on Bolivar Heights, Miles's key defense line.[26] This was a ridge of high ground, about a mile and a half west of Harper's Ferry, which stretched like a huge dike most of the two miles from the Potomac River on the north to the Shenandoah River on the south. Only at its very north and very south ends did it drop off, leaving narrow but defensible passageways between mountain and river. Its forward slope, up which any invader from the west must fight his way, rose about

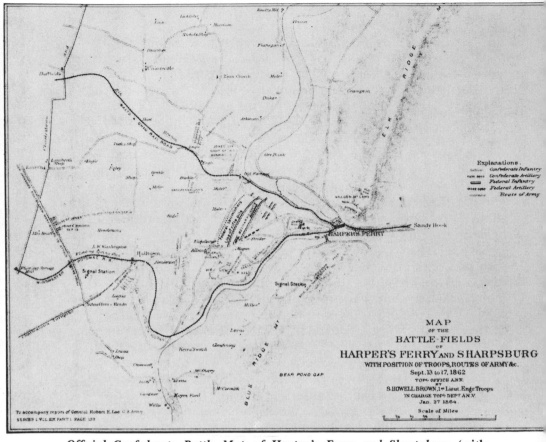

Official Confederate Battle Map of Harper's Ferry and Sharpsburg (with Sharpsburg deleted)

Prepared on 1/27/64 to accompany Lee's report on the Maryland Campaign. (See WR/OR, series, I, vol. IX, pt. I, p. 139.)

two-hundred feet in less than half a mile. Well fortified and properly manned, Bolivar Heights could have posed a very difficult challenge to an attacker from the west.

As we have seen, however, Dixon Miles had concentrated his attention almost entirely on the northern half of the Bolivar Heights line, where a slight earthwork had been constructed to protect the men of the batteries.[27] In this area, from the Potomac to the midpoint of the line (i.e., where the Charlestown Pike [now I-340] crosses Bolivar Heights) Miles had stationed nearly all his infantry and artillery.[28] Even along this northern half of Bolivar Heights he failed to build the effective fortifications that General Wool had ordered in August.[29] However, some of Miles's troops had made up for his deficiency by taking it upon themselves at the last moment to abatis part of the westerly slope (i.e., to cut down its standing timber) and to dig two lines of rifle pits, one along the ridge and another parallel to it and halfway down the western slope.[30] It was no mighty fortress but it was not a bad defense line, either—as far as it went. The real trouble was that (like France's Maginot line in World War II) the Bolivar Heights "fortified" line did not extend far enough.

To guard the rest of Bolivar Heights—the entire half of it south of the Charlestown Pike intersection—as late as mid-afternoon on Sunday the fourteenth Miles had only one of his dozen regiments, Downey's Third Maryland (PHB), assigned to defend this half of the whole.[31] It is true that this southern half of the Heights, which culminates in a circular eminence, called Bull's Hill, is rugged terrain, overgrown with brush and trees, and that the slope of Bull's Hill is much steeper than the slope along the northern half of Bolivar Heights. It is barely possible that an untrained, inexperienced civilian soldier might have thought this part of the line needed no defense. It is inconceivable, however, that a West Point–trained veteran of forty years service, including two wars and a great deal of guerrilla fighting, could have been so blind to elementary tactical considerations as to leave the southern half of his line almost undefended.

Nor, as we shall now see, was there any lack of advice from his lieutenants that something should be done about this gaping hole in the Bolivar Heights defense line. Miles, however, stubbornly insisted that the Bolivar Heights line, which Saxton had already found out the hard way was too long to defend, was going to remain just as it was. Such, for example, was the testimony before the Harper's Ferry Commission of Colonel Trimble of the 60th Ohio, to whom Miles had assigned command of the southern half of Bolivar Heights:

Q. [by General White] Did Colonel Miles ever say to you that the line on [i.e., along] the summit of Bolivar Heights, stretching from the Potomac to the Shenandoah was to be the line which he proposed to defend—the line we occupied?
A. Yes, sir; he told me from the first that was to be the line.
Q. Do you know of its having been suggested to him that that line should be contracted, in order that proper support to the front might be had . . . ?
A. . . .I did hear of others making that suggestion and I suggested to him, myself, that it was so long a line for the number of troops we had, that I did not see how we could defend it, unless there was some effort made to give us the advantage by throwing up breastworks and making rifle pits from the Charlestown Pike to the Shenandoah and [at] Bolivar Heights. Colonel Stannard [of the 9th Vermont, which, with the 60th Ohio, made up Trimble's brigade] and myself had taken every pain the first day I was appointed to command the brigade [Friday, September 5th], to examine the country and see what was necessary for the defense of the left flank, as we thought it a weak point, and it was generally so regarded. We suggested to Colonel Miles the cutting down a belt of forest only about a half-mile from our front, in which the enemy could conceal themselves, and the cutting down also the cornfields between that forest and our front line. *He objected to both.* (Emphasis added)
Q. This was before the siege commenced?
A. Yes, sir.[32]

It further appears that shortly before Trimble took command of this section of the line Captain Powell, Miles's own West Point–trained engineer, had equally unsuccessfully urged him to better prepare for an attack on this vulnerable left flank:

Q. Were any of those things done which were then recommended?
A. No, sir; I spoke of it several times to Colonel Miles, but *he said there was no necessity for doing so.* I even wanted to have the woods cleared off Bolivar Heights but he said it was

unnecessary; that we wanted to keep the woods there to mask what we were doing; whereas, instead of that it was a shelter for an attack on their part. The woods that were cut down on the left of Bolivar Heights was done by the consent of Colonel Miles, after a great deal of persuasion from me and others. If it had not been for that woods being cut down, I think they would have taken that battery [where the Charlestown Pike crosses Bolivar Heights] when they made their attack on the left flank. . . . (Emphasis added.)[33]

General White, too, was much concerned by this hole in the Union defense perimeter. After he returned to Harper's Ferry from Martinsburg on Friday, September 12, he studied the proposed defense line and became convinced that it would be impossible to hold the long, unfortified, and thinly defended southern sector of Bolivar Heights. Sometime Saturday or Sunday he went to Miles's headquarters and, according to Miles's aide, Binney,

proposed to contract the lines, throwing back the left wing into a deep ravine, nearly a quarter of a mile from the left flank of the heights, to the left of the Shenandoah road, going from the Ferry to the Heights . . . [arguing that] he thought by contracting the lines it would make the place more defensible in case of an assault.[34]

The White plan to swing the Union left flank 90° to run southeast to the Shenandoah River (instead of southwest to the river) would have materially shortened the line, and the ravines along White's proposed line would seem to have been easier to defend than the southwestern continuation of the ridge.

Miles, however, "represented that if the enemy should plant a battery on the plateau at Loudon Heights [directly across the Shenandoah River] it would enfilade [White's proposed] position.[35] White argued in reply that if they (the garrison) should await an assault on the heights it would then be impossible to withdraw the line to the ravine."[36] (Binney later added his own opinion that the contracted line would have been more advantageous because it would have been within range of supporting Union artillery positioned on Camp Hill.)[37] Yet the recommendation of White had no more effect on Miles than the recommendations of Trimble and Powell. Miles was determined to "defend" the ridge of Bolivar Heights all the way to Bull's Hill and the Shenandoah River: "That was where he proposed to fight it out in case he was obliged to. . . ."[38]

Miles's tactical decision to "defend" Bolivar Heights (and particularly to "defend" the Bull's Hill area south of the Charlestown Pike) was entirely consistent with most of the other mistakes he made in his "defense" of Harper's Ferry in that, whether intentional or not, such mistakes always seemed to redound to the advantage of the Rebel attackers. Moreover, the fact that he regularly made such mistakes in spite of generally unanimous advice to the contrary eliminates any possibility that his "mistakes" were not deliberate. Finally, we must note a particularly suggestive piece of evidence that defeat may have been as much the *purpose* as the *result* of Miles's insistence on defending the indefensible southern portion of Bolivar Heights.

In the incredibly lax security conditions that existed at Harper's Ferry under the Miles regime,* Stonewall Jackson must no doubt have had some idea of Miles's troop dispositions in any event. As we have already noted, however, it was Miles's surprising custom, at least from the time Lee invaded Maryland[39] until the next to last day of the siege,[40] to release captured Rebels for return to their units through Miles's own front lines, unblindfolded, simply on their signed promises not to reveal whatever they might see of Union troop positions or movements on their way out.[41]

On Friday, September 12, for example, with the Rebels already atop Maryland Heights in force, a group of sixteen paroled Rebel prisoners were sent out of Harper's Ferry *twice*.[42] First they were marched through the Union pickets in *front* of Bolivar Heights' southern sector. After being returned to Miles for a proper pass by suspicious Union sentinels, the Rebels were again marched out, this time by way of a completely unguarded wagon road that ran *around* the southern sector alongside the Shenandoah River, paralleling the tracks of the Winchester and

---

*A Federal Secret Service operative named Lawrence reported to his chief, Col. Lafayette Carlos Baker, about a month after Miles assumed command of Harper's Ferry (April 16, 1862): "There seems to be no authority here. Men of Rebelist [sic] stamp are coming every day into Bolivar and Harper's Ferry, stay and go at pleasure; men that have operated as spies for months are here and ready to go again when they see fit." National Archives, Record Group 153, Congressional Investigation of Subversive Activities (commonly known as "the Turner-Baker Papers"), Baker file, item #14.

Harper's Ferry Railroad.[43] Between these two guided tours the sixteen rebels must have seen virtually everything they should not have seen.[44] With such valuable knowledge of Miles's disastrous troop dispositions thus served up to him on a silver platter, Jackson might be expected to concentrate his attack largely on the ill-defended southern sector of Bolivar Heights around Bull's Hill—and that is exactly where he struck.

Jackson's order of the day on Sunday the fourteenth assigned to his left wing under Jones a feint designed simply to keep Miles's right wing under D'Utassy from joining in any effort to relieve Miles's left wing.[45] Jackson's center, under Lawton, would approach Bolivar Heights from the west along the Charlestown turnpike to occupy the attention of Miles's left wing under Trimble to the extent possible.[46] But the real action—a run around Miles's left end—would belong to Jackson's right, under A. P. Hill, which was to march south from its Saturday night bivouac at Halltown to the little village of Millville, located about a mile down the Shenandoah River.[47] Thence Hill would turn northeast and follow the Winchester and Harper's Ferry Railroad tracks paralleling the river, around the cliffs of Bull's Hill, and "thus turn the enemy's left flank and enter Harper's Ferry."[48]

When A. P. Hill's division reached Bull's Hill he sent two of his brigades (Pender and Archer) northerly up the hill along an old road toward the southern end of Miles's "fortified" defense line.[49] Archer, on the right of the road, became hopelessly entangled in the abatis which Miles had finally permitted Trimble and Powell to cut down on that part of the Bull's Hill area.[50] Indeed, Archer was so thoroughly ensnared that his troops were still cutting their way through this abatis when Miles surrendered next morning.[51] However, Pender's troops, on the other side of the road, were not troubled by any abatis and swiftly fought their way north over Bull's Hill against scattered opposition by Downey's badly outnumbered 3rd Maryland.[52] Realizing he was in serious trouble, Downey called on Trimble for reinforcements.[53] Unable to locate Miles at this critical moment, Trimble's messenger finally found White, who quickly joined Trimble in personal charge of the southern sector.[54] The 125th New York, huddled in their ravine, were still too panic-stricken by the Rebel bombardment from Loudon Heights to be of help.[55] However, White promptly ordered

Stannard's 9th Vermont and later Ford's 32nd Ohio to join the defense of Downey's sector.[56] What happened thereafter depends on which battle report one reads.

According to Rebel General Pender's account,[57] his advance had penetrated to within about 60 (150?)[58] yards of Rigby's key Union battery (at the point where the Charlestown Pike crosses Bolivar Heights) before he (Pender) caught up with his own troops. Knowing that no other Rebel units were within supporting distance, according to his own report Pender promptly ordered his brigade to fall back to a position 400 yards south of the south end of the "fortified" part of the Union line.[59] In contrast, the Union version, while agreeing that the Rebels had almost reached the main Union line before stopping about dusk, denied that the Rebel pullback from that advance position was voluntary.

According to the historian of the nearby 115th New York, the Rebels had reached far enough north to make a "desperate bayonet charge" on Rigby's Indiana battery (at the point where the Charlestown Pike crosses Bolivar Heights):

> The gallant Captain [Rigby] saw them stealing up and quickly ordered the guns to be double-shotted with grape and canister. He then mounted one of the pieces and, with swinging sword, cautioned his men not to fire until the whites of their eyes could be seen.
>
> The command to fire was given and executed. The awful storm of iron swept like a dreadful tornado through the enemy's ranks. When the smoke of battle lifted, swaths of rebel dead and wounded lay on the ground; while their comrades, uninjured, were hurrying from the field of carnage.[60]

The *New York Times* correspondent confirmed that "an attempt to storm Rigby's battery about 8 o'clock, which did fearful execution, signally failed."[61] General White's official battle report told how A. P. Hill's late afternoon assault on "the extreme left" was made "with great spirit . . . the firing being very sharp and the troops involved behaving very handsomely, when the enemy was repulsed."[62] And Binney's report (after Miles's death) told of Pender's attempt to turn the Union flank, "which move Brig. Gen. White shrewdly anticipates and repels with much slaughter."[63]

The unanimity of the Northern sources on this point

suggests that Pender's 250-yard withdrawal from his troops' most advanced position in the late Sunday afternoon fighting was something less than voluntary. Even so, however, Pender was still in control of most of the Bull's Hill area, and as soon as night fell A. P. Hill began moving artillery onto a little knoll behind Pender's troops for use when the attack would resume next morning.[64] It is thus clear that Rigby's late afternoon success in stopping Pender was not enough; there should have been an immediate follow-through to drive Pender's troops right off Bull's Hill. But that would have required more troops and White apparently realized this, as what followed made plain.

Back in the trenches on Camp Hill, right above the village of Harper's Ferry, was Ward's 12th New York Militia. Camp Hill, as we have seen, was strictly an interior defense position. Functionally the 12th New York was merely a reserve force. And the preferred use of a reserve is not to retrieve a defeat but to exploit a success. In accord with this elementary rule of military tactics, White now correctly ordered the 12th New York forward to join the Sunday afternoon counterattack on Pender.[65] What happened the regimental historian later described as follows:

> On the following Sunday the command was ordered to the front and attack the enemy. Every man in the regiment seemed electrified at the thought of having a hand-to-hand fight with the foe.
> The Regiment formed with the greatest promptness and forthwith proceeded to Bolivar Heights. On reaching there the 12th found the other regiments in great confusion. But it marched on till it came within musket shot of a Confederate regiment in ambuscade. They reserved their fire, expecting that the 12th had been ordered up to clear them out.
> Just as the Twelfth was about to charge on the rebels, Colonel Miles' orderly rode up in hot haste and ordered it to return immediately to Camp Hill. It seems the Regiment had been sent out by mistake, at which Colonel Miles manifested great indignation.[66]

That the 12th New York was *not* sent out "by mistake" was made crystal clear in General White's amended battle report, wherein he took full responsibility for ordering that regiment up to the left front on Sunday afternoon but explained that "it was ordered back by Colonel Miles, as I am informed, on the ground that Camp Hill must be held by a part of our force."[67] White then commented simply: "This position [Camp Hill] was protected on all sides by our outer lines."[68] Miles's affirmative act recalling the 12th New York to "protect" an interior position just as the 12th was about to try for what could have been the first Union success of the day is so totally foreign to any reasonable exercise in military science that it cannot be explained by mere incompetence or emotional stress. Like Miles's deliberate refusal to fortify and defend the southwest sector of Bolivar Heights, his active intervention to stop White from exploiting a Union success there suggests that Miles's real concern was to ensure not victory but defeat.

The arrival of dusk did not prevent continued maneuvers by Hill's other brigadiers to reach good springboard positions for next morning's assault on Bolivar Heights. While Pender and Archer had peeled off from A. P. Hill's line of march to climb Bull's Hill, Branch and Gregg had continued down the left bank of the Shenandoah to the foot of deep ravines *behind* the Union position.[69] Held at bay for several hours where the passage between ravine and river was uncomfortably narrow,[70] it was well into the night before Branch and Gregg finally scaled their assigned heights.[71]

That the Rebels managed to fight their way up the steep slopes of the ravines along the Shenandoah River was probably as much a tribute to Union disorganization as to Rebel valor. After the war the historian of Gregg's Brigade wrote:

> Why we were allowed to climb the precipitous heights I never could understand. A handful of the enemy could have beaten back an army here, for it was so steep that a man could hardly carry his arms up it. And they [the Union defenders] had night to assist them also.[72]

This phenomenon might have been more readily understood if the Rebel historian had had access to a Union captain's description of the confusion among the defenders:

> We [the 9th Vermont] held the line in the woods with some little fighting until about 9 o'clock in inky blackness. My Company B, on the extreme left flank, was deployed down the side of the bluffs overhanging the river and railroad. As I was in a measure isolated in the darkness, the company [of

the 125th New York] connecting my right to the main line had orders to keep up a careful contact with me. After a while the firing seemed to drop back, as though our line had given way and I heard great confusion. Creeping carefully up I found myself among the advancing rebels and our line gone. I slipped back and whispered to my men to slide silently down the slope. This was safely done and we made our way back to the new line after we were supposed to be captured.[73]

It is important to note, however, that the ultimate success of Gregg and Branch in reaching positions in the rear of the Union line could not have been appreciated at dusk—Gregg and Branch then being, in fact, stalled at river level. Archer was still trying fruitlessly to work his way through a partial abatis on Bull's Hill. Pender, in the last fighting of the afternoon, had just been forced to retreat from his most advanced position (although saved from further retreat by Miles's intervention). It is plain that the tactical situation from the Rebel viewpoint at eight o'clock Sunday night was neither better nor worse than when Walker had fired the first Rebel shell some six hours earlier. The subsequent battle report of A. P. Hill, boasting that with Pender's seizure of Bull's Hill "the fate of Harper's Ferry was sealed,"[74] is probably not correct and it is 20–20 hindsight at best. In light of the tactical situation as it actually existed about 8:00 P.M., an exchange of messages between Lee and Jackson about that time takes on considerable interest.

Shortly before 8:15 P.M. Jackson received a message from Lee (now lost) "respecting the movements of the enemy, and the importance of concentration."[75] The "movements of the enemy" to which this message referred had to be the eminently successful Sunday afternoon assaults by McClellan's forces on South Mountain—Burnside almost atop Turner's Gap (the National Road) and Franklin, a few miles south, over Crampton's Gap. Both engagements had been Rebel disasters and the Rebel position in Maryland suddenly appeared desperate, forcing Lee to call for the immediate reconcentration of his now widely scattered forces. Inglorious retreat to Virginia seemed the only Rebel alternative, as indicated by this urgent message Lee sent to McLaws about 8:00 P.M.:

The day has gone against us and this army will go by Sharpsburg and cross the river. It is necessary for you to abandon your position tonight. Send your trains not required on the road to cross the river. Your troops you must have well in hand to unite with this command, which will retire by Sharpsburg. Send forward officers to explore the way; ascertain the best crossing of the Potomac and if you can find any between you and Shepherdstown leave Shepherdstown Ford for this command. . .[76]

It was apparently in response to a similar dispatch from Lee to Jackson that the latter, at 8:15 P.M., sent off to Lee a message which seems a good deal more optimistic than the objective facts of the situation at Harper's Ferry would really seem to have justified as of dusk on Sunday the fourteenth:

Through God's blessing, the advance, which commenced this evening, has been successful thus far, and *I look to Him for complete success tomorrow.* The advance has been directed to be resumed at dawn tomorrow morning. . . . (Emphasis added.)[77]

Of course Jackson had obvious reason to want to complete the exercise in which he was then engaged, but eminent authority agrees that the great general was the kind of man who "characteristically refrained from incautious promises."[78] If we accordingly assume that Jackson really believed what he was telling Lee and if the objective facts of the situation hardly seem to justify such optimism, this suggests that Jackson must have known more than he wanted to say in explanation of his optimism. Finally, we cannot disregard the possibility that the words "I look to Him for complete success tomorrow" were, in fact, Jackson's prearranged assurance to Lee that Miles could still be relied on to deliver up Harper's Ferry on the morrow.[79] Unlikely though such a possibility might have seemed on Sunday night, the events of Monday morning would provide striking confirmation that such a speculation *could* have hit close to home.

21

The Brink of Disaster

The events of Sunday afternoon had demonstrated graphically the ways in which Miles would manage to lose the Battle of Bolivar Heights. The events of Sunday night demonstrated with equal clarity his vigilance, if only partial success, in making sure that neither his cavalry and their 1,500 fine horses—which Jackson himself deemed the chief prize of Harper's Ferry[1]—nor any of the rest of the garrison should manage to escape the trap in which they now found themselves.

As early as the preceding (Saturday) evening, following the evacuation of Maryland Heights, a dashing young West Pointer, Colonel Benjamin F. ("Grimes") Davis[2] of the 8th New York Cavalry, thought he had persuaded Miles to let the Union cavalry try to break out of the now surrounded camp, ford the Shenandoah River about a half mile above the village of Harper's Ferry, and escape eastward at river level around the base of Loudon Heights, whence they would race down the south bank of the Potomac River to Washington.[3] After all arrangements had been settled, however, Miles had rescinded his permission on the ground that potholes in the river made a cavalry crossing "impracticable."[4]

The same question arose again late Sunday afternoon because the cavalry was particularly vulnerable to the Rebel bombardment, yet seemed to serve little purpose in remaining at Harper's Ferry. That afternoon a breakout through the enemy lines was discussed by most of the cavalry unit commanders, who unanimously agreed on its feasibility and appointed a committee led by Davis to obtain official consent.[5] White's approval was successfully sought and he accompanied Davis and another officer to Miles's office,[6] where Davis made his argument to Miles. According to Miles's aide, Binney:

> Colonel Davis represented that the cavalry was of no use there and if we were obliged to surrender the place eventually, they would be as great a prize as the enemy could get. . . .[7]

While Binney's testimony before the Harper's Ferry Commission minimized mention of Miles's initial opposition to what would eventually prove an extremely successful venture, we know from postwar sources that:

> Colonel Miles was at first opposed to the movement, deeming it impractical and involving too much risk; but after consulting with General White and other officers he finally promised his consent, if a practical route could be found.[8]

Colonel Voss of Illinois, the nominal cavalry commander, later described Miles's opposition rather more strongly:

> At first he [Miles] would not listen to such a proposition at all, denouncing it as wild and impracticable, perilling the lives of the whole command; but finally yielded and assented to the expedition.[9]

A Rhode Island cavalryman wrote similarly:

> Col. Miles was strongly opposed to the project, pronouncing it extremely hazardous, if not impossible, and saying that "he would not be justified in giving his consent to a movement which would almost inevitably result in serious loss to the government." The almost inevitable certainty that these troops would be captured, with the rest of the garrison, if they remained at Harper's Ferry, was urged by the cavalry officers as a reason for attempting to escape and at length Col. Miles was induced to give his consent to the proposed plan.[10]

Miles's "consent" may also have been extracted in part by Davis's warning in no uncertain terms that he was going to take his men out with or without Miles's approval.[11]

After approval of the project in principle, Miles switched tactics and called a meeting of all the cavalry leaders in his office about 7:00 or 7:30 P.M. to pick the best route.[12] According to Binney:

> There was considerable disputing as to the road they should take. Colonel Davis represented that he wanted to go up on the western side of the Potomac as far as Kearneysville, and then cross the [Potomac] river at Shepherdstown. Colonel Miles represented that there was extreme danger in their going that way. He and Colonel Davis had considerable talk about it, until finally Colonel Miles issued an order directing them to go across the pontoon bridge [over the Potomac at Harper's Ferry], then go up the Maryland side and take the Sharpsburg route, which they did.[13]

Once the decision was made, Miles issued a written order for the cavalry to leave Harper's Ferry at 8:00 P.M.[14] Although stating generally that "no other instructions can be given to the Commander [Voss] than to force his way through the enemy's lines and join our own army,"[15] Miles did pin down in writing—surprisingly from a security viewpoint—the route which he had insisted be taken: "crossing the Potomac over the pontoon bridge and taking the Sharpsburg road."[16] Meanwhile, none but the cavalry were to know of the planned escape.[17]

Between 8:30 and 10:30 that Sunday night[18] 1,500 Union cavalrymen rode off over the Potomac pontoon bridge in column of twos, into a pitch black night for a Hollywood-style gallop through some fifty miles of Confederate-occupied territory—capturing forty wagons of Longstreet's ammunition train in the process—before safely reaching Union-held Greencastle, just across the Pennsylvania border, about nine o'clock next morning.

While numerous Rebel pickets were encountered and avoided or disposed of one way or another, in only one place was there anything that might be thought a prepared opposition. That was at Sharpsburg, the town Miles had been so insistent must be included in their escape route. There a "sheet of flame," apparently from massed troops, met the first Union arrivals:

> Suddenly a sheet of flame illumined the darkness for an instant, followed by the report of at least a hundred rifles sending their leaden message about our ears. This came from

a strong outpost placed at the entrance of the Hagerstown Road into the City of Sharpsburg, not more than 150 paces ahead of us, furnishing the most conclusive proof that the rebels were in strong force in that direction. Before allowing the alarm to spread, the head of the column was turned in another direction, towards Falling Waters on the Potomac, to find, if possible, a weaker point to pierce their lines.[19]

The quick reaction of Davis and his scout, Tom Noakes, to desert Miles's enforced route through Sharpsburg undoubtedly saved the Union cavalry; the few shells sent after them in the darkness did them no damage.[20]

Once clear of Sharpsburg, there were no more serious encounters. Indeed, as just noted, near Hagerstown as dawn was breaking, Davis's men, in the best Hollywood tradition, actually stumbled onto a sixty-wagon supply train of Rebel General Longstreet and successfully "re-directed" forty wagons loaded with ammunition to the North instead of the South—one of the most colorful Northern exploits of the whole war.[21]

Without regard to how much significance should be attached to Miles's insistence that the cavalry take the Sharpsburg route,[22] it is clear that Miles's original resistance to *any* effort to spring the cavalry from this trap is quite significant for present purposes. No useful purpose could have been served by holding the cavalry in Harper's Ferry, and the capture of 1,500 horses by Jackson next day would have been an invaluable addition to his cavalry. For the Union cavalry there was everything to gain and nothing to lose by making the effort to escape. The brutal fact is that there was only one logical reason for Miles's opposition to the escape of his cavalry: to ensure that when Jackson opened the henhouse door an important portion of the chickens had not already flown the coop. But that was a Rebel goal, not a Union goal.

While Miles's opposition to the escape of his own cavalry is important evidence against his loyalty, it is as nothing compared to a simultaneous event of the most damning character, to which we must now turn. It will be recalled that shortly after noon on Sunday, General McClellan had persuaded Captain Cole to try to make his way back to Harper's Ferry, if possible, to give Miles McClellan's crucial message that he was "approaching rapidly and felt confident [he] could relieve the place."[23] It can be assumed that a daylight ride the dozen miles from Middletown to Harper's Ferry, while more dangerous than a night ride, would take somewhat less time. From the fact that no mention is made of Cole's presence in any account of Miles's 7:00-7:30 P.M. meeting with his cavalry officers,[24] we may postulate that Cole had not yet returned by then.

We know, however, that Cole did return—and therefore presumably delivered the message to Miles which was the whole raison d'etre for his extremely dangerous ride—sometime before the departure of Cole's Cavalry from Harper's Ferry about 10:00 P.M.[25] Sunday. We know this with certainty because the post–Civil War history of Cole's Cavalry (not published until 1895 and not reprinted until 1970) *expressly so states:*

> . . . General McClellan personally thanked Major Cole and sent him back with a reply to Colonel Miles at Harper's Ferry, *where he arrived in due time to take his command and other cavalry out of the besieged garrison.* (Emphasis added.)[26]

Other passages of this regimental history reaffirm that Cole was back with his troops when they left Harper's Ferry that night,[27] and Cole personally endorsed the accuracy of the history.[28] It is thus clear from the passage just quoted—and confirmed by Cole himself—despite the deliberate failure of the anti-McClellan Harper's Ferry Commission to subpoena Cole as a witness,[29] that he must have reached Harper's Ferry and given Miles the crucial message from McClellan sometime between 7:30 and 10:00 P.M.—shortly thereafter riding off with the cavalry as it escaped from Harper's Ferry.

Whatever the military merits of George B. McClellan (and they have been debated for over a century), no one has ever questioned the strength of his hold on the hearts and minds of his soldiers, to whom he seemed a demigod.[30] The news that the Army of the Potomac was "approaching rapidly" and that Little Mac "felt confident [he] could relieve the place" could well have revitalized the morale of the sorely pressed Union garrison at Harper's Ferry. Instead of announcing this news to his officers and men, however, Dixon Miles did all that Stonewall Jackson could have asked under the circumstances. *Cole having quickly and conveniently departed with the Cavalry, Miles simply kept the crucial message entirely to himself.* Miles's aide Binney, for example, testified before the Harper's Ferry Commission that he had never heard anything of either Russell or Cole after they left on their missions to McClellan and stated flatly: "They never came back again."[25] Miles's omission to reveal his message from McClellan, as distinguished from various others of his acts and omissions, was utterly unambiguous: it could *only* have been the act of a traitor.

Indeed, McClellan's unexpectedly swift approach, making it advisable not to await Monday evening before surrendering, as planned, now evoked another suspicious act on Miles's part. The Washington *Star* later reported that *"during Sunday night, after the firing had ceased,* Col. Miles announced his intention of surrendering next morning by 9 o'clock if assistance did not arrive . . ."* (emphasis added).[32] From this evidence we infer that Miles's pronouncement was made *after* dusk Sunday night, when the firing had ceased. On the other hand, it appears that the pronouncement was made *before* the cavalry left Harper's Ferry (because the cavalry leaders apparently knew of this pronouncement when they reached Greencastle, Pennsylvania, on Monday morning).[33]

Since the timing of Miles's shift from a Monday *evening* to a Monday *morning* surrender plan coincides so closely with Captain Cole's brief return to Harper's Ferry, it seems a fair inference that it was Cole's return which triggered Miles's change of plan. To put it simply: when Miles was suddenly and unexpectedly faced with the prospect of relief by McClellan, his immediate reaction was to *change his own surrender schedule to beat McClellan's relief schedule.* Stonewall Jackson could have asked for no more.

As might be expected, circulating rumors of probable surrender next morning and the news that the cavalry had already left Harper's Ferry not only decimated morale but prompted all sorts of similar last-minute escape proposals for the infantry and artillery, ranging from the reoccupation of Maryland Heights to a dash down the Potomac toward Washington. In every case Miles was able to beat back these threats to his plans—but with a logic that will not withstand analysis.

Miles had correctly taken the position that he had received standing orders (before communications with Baltimore and Washington were broken) to hold Harper's Ferry to "the last extremity" (Wool)[34] and "the latest moment" (Halleck).[35] This much was true but Miles also took an absurdly strict-constructionist viewpoint that "Harper's Ferry" did not include Maryland Heights.[36]

Whatever the abstract merits of Miles's logic—and his West Point–trained engineer testified that there was no logic to it[37]—Miles knew perfectly well from his preinvasion conversation with Halleck's chief of staff (General Cullum) that the high command in Washington deemed Maryland Heights not only a part but *the most important part* of the Harper's Ferry defense complex and that Miles should, in fact, "mainly confine his defense, in case he was attacked by superior forces, to the position of Maryland Heights."[38] Moreover, it is not impossible that one or more of McClellan's three couriers other than Cole somehow managed to get through the Rebel lines and deliver McClellan's written message. (If Miles concealed one, he probably concealed any others.) In such case Miles knew that McClellan, too, wanted him to "re-occupy Maryland Heights with his whole force."[39] Be that as it may, Miles knew from Cullum, at least, that the general-in-chief would have no objection to his reoccupying the heights to which Cullum had instructed Miles to "mainly confine himself." Miles's transparent effort to stymie any escape of his troops to Maryland Heights by a ridiculously strict construction of what constituted "Harper's Ferry" is a significant circumstance in this case.

Rather different considerations must govern, however, in assessing Miles's similar recourse to the same orders (to hold Harper's Ferry "to the last extremity" and "to the latest moment") for the different purpose of beating back more general proposals to escape in any direction (i.e., without reference to reoccupying Maryland Heights). There was persuasive testimony before the Harper's Ferry Commission by Colonel Davis, who led the cavalry escape,[40] and scout Noakes, who guided it,[41] that it would have been almost impossible for the infantry and artillery to have accompanied the cavalry or even to have taken the same route at a lesser pace.

On the other hand, young Captain (later Brigadier General) Ripley of the Ninth Vermont thought it might have been practical to swing the Harper's Ferry pontoon bridge* from the

---

*Although Miles first ordered the pontoon bridge to Maryland destroyed as soon as the last cavalryman had made it across (WR/OR, series I, vol. XIX, pt. I, p. 558), he thereafter countermanded his own order, ibid., and the bridge remained intact, ready for McLaws's use in escaping from his trap in Pleasant Valley on Monday after Miles surrendered Harper's Ferry. Miles's unexplained decision to maintain the pontoon bridge intact may well have been the second most important aid—knowing or not—that he rendered the Rebels during the entire siege of Harper's Ferry.

Potomac River to the Shenandoah River, dispose of Rebel General Walker's guard at the base of Loudon Heights (Walker had only 4,000 troops, *in toto*) and then make a forced march downriver toward Washington, D.C.[42] Walker himself agreed that "it would have been practicable for Colonel Miles to have escaped with the infantry of his garrison during the night of the 14th–15th. . . . "[43] Colonel Trimble made it clear to the Harper's Ferry Commission that there was widespread support as early as Sunday afternoon for such a tactic:

> We had no knowledge at all of the position of the enemy. It would have been venturing upon blind chance. But if Colonel Miles had consented to it or listened to the proposition and held a military consultation, I believe that nine tenths of the officers would have voted for venturing the attempt to cut our way out; that was the feeling. I know it was my own feeling. I asked Colonel Miles at 2:30 [p.m.] Sunday whether we had not better attempt to fight our way out in some direction. He said *'No, he could not listen to any such proposition; he was ordered to hold Harper's Ferry at all hazards.* (Emphasis added.)[44]

Viewed in a vacuum, Miles's repeated Sunday night refusals to let the garrison cut their way out in some direction[45] would hardly seem suspicious; they might even be deemed the mark of a loyal and courageous commander. It is also true that there was, of course, room for the exercise of discretion as to whether "the last extremity" referred to in all Miles's orders was really at hand. *However, Miles could not have it both ways.* His surrender early Monday morning was fundamentally inconsistent with his refusal to consider letting the garrison "cut its way out" just the previous (Sunday) night. It casts serious doubt on the good faith of his purported adherence to his orders. Like his refusal even to consider the reoccupation of Maryland Heights, his successful prevention of a general escape into the night looks much more like the implementation of a Rebel goal than a faithful adherence to his own superiors' orders.

The implications of Miles's strange reactions and orders were not lost on his men. While they obviously did not then know enough to appreciate fully the real import of his specific acts and omissions, an aura of widespread mistrust—not merely of his competence but of his loyalty—now pervaded at least the lower echelons of the Harper's Ferry garrison.[46] Such mistrust found its most striking expression in an unofficial Sunday night council of war among regimental commanders defending the southern sector of the Bolivar Heights line, which had thus far suffered much more from Miles's misfeasance than had the northern sector.

Colonel George Willard was the commander of the 125th New York Infantry, the raw recruits who had panicked so badly and fled to the ravines above the Shenandoah River when the Rebel bombardment started that afternoon.[47] They had thereafter done a very poor job of trying to stop Gregg's and Branch's Rebel brigades as both scaled those steep ravines to the open plateau behind the main Union line about 9:00 P.M.[48] Now Willard could see and hear the Rebels erecting new batteries on a plateau just across the Shenandoah River (half way up Loudon Heights) from which to enfilade the Union defense line.[49]

By 11:00 P.M., Willard later told the Harper's Ferry Commission, he felt

> that our position was exceedingly desperate; that the line was very extended; so far as I could judge, but a thin deployed line of men on our left. The battery on Bolivar Heights, the earthwork, was of a very simple character. There was nothing to defend us in front [of the main line]: the trees had not been felled; there were no rifle pits and other things and the knowledge that I had that the enemy were erecting these batteries that I mentioned on the south side of the Shenandoah, which enfiladed the line I was on, induced me after some reflection, to see Colonel Downey [commanding the 3rd Regiment (PHB), which was positioned on Willard's immediate right]. I mentioned these things to him. He felt as I did. We went to see Colonel Stannard [commanding the 9th Vermont, on Downey's right]. Colonel Stannard seemed to feel as we did. We sent [a messenger] for the Commander of the brigade, Colonel Trimble [who very soon made his appearance].[50]

Willard further testified at the hearing that he told Trimble he thought their lines were "entirely too extended" and that they were "trying to defend a position which, unless there were some other means taken, would take 50,000 men to defend."[51] Questioned about what he had proposed to do, Willard explained to the Commission that his "idea" was to withdraw the force entirely into Harper's Ferry and retake Maryland Heights, if it was possible":

> Harper's Ferry is down; in the town were many old walls, stone walls, bridges and rocks which I thought could be made available. That might have been done at that hour, possibly. . . . [52]

Basically, he argued, it was not so much a question of successful resistance as of prolonged resistance for twenty-four or forty-eight hours.[53] Trimble, however, replied distinctly that Colonel Miles's order was to hold the position then occupied.[54]

Willard's testimony before the Harper's Ferry Commission went no further than this. However, headstrong young Colonel Downey of the Potomac Home Brigade, protege and law partner of Western Maryland's radical reconstructionist Congressman, Francis Thomas, was thinking of more than a withdrawal into Harper's Ferry and an attempt to reoccupy Maryland Heights. Always doubtful that White should have renounced the command of Harper's Ferry,[55] Downey was now "fully convinced that Colonel Miles was not the officer for the position" and stated frankly to Trimble, Willard, and Stannard that he thought it would have been better for White to have assumed the command.[56] They agreed, Downey testified, that Miles was incompetent to command.[57]

Although it is not clear that there would have been anything wrong with a conspiracy to persuade a general officer to assume his proper command, none of the witnesses before the Commission at the time testified to discussing such a radical step. Forty years later, however, Downey wrote that not only did they "all" believe Miles to be "incompetent" but that

> I did advise at this council that *the command be taken from Colonel Miles. . . .* We talked in particular of General White being placed in command. (Emphasis added.)[58]

The record shows that shortly before midnight White was at Trimble's headquarters, calling for D'Utassy to join them.[59] When D'Utassy arrived, White asked, "What is your opinion? What do you think we can do?"[60] D'Utassy said: "Nothing but fight" and White acquiesced: "Well, make your arrangements accordingly."[61] While there is no testimony in the record that

Colonel Stephen W. Downey (1839–1902)

Commanding officer of the 3rd Infantry Regiment of the Potomac Home Brigade. Grandfather of the author.

White expressly turned down a proffered crown, the record is clear that he did not, in fact, assume his proper command. This decision by White, a brigadier general, obviously made it impossible, as a practical matter, for any of the lesser officers to assume command and any thoughts of deposing Miles died aborning.

Downey made it clear nearly forty years later, however, that:

> *We did not know* that General McClellan, with the Union Army, was in pursuit of the Confederate Army and following them up. Of course *had we known* the situation then as we found it out afterwards, no doubt one of the commanders of brigades would have taken command. (Emphasis added.)[62]

Again the critical importance of McClellan's message to Miles and the latter's failure to reveal it to anyone else— even his top officers—becomes clear. Had the participants in this midnight council of war been privy to Cole's report that McClellan was "approaching rapidly and believed he could relieve Harper's Ferry,"[63] an entirely different atmosphere could be postulated.

As it was, however, there was universal ignorance of that key fact. Harper's Ferry knew only the despair of the deserted. Wrote the Ninth Vermont's young Captain Ripley of that miserable night:

> All night we could hear the voices of the Rebels getting batteries into position on the extension of our plateau across the Shenandoah to our left and rear. As far as the eye could reach, in the circle from the Potomac to the Shenandoah, was the lurid glare of Jackson's camp fires close up around us. How we welcomed the night that brought protection from that powerful artillery fire and the cessation for the time of hostility; those blessed hours when the wicked cease from troubling you and, weary, you try to rest. Six months of arctic night would have suited our needs just then, so terrible, so inevitable was the hopeless struggle to come with the dawn.[64]

Of the ten thousand Union troops at Harper's Ferry who waited out that night in silent misery, only one knew that relief was now just hours away. And he—incredible as it may seem— had elected not to share this crucial intelligence with anyone on the Union side.

22
Surrender

(I) As the Commission Saw It

It was not long after dawn on Monday, September 15, while the characteristically pervasive morning mist had yet to rise above the upper reaches of Maryland Heights and Loudon Heights, that the Rebel bombardment of Harper's Ferry was resumed.[1] With the strategic new Rebel gun positions to which we have just referred on Bull's Hill and across the Shenandoah River, Jackson now had a total of some fifty artillery pieces converging their fire on Bolivar Heights from front, flank, and rear.[2]

The principal targets of this bombardment were Rigby's and Potts's batteries, both guarding the critical point where the Charlestown Pike (now Highway I-340) cuts through Bolivar Heights (the Union position that Pender had almost taken before being thrown back the previous afternoon).[3] Both Pender, now waiting in the Bull's Hill area to resume his flank attack, and Ewell, waiting on Schoolhouse Hill to lead a frontal assault on the southern sector of Bolivar Heights, recognized that Rigby's and Potts's batteries "had to be taken if it cost a thousand lives."[4]

Poised for an attack on the rear of Bolivar Heights from the top of the ravines along the Shenandoah River were Gregg's and Branch's brigades. The potential danger to the garrison from an attack on the Union rear was indubitably serious but it was far from an open-and-shut case. A large plateau which Gregg and Branch must cross from their ravine starting points to reach the main Union line ran upslope over open ground for over a half-mile. Moreover, while Gregg and Branch would

185

have some support from the newly planted Rebel artillery across the Shenandoah River, they would be subject to serious harassment by Graham's New York battery atop Camp Hill as they (i.e., Gregg and Branch) tried to advance over the upslope open plateau toward Bolivar Heights.[5] In short, the outcome of Jackson's plans for a pincers movement against the southern sector of Miles's Bolivar Heights line[6] could not, we think, be fairly predicted when the preparatory Rebel bombardment began on Monday morning.

The Rebel bombardment lasted something like an hour and a half[7] and it was impressive. "Perfectly terrific" was the way Colonel Trimble, commanding the southern sector of the Union line, later described it,[8] and Miles's aide Binney exclaimed in his retrospective "journal" that "nothing could stand before such a raking cannonade."[9] There were, indeed, some losses but, like the losses of Sunday afternoon, their significance was probably chiefly psychological.

The morning's loss for D'Utassy's whole brigade was only twenty killed and wounded.[10] Trimble's own regiment (the 60th Ohio), which was positioned immediately on the right of Rigby's battery, lost eight or ten men when a shell burst in a rifle pit just before the surrender,[11] yet Trimble himself was constantly riding his horse along the ridge of Bolivar Heights with impunity the whole morning.[12] Perhaps the best indication of what the bombardment was really like is the fact that while Rigby and Potts were at the center of the bombardment and each characterized the Rebel fire as the "heaviest" he had ever seen,[13] neither had more than three men wounded—and those only "slightly"—while none were killed during the whole morning.[15] Phillips's battery lost only one man during the whole siege, a fact Phillips attributed to overlong Rebel fusing which kept nine out of ten shells from bursting.[15] It should be remembered, too, that most of the Bolivar Heights area was outside the range of the Rebel guns on Maryland and Loudon Heights.[16] Moreover, the fog never did disappear from Loudon until after the surrender, so that even as to targets within range (such as Camp Hill) the Rebel gunners on Loudon Heights were largely firing blind (on the basis of Sunday afternoon's settings).[17] This does not mean that they were totally ineffective; the historian of the 126th New York thought that two successive shells which cost the lives of seven men of that regiment came from the Heights.[18] If so, however, there must have been a large element of luck in the hit.

Most of the Union infantry along the southern sector were able to obtain the protection of cover in a ravine.[19] Those that could not do so, moreover, found other ways to avoid serious injury. How one Union infantry regiment escaped damage (and incidentally kept the men's minds off their troubles) is told by young Captain Ripley of the 9th Vermont, whose mission to support Rigby's battery necessarily kept it in the hottest spot on Bolivar Heights:

> We thought there was no regiment there tried as severely as the 9th Vermont. . . . We were in a straight line between Rigby and the batteries across the Shenandoah and in a straight line between Potts and those westward on either side of the Charlestown Pike, while the sabots of Rigby's guns under which we lay annoyed us not a little. We were in a freshly plowed field of red earth on our bellies, a very conspicuous line of blue on red as seen from above, and there was no tree in the orchard over an inch in diameter, or with foliage enough for a screen. All we could do was to lie still and wait until they got a range upon us, and then [Colonel] Stannard would order us to jump, double quick as far to the front as possible, and drop flat, then back again under Rigby's guns. This was repeated several times with perfect steadiness.[20]

With the benefit of such protective action the total casualties of the Ninth Vermont during the entire siege were only three men wounded and none killed.[21]

Gradually the Union firing grew slower and more sporadic, as Miles's batteries began running out of long-range ammunition. The note below indicates that they were also running low on antipersonnel ammunition for use at short range against an infantry assault on the Union works, *but they were by no means out of it.** It was apparently this gradual silencing of the Union guns

---

*At the moment of surrender, Captain von Sehlen's battery, on the right of Bolivar Heights, had an undetermined amount of ammunition, mostly shrapnel (WR/OR, series I, vol. XIV, pt. I, p. 664). Captain Phillips, in the same sector, had no long-range ammunition but 40 rounds of canister (ibid., p. 684). On the left, both Rigby and Potts were nearly out of everything but canister, of which Potts had 12 rounds to the gun (ibid., p. 654) and Rigby had 21 (ibid., p. 651). On Camp Hill Captain Graham's two guns apparently still had something like 100 rounds of all kinds of ammunition except long fuses (ibid., p. 662).

that led Jackson to order the Confederate artillery to desist.[22] (By previous arrangement the silence of the Rebel guns had been made the signal for storming the Union works.)[23] Pender had just started his advance north from Bull's Hill when a resumption of firing by some Union guns led to a similar resumption by two Rebel batteries in advance of Pender's men.[24] While the artillery duel resumed, the Rebel assault halted.[25]

Meanwhile, however, the same Union shortage of long-range ammunition which had triggered Jackson's decision to order the assault had simultaneously triggered a decision by Miles to inaugurate surrender negotiations. According to the testimony of Miles's aide, Binney, before the Harper's Ferry Commission, Miles and his aides arrived at the front sometime after the Rebel shelling began; observed the enfilade of the extreme Union left by the new Rebel batteries planted during the night; found White repositioning some artillery; moved north beneath the ridge of Bolivar Heights to the crest of the extreme right where they stayed fifteen to twenty minutes watching D'Utassy fight off Jones's feint; and finally started back south along Bolivar Heights.[26] Binney's testimony continued:

> We met Captain von Sehlen, who reported that his [artillery] command was entirely exhausted, and we met Captain Phillips [another artillerist] who stated that his ammunition was expended.[28] About the center of Bolivar Heights Colonel Miles met General White and remarked to him that the artillerists had reported that they were out of ammunition and he did not know what he should do; that he did not see that he could hold out any longer without the butchery and the slaughter of his men as the heights were being completely enfiladed. He asked General White's advice in the matter. General White did not seem inclined to recommend a surrender or anything of that sort. It was by Colonel Miles's proposition entirely, his first proposition, to raise a white handkerchief and ask for a cessation of hostilities.
>
> . . . .
>
> He [Miles] asked your [White's] advice and after some time you [White] proposed that the best thing we could do was to have a consultation of his officers. He [Miles] sent Lieutenant Willmon [an aide] to the right for Colonel D'Utassy and sent me to the left for Colonel Trimble.[29]

White's aide, Curtis, confirmed Binney's memory:

> "He [Miles] remarked, in the first instance, that it would perhaps be necessary to surrender, and you [White] suggested to him that it would be better to call together the commanders of brigades, and see what they thought on the subject.
>
> . . . .
>
> The commanders of brigades were sent for, according to your [White's] suggestion, and appeared, at least some of them; I recollect distinctly Colonel D'Utassy and Colonel Trimble being there; I do not recollect personally the others. . . . [30]

Unfortunately we have no tape recording of the surrender council, which reached a formal decision to raise the white flag. By the time of the Harper's Ferry Commission's hearings, Miles was, of course, dead. Colonel D'Utassy, however, gave considerable testimony as to what was allegedly said at the surrender council.[31] Other information comes from Colonel Trimble's testimony elaborating retrospectively on his own reason for agreeing to the surrender.[32] And although the rules of evidence in force at the time did not permit General White, as the one calling for the Court of Inquiry,[33] to testify in his own behalf,[34] his reasons for agreeing to a surrender may be found in his battle report and a carefully prepared amendment thereto,[35] as supplemented (and somewhat altered) by a memoir written many years later.[36] Recognizing the limitations placed by time and circumstance on the credibility of these retrospective accounts of what was said in the surrender council, it is nevertheless of prime importance to know what the three surviving participants claimed was said.

D'Utassy, the colorful Hungarian horse-thief, who would end up in Sing Sing Prison and whose military leadership qualities have been seriously questioned,[37] was the last to arrive at the hastily called council. This is the way he remembered it:

> Colonel Miles said, "Well, my boy, we meet again under unpleasant circumstances." I said, "Why?" He replied, "Well, we don't know what to do." I asked, "In what regard?" "Well," said he, "we must surrender." I looked at him a moment and then said, "What! Surrender?" "Yes, sir," he

said. "What do you want to do?" I told him, "Cut our way through." "Poh," he said, "Bosh! Nonsense! Today it is too late." I said to him, "Colonel, I offered to do the same yesterday, and I suggested it to Colonel Davis, who, as you see, did it." "Well," said he, "yesterday is not today; what shall we do today; what shall we do today?" I said, "Is it a council of war or is it a mere private conversation?" He replied, *"Well, I have half determined what to do but General White said to call you all together."* I said to him, "Then let the junior give his advice." Colonel Trimble was the junior, and he said, *"Under actual existing circumstances, nothing else is to be done but to surrender."* General White stood near us but did not say one word. Colonel Miles went over to him [White] and said, "Well, you hear what he says." General White said, "Hear Colonel D'Utassy's opinion." I replied, "You know it; *I will never surrender as long as I have a shot."* Colonel Miles then began to curse and said, "How many shots have you?" I sent for Captain Phillips and Captain Von Sehlen; the one had three shots and the other had one, long-range emmunition. When I heard that, I said, *"I can do nothing else but surrender, particularly as you are averse to cutting our way out,* but I will surrender only on honorable conditions. . . ." (Emphasis added.)[38]

D'Utassy's statement of his own initial opposition to surrender was corroborated at the hearing both by Miles's aide, Binney, who had not heard all the surrender discussion but said he did hear D'Utassy's remark that he "did not see any reason for surrendering.[39] and also by one of D'Utassy's company grade officers, Bacon, who, although not present, "always understood that you [D'Utassy] agreed to the surrender only upon the understanding that the ammunition was entirely out."[40] It is important to note two things about D'Utassy's position.

Firstly, in the end he expressly agreed with Miles that an outage of *long-range* artillery ammunition was critical and that fairly implies that he did not attach much importance to the remaining stock of *short-range* ammunition, which would seem to have been of at least as great concern if he was prepared to await an enemy assault. Apparently, he was not really prepared for that extremity.

Secondly, however, he was still prepared to attempt a break-out. This might not—as Miles asserted—have been very practical if the nearby presence of Franklin's relieving column were ignored. However, if all present—and not just Miles—had known that Franklin was only a half-dozen miles away in Pleasant Valley and had McLaws hopelessly trapped, D'Utassy's proposed breakout, while still risky, would necessarily have appeared a good deal more practical. The importance of Miles's failure to reveal Cole's dispatch from McClellan to anyone else is once again apparent.

Analysis of Trimble's account reaches a similar result. Before the Harper's Ferry Commission he testified to about the same things D'Utassy had quoted him as saying on Bolivar Heights:

> There was no difference of opinion. A point made and which all acquiesced in, was to make honorable terms. It seemed to be generally conceded[41] that there was nothing left for us but to surrender or see our men slaughtered without being able to do any public good.[42]

Here again, as with D'Utassy, we must conclude that under the circumstances Trimble was not prepared to withstand an enemy infantry assault, even though there was still some canister for the artillery to aid a musketry defense by the Union infantry. He explained to the Commission in some detail:

> I believe that whenever the troops rose from their cover . . . the very moment they rose from their position I think there would have been such a destruction of human life without the accomplishment of any public good that we would have been held morally responsible by the country for having permitted it. That is my view of the matter.

> . . . .

> I do not think we could have held out an hour. The enemy were there almost within rifle range.

> . . . .

> I do not think they could have destroyed us in an hour or a half day or even a day by their artillery alone, because we could have kept the men under cover, but the very moment they advanced with their infantry in such superior numbers*

*The actual ratio of attackers to defenders reflected little, if any, "superiority." Nearly 12,000 (J. V. Murfin, *The Gleam of Bayonets* (New York and London: Thomas

and our men rose to engage them we would have been swept from the very face of the earth by their artillery, being such close range, in full view, and taking the regiments on the flank, as would have been the case. . . . There were some regiments there that would have stood until they were cut to pieces but some of those new regiments, not three weeks from home could not have been expected to stand.[43]

However, Trimble expressly qualified this pessimistic view of any further defense with a ringing declaration that *nothing would have led him to countenance a surrender if he had thought that relief was a real possibility:*

If I had thought there had been a possibility of holding out against the enemy until we were re-inforced or of defeating the enemy, I would not have consented to surrender if all the men in the universe had asked me to do it. I do not think any officer there would [have consented].[44]

Clearly, then, even Colonel Trimble's views on surrender, soundly based or not, must have been vastly different if he had been allowed to know—as only Miles knew—that Little Mac had promised relief which was now, in fact, no more than a half-dozen miles away. The failure of Miles to share Cole's message from McClellan with anyone else once again looms as principal factor in the surrender of Harper's Ferry.

This leaves only White's part in the surrender to be explored. D'Utassy's above mentioned description of the council paints the Chicago politician in a familiar, Pilate-like role, initially refusing to accept the surrender planned by Miles yet eventually going along with the decision (already "half made" by Miles) when the proposed consultation seemed to go Miles's way. Indeed, White's subsequent battle reports reveal no doubts but only a defense of the team's "collective decision."

White's first report to his superiors on Miles's surrender to "at least 40,000 rebels" (dated September 16, 1862) stated

Yoseloff, 1965; New York: Bonanza Books, 1968), p. 135, 143, of Jackson's 24,000 men (ibid., p. 126) were positioned beyond the Potomac and Shenandoah Rivers, where they could be of no assistance in an assault on Bolivar Heights. This left less than 12,000 Rebels (ibid., p. 135) available for such an assault. As for the Union garrison, Miles had between 11,000 and 12,000 men available for the defense (WR/OR, series I, vol. XIX, pt. I, pp. 549, 955). Note further that the Rebel assault must have been all uphill, except for Pender's flank attack.

merely that "after expending all our artillery ammunition, *except that for short-range,* and defeating two attacks of the enemy's infantry [apparently referring to Pender's Sunday night attack and withdrawal] Colonel Miles, with the advice of his brigade commanders, reluctantly surrendered" (emphasis added).[45] White's official report on September 20, 1862, amplified the theory that running out of long-range artillery ammunition had really left Miles no choice but to surrender:

> The long-range ammunition had now almost entirely failed and it became evident that, from the great preponderance of the enemy's artillery* and his ability to keep up a fire at long range to which we were no longer able to reply, our ability to hold the position became a mere question of time and that our defense could only be continued at a great sacrifice of life without any corresponding advantage.
>
> . . . .
>
> It was the unanimous opinion of the officers present [at the council] that it was useless to attempt to hold the position longer and that if reasonable terms could be obtained, it was best to surrender at once.[46]

Commending the late Colonel Miles as a "brave and loyal officer." White again emphasized that:

> The surrender was determined upon unanimously by a council of war when further resistance seemed useless, inasmuch as the commanding positions were held by the enemy in a force of not less than 40,000** of all arms in front, on both flanks, and in rear.[47]

Finally, on September 25, 1862 (five days later), White amended his report—with the "permission" of his superiors—to expand the reasons for the surrender beyond the expenditure of most long-range artillery ammunition, the alleged overwhelming manpower superiority of the Rebels, and the

*The fact is that the garrison had at least as much artillery as the attackers. White estimated fifty Rebel pieces (ibid., p. 527). Jackson reported capturing seventy-three Union pieces (ibid., p. 955).

**The effective strength was about 12,000. Murfin, *The Gleam of Bayonets*, pp. 135, 143.

council's desire to avoid useless sacrifice of life, *for the first time incorporating McClellan's failure to relieve Harper's Ferry as a reason for the surrender:*

> The considerations which prompted me to concur in the judgment of the council of war, when the surrender was decided upon, were as follows:
> 1st. The loss of Maryland Heights and their occupancy by the enemy in a force greatly superior to our own entire force.
> 2nd. The commanding officers of the batteries composed of our best guns reported their ammunition expended, except canister, etc. for short range.[49]
> 3rd. All hope of re-enforcement had departed, the firing during the engagements of Major General McClellan's forces with the enemy having, day by day, receded northwesterly.
> 4th. The enemy in front, exclusive of his strength on Loudon and Maryland Heights, was double our own,[50] preponderance of available artillery being still greater.[51]
> 5th. There appeared no good object to be attained by the sacrifice of life without a reasonable hope of success.
> 6th. The council of war was unanimous in the opinion that further resistance was useless.[52]

The third of these six considerations which "prompted (White) to concur" makes it plain that White was never made privy to Cole's dispatch from McClellan[53] and shows that White was influenced as much as D'Utassy and Trimble by McClellan's apparent lack of concern for the Harper's Ferry garrison. The crucial significance of Miles's deliberate concealment of what he had learned from Cole—and that would almost certainly include the news that Franklin was already in Pleasant Valley—is not left to inference. The third reason for the surrender is repeated in White's postwar apologia where he wrote that:

> The hope of relief from McClellan, which the proximity of the firing had inspired, was abandoned. Harper's Ferry was doomed.[54]

The decision to surrender having been reached and General White having been dispatched to seek "honorable terms," Miles took out a large white handkerchief and directed his aides to do the same. While the brigade commanders promptly carried the shocking news to their regimental commanders and the troops, none of whom had been consulted, Miles and Binney started to ride southward along the crest of Bolivar Heights, waving their white handkerchiefs as they rode, seeking to attract the attention of Rebel artillerists to stop the cannonade.

Whether most of the garrison really agreed with the decision to surrender when it was made is by no means clear. If we consider only the record of the Harper's Ferry Commission, that record gives an impression that most of Miles's officers— no enlisted men testified—agreed on the necessity for surrender at the time it occurred. To some extent this is true; although it should be noted that much of such evidence is accounted for by the testimony of participants in the surrender council[55] or their aides.[56]

Among the other officers who testified, there were varying opinions as to whether the surrender was too precipitate, turning largely, it seems, on whether the witness had been on the left or right of the Union line. Colonel Downey of the 3rd Maryland (PHB), who noted that his regiment was facing two Rebel brigades, said flatly that at the time of surrender "it would have been impossible to have held out, in the condition of things."[57] Colonel Willard of the 125th New York, who was also on the left, thought that the time for retreating to a more defensible line (as he had urged the night before) was past by Monday morning and thought he could have held his position only "about three minutes."[58] Major Hewitt of the 32nd Ohio had "no idea at all that we could have made any resistance but a short time longer; that is, successfully."[59]

While Stannard of the 9th Vermont was not called to testify before the commission, his view was probably fairly expressed by one of his captains in a postwar reminiscence: "In fifteen minutes more A. P. Hill's and Lawton's overpowering forces would have swept over us easily, we having no works to defend, and the result would have been virtually immediate."[60] It is probably a fair conclusion that Miles's regimental commanders on the southern sector of Bolivar Heights, in the line of the main Rebel attack, would have agreed with the surrender decision at the time it was made—assuming, of course, that they were no more aware than White, D'Utassy, and Trimble of the relief message from McClellan which Miles had seen fit not to share with any of them.

In contrast, those regimental commanders who had been positioned on the right of the Union line, where the Rebels never made more than a feint,* naturally did not feel the same sense of urgency. Thus Colonel Segoine of the 111th New York, while agreeing that the surrender "could not have been avoided very well" after the evacuation of Maryland Heights and after exhaustion of the long-range artillery ammunition, nevertheless believed that

> We could have held our position a few hours longer and I supposed we were going to make the attempt on Monday morning.[61]

Colonel Cameron of the 65th Illinois testified that:

> Informed as I was, subsequent to the surrender, that the ammunition was exhausted—that the enemy were massing their men on the left, and that a great many of our regiments now in the service were not to be relied upon in a close encounter—if I had been consulted, I should probably have acted [i.e., voted] in the same manner that the other officers did.[62]

However, Cameron was convinced that the surrender was too precipitate:

> I do not think it was the last extremity. My impression is that we would have driven the enemy back in the first assault with heavy loss and they would probably have slaughtered us in the second.[63]

---

*Jackson's aide, Kyd Douglas, tells in his memoirs how Jackson, about 3:00 A.M., sent him to get General Jones, commanding on the Rebel left (i.e., the Union right), to make "as imposing a demonstration as possible": "I knew of course, that General Jackson did not expect Jones to attack seriously the steep bluffs of Bolivar [at the Potomac end of the line] but that he desired a very decided demonstration. But Jones carried out his order strictly and in the early morning filled the air with a din of war that echoed along the Potomac and reverberated in multiplied repetitions against the rocks of Maryland Heights. It seemed a very transparent feint but it had its effect, for I soon discovered a column of Federal troops hastening to the defense of those unscalable heights." H. K. Douglas, *I Rode with Stonewall* (Chapel Hill, N.C.: University of North Carolina Press, 1940; Greenwich, Conn.: Fawcett Publications, Inc., 1965), p. 160.

Of special interest is the testimony of the artillerists. Rigby and Potts had commanded batteries on the left. Rigby, called as General White's witness, testified that by the time of the surrender he had expended all the hundred rounds of long-range ammunition per gun with which his six pieces had arrived at Harper's Ferry but still had twenty-one rounds of canister left for close-in antipersonnel firing.[64] While he doubted that the infantry could successfully have repulsed the enemy force he saw at Harper's Ferry,[65] he was never, in fact, asked whether he would have surrendered when Miles did.

Potts, also called by White, testified that when firing ceased he had no ammunition left except twelve rounds of canister per gun.[66] A former infantry officer, Potts, like Rigby, doubted that "with the force we had under the fire of the enemy's guns, that we could have repulsed them at all."[67] However, Potts, like Rigby, was never asked whether he thought Miles had really reached "the last extremity" before surrendering.

Von Sehlen and Phillips had commanded batteries on the right. Von Sehlen, called as a White witness, testified merely that he could not say how much ammunition he had left at the time of surrender but that what he had was "mostly shrapnel."[68] He was not asked about the timing or propriety of the surrender. Phillips, another witness for General White, was the only one of the artillerists to defend the surrender without substantial qualification. Asked for his opinion as to the "propriety" of the surrender and whether, in light of the rawness of the troops and the shortage of (long-range) artillery ammunition, a successful defense could have been made for "any length of time," he answered:

> I had no ammunition [other than forty rounds of canister].[69] I could not do any more myself. My guns were rendered useless, and, as far as I was concerned, I supposed it [i.e., the surrender] was necessary.
>
> . . . .
>
> From what I had seen, from what information I could gather from some of the rebel officers that I was speaking to there [after the surrender], I considered that any longer defense, as I understood they were about to make an attack, would have been with a great sacrifice of life as the consequence and we finally would have been overcome.[70]

It is not surprising to find, as we shall see shortly, that Phillips, the only artillerist to endorse Miles's surrender decision so unequivocally, had powerful reason to avoid throwing any stones at anybody and, indeed, must have wanted badly to ingratiate himself with the Washington military establishment. Judgment as to his credibility must be suspended for the moment.

The ranking artillerist at Harper's Ferry was Major Henry McIlvaine, Miles's chief of artillery. Called as a witness for the Government, McIlvaine gave it as his opinion that the surrender was "necessary for the saving of life" because

> the position was weak to stand against an assault from the enemy, from the fact that they could take a position out of range of what ammunition we had and open their batteries effectually upon us and it would just have made a slaughter house of our position.[71]

Perhaps not expecting the answer he would get, the judge advocate then asked how long McIlvaine thought the position could have been held at the time of surrender. McIlvaine replied:

> I think it might have been held *that day,* no longer; but do not think it would have been [good] policy in any commanding officer to have sacrificed his command [in this way]. It [Harper's Ferry] could only have been held by the retiring of the forces in a condensed position as it were, and dreadfully exposed; but the result, in my opinion, is the same. (Emphasis added.)[72]

Presumably after making sure what kind of answers he would get, General White the following day recalled McIlvaine to the stand to show that the word "might" in the first line of the above testimony was intended to refer only to a "possibility," not a "probability." McIlvaine tried hard to oblige the general:

> Well, Sir, I meant this, that it could only have been held that day by desperately disputing the ground by an almost hand to hand conflict, disputing the ground inch by inch and hardly that. My mind has always been made up that the place was untenable.[73]

Plainly Major McIlvaine had spoken truth the first day he was on the stand, and his second day did *not* change the *substance* of that truth. He clearly believed that while it would have been at a terrible cost, Harper's Ferry *could* have been held several hours longer than Miles's precipitate action permitted.

Such, too, was the essence of the testimony of old Major General John Wool, hero of both the War of 1812 and the Mexican War,[74] and now Miles's immediate superior as commanding general of the Middle Department at Baltimore:

> I had no idea, after my instructions to him that he should defend Harper's Ferry to the last extremity that he would give up without resistance; in fact when no assault had been made. His men could have got out of the way of the enemy's long range cannon, if they were enfilading his works. Indeed, I think that musketry would have kept them back if nothing else. Camp Hill is very steep and the flanks are nearly perpendicular. Colonel Miles himself never seemed to doubt his ability to defend the place.[75]

. . . .

> If Colonel Miles had held out there for a few hours longer, I have no doubt General McClellan would have reinforced him. At any rate, my opinion was that 10,000 men could have defended that place against 40,000, and I do not think the enemy had half that number; not over 30,000 at all events.[76]

23
Surrender

(II) As the Troops Saw It

When now we turn from the testimony before the Harper's Ferry Commission to the contemporary public prints and other nonofficial sources, a strikingly different picture emerges. The *New York Times* correspondent, for example, reported:

> *A murmur of disapprobation ran along the whole line when it became known that we had surrendered* [emphasis in the original]. Captain McGrath [an Irish-born artillerist from New York City] burst into tears, exclaiming, "Boys, we have got no country now." Other officers exhibited a corresponding degree of grief, while the soldiers were decidedly demonstrative in their manifestations of rage.[1]

A veteran who considered the surrender "the crime of the war" some forty years later described the scene thus:

> *The indignation of Union men and officers at the surrender was terrible*—some sobbed like children, some swore, some were angry beyond words. (Emphasis added.)[2]

Another veteran, from the 111th New York (on the Union right), later recalled:

> We were all expecting an order to attack this [Rebel] line, when the Colonel [D'Utassy] commanding our brigade came riding behind our lines, repeating in a loud voice, "There will not be one shot fired. You are surrendered." If these men had been veterans instead of recruits of yesterday, there

would have been trouble. *I have never seen ten thousand men all terribly angry in my life but this once.* (Emphasis added.)[3]

The Frederick, Maryland, correspondent of the Baltimore *American* described

the feeling of *mortification, anger and earnest denunciation* which prevails in the ranks of the late garrison of Harper's Ferry. (Emphasis added.)[4]

The Baltimore correspondent of the New York *Tribune* wrote:

It was a sad blow to our troops, who had looked forward to a desperate fight in which they did not intend to come off second best. . . . The case looked pretty desperate unless reinforcements arrived but *all the officers and men were confident of their ability to hold the place for another day . . . and no one thought of a surrender* until Miles, soon after 8 o'clock in the forenoon ordered the stars and stripes down and the white flag up. (Emphasis added.)[5]

As already said, almost none of this seething indignation comes through in the record of the Harper's Ferry Commission. Indeed, the only suggestion of this massive discontent is a brief mention by Miles's aide Binney that:

after the council of officers had broken up, Colonel Miles remarked to some infantry who were manifesting some dissatisfaction at the hoisting of the white flag, that it was merely for a cessation of hostilities [i.e., not a surrender].[6]

Although Binney, in a second reference to the same incident, substituted "began to use some pretty harsh language" for "manifesting some dissatisfaction,"[7] a reader of the Commission record would otherwise find little evidence therein of the wrath turned on the man who, most of the troops were now convinced, was the deliberate author of their troubles. Examples to be gleaned from other sources make this crystal clear.

The historian of the 126th New York tells how Miles, passing Captain Philo Phillips of Company D, a lawyer in civilian life,

orders him to raise something, *anything* white, in token of surrender. Phillips says "For———'s sake, Colonel, don't surrender us. Don't you hear the signal guns? Our forces are near us. Let us cut our way out and join them." Miles replies that the situation of things renders this impossible. He says, too, "they will blow us out of this in half an hour." Phillips still expostulates; says that even with the loss of a thousand men, the place with its valuable stores can be held till relief comes; it ought to be done. Miles said, "Do you know who I am?" Phillips said, "I do; you are Colonel Miles," and turned to walk away, when a fragment shell struck Miles's leg, tearing the flesh from the bone. Miles fell and Phillips was heard to say, "Good!" and the rest felt it if they did not say it. It was difficult to find a man who would take him to the hospital.[8]

A similar (and not impossibly the same)[9] incident is told by a veteran of the 111th New York:

When we came up the [west slope of Bolivar Heights] we found one of our batteries firing and two or three rebel guns replying. It seems this battery had refused to surrender and began to fire [again]. Col. Miles rode up in person and ordered a sergeant to put up a white flag. The sergeant refused with an oath. Col. Miles jumped from his horse, tied his white handkerchief to his sword blade and climbed on one of the guns to wave his white flag. Just at that moment a shell from the enemy struck one of his legs and he fell to the ground. As my company marched by he was being carried off the hill. Miles was so hated by the soldiers that it was hard work to get men to help carry him.[10]

General White's official report on the death of Miles,[11] of which White was *not* an eyewitness (being then engaged in front of the Union lines as Miles's emissary to negotiate a truce with Stonewall Jackson),[12] plainly implied, without expressly so stating, that Miles was wounded by a stray enemy shell, probably fired by some Rebel battery which had not yet gotten the word that Miles had surrendered:

The enemy did not cease firing at once upon the display of the white flag, probably not perceiving our signals, and some time after the flags were exhibited Colonel Miles was struck by a shell in the leg and mortally wounded. . . . Many others were struck at about the same time and before the most distant batteries of the enemy had ceased.[13]

The Rebels themselves, although they could not have had

any firsthand knowledge, generally assumed responsibility for Miles's death. Thus General Walker later wrote:

> owing to the fog I was ignorant of what had taken place [i.e., the surrender], but surmising it, I soon ordered my batteries to cease firing. Those of Lawton, however, continued some minutes later. This happened unfortunately, as Colonel Dixon S. Miles, the Federal commander, was at this time mortally wounded by a fragment of shell while waving a white flag in token of surrender.[14]

Although Walker was ready to lay the blame on Lawton, who was located about a mile *southwest* of the center of the Union line,[15] a leading Rebel artillerist (Poague), about a mile *northwest* of the same point,[16] thought that *his* were the guns of death. In his memoirs Poague tells of seeing a white flag appear on the enemy's works. His brigade commander, however, "either could not or would not" see the flag and ordered: "D——n their eyes, give it to them." Although Poague thereafter contrived to fire his cannon as slowly as possible, he later expressed fear that it had not been slow enough:

> We afterwards learned that the commanding officer was killed by a shell after he had capitulated. Under the circumstances we all thought the shell went from either our battery or Carpenter's (or whatever battery was engaged along with us).[17]

Despite the inherent improbability of an overtime Rebel shell just happening to hit—of all people—the Union commander* the record of the Harper's Ferry Commission was barren of any suggestion that Miles might have died at the hands of his own men. Moreover, for over four decades—understandably—no one stepped forward to confess to Miles's murder or to involve anyone else. In 1895, however, the historian of Cole's Cavalry stated flatly that "after the capitulation Colonel Miles was shot and killed *and it was generally supposed by one of his own men*" (emphasis added).[18] Ten years later came the first solid evidence to support the "general supposition."

---

*The improbability seems increased by the circumstance that Miles was one of only five Union officers killed or mortally wounded during the entire siege of Harper's Ferry, including the battle of Maryland Heights. WR/OR, series I, vol. XIX, pt. I, p. 549.

In 1905 a missionary from Harper's Ferry named New-comer,[19] serving a tour of duty near Mancelona in northern Michigan, was called to the home of a dying farmer named Parks. Parks told Newcomer of being present at the battery of Captain John Phillips (2nd Illinois Light Artillery, Battery M) on Bolivar Heights on the fateful morning of Monday, September 15, 1862. Parks's dying declaration, as then relayed by Newcomer to her family in Harper's Ferry, was as follows:

> Yesterday afternoon Curt and I went to see Mr. Parks who witnessed the shooting of Miles following the surrender at H.F. He is a tall, fine looking, rather cultivated appearing farmer, having one of the best homes west of the town. He is a great sufferer, however, and a trifle difficult to follow in conversation, owing to a terrible rose cancer in the cheek, with which he is doomed to die.
>
> He [Parks] says that after the white flags had been hoisted an Illinois battery of light artillery, stationed across the road to the right (as you face Charles Town) continued a lively fire. Colonel Miles rode up to the captain and ordered him to stop firing, adding angrily, "Can't you see the signals—we've surrendered." Captain Phillips was an immensely tall man who looked like an Indian, with eyes like steel traps. It had been remarked that he had been drinking.* He turned to the Colonel and damned him in terrific language, at which the Colonel repeated his order and turned away, riding straight along the crest of the Heights toward Jackson's forces massed at the Shenandoah end. Captain Phillips watched him, cursing, and after a moment's pause shouted the order "Gun number three:—half-a-second fuse shell."—then "Gunner number three: See that man on the horse? You fix that man! Miss your mark and you die in your boots!" The gunner fired and the shot exploded under Miles' horse, killing the horse and wounding Miles in the leg—terribly mangling the calf, he heard. The Colonel was carried to a brick building which Parks thought had been a seminary, and which was a Union Hospital. A Confederate surgeon was detailed to attend him. "Not a Union surgeon would go near him." Parks said the

---

*Parks was probably wrong when he stated that Phillips had been drinking. The latter's military pension file (National Archives, Record Group 79) indicates that he was not a drinker. However, the same file also reveals that prior to the surrender Phillips had been forcibly knocked to the ground by a shell which barely missed him and deafened him in one ear for the rest of his life. A man who had just been through such a traumatic experience could well have given an impression that he had been drinking.

indignation of Union men and officers at the surrender was terrible—some sobbed like children, some swore, some were angry beyond words. He considered it the crime of the war. "For Harper's Ferry was the key to the situation." "If Miles had done his duty the war would have ended then and there," he declared. He stood within ten feet of Captain Phillips when he gave this order, and when the shot was fired—he heard every word and saw every action.[20]

No one will ever know the truth of Parks's dying declaration with certainty but in the absence of affirmative proof to the contrary there is no good reason to doubt the man. And if Miles was so mistrusted by his own men that they assassinated him, that shocking fact cannot be irrelevant to whether he was, in truth and fact, a traitor.

Meanwhile, the same act of surrender which was evoking such wrath, despair, and mistrust on the part of the Union garrison was evoking quite contrary emotions among Harper's Ferry's Rebel besiegers. To the latter a Southern victory had seemed by no means as certain or as cheap as it had to the Northern surrender council. From the Rebels the white handkerchief brought cheers of relief as much as of victory. Thus Jubal Early, poised on School House Hill, whence he was supposed to storm the strong westerly front of Bolivar Heights, later wrote:

> In front of the position occupied by Ewell's Division [of which Early's brigade was a part] was a deep valley between School House Hill and Bolivar Heights, the whole of which was cleared. On the opposite side the ascent to the enemy's works was steep and over thick brush that had been felled so as to make a formidable abatis. It was over this ground we would have had to move to the assault and *the prospect was by no means comforting.*

> . . . .

> Hill's division . . . was moving to the assault when the white flag was hoisted on Bolivar Heights. This indication of the enemy's surrender was received with very hearty and sincere cheers all along the line, *as we were thus saved the necessity for an assault, which, if stubbornly resisted, would have resulted in the loss of many lives to us.* (Emphasis added.)[21]

Nor could there have been much less cheering among Gregg's and Branch's Rebels, poised near the tops of the steep ravines above the Shenandoah, ready to charge across the broad, open central plateau to attack Bolivar Heights from the rear. A Rebel officer who had crept up at sunrise from the ravine where his men were waiting, in order to observe the lay of the land, was asked when he returned: "How is it?" He replied: *"We will say our prayers and go in like men"* (emphasis added).[22] Here, too, all need to pay a price for victory vanished with what old General Wool would later call a "disgraceful surrender and not to be justified or excused."[23]

Five miles from Harper's Ferry, over in Pleasant Valley, where Franklin's relieving army of 18,000 men was about to join issue with McLaws's defeated and trapped 8,000 men, the news of Miles's surrender came suddenly and stunningly, revolutionizing the strategic situation. One of Rebel General Stuart's cavalry officers later recalled:

> After dark [on Sunday night] a vigorous attack was made by the enemy upon the passes above, which resulted in his getting possession of the valley road and placed us in a most critical position between them and the garrison, closing the only outlet southward. The morning of the 15th opened with heavy cannonading from the Ferry five miles below us, where Jackson was beginning his bombardment. Up the valley we could see heavy masses of Union infantry bearing down upon us, their lines of skirmishers extending clear across [the valley] from mountain to mountain, as they came hastening down to the relief of the beleaguered garrison. If they had continued their advance with vigor they would inevitably have succeeded in relieving the place but they halted and delayed.

> . . . .

> Their skirmishers were within two hundred yards of our lines when the roar of Jackson's guns suddenly ceased. There followed a few moments of painful suspense. The enemy halted, evidently arrested by the significant quiet. Then from away [*sic*] down the valley came rolling nearer and nearer, as the news reached the troops, ringing cheers and we knew the Ferry had surrendered and soon a courier came spurring in hot haste with the official information of the fact. A skirmisher of the enemy, as our cheers rang out in response,

sprang up on a stone wall and called over to us, "What the hell are you fellows cheering for?" We shouted back, "Because Harper's Ferry is gone up, G——d d—— you." "I thought that was it," shouted the fellow as he got down off the wall.[24]

Almost immediately McLaws's heretofore trapped soldiers began pouring into Harper's Ferry over the captured pontoon bridge,[25] on their way, with Jackson and Walker, to rejoin Lee and fight McClellan to a bloody standoff at Antietam two days later. The siege of Harper's Ferry was over. Before the Harper's Ferry Commission crusty old General Wool put it simply:

If Colonel Miles had held out for a few hours longer I have no doubt General McClellan would have reinforced him.[26]

But the relief of the Harper's Ferry garrison—only hours away if Miles had kept his promise to hold out until Monday night—was never to be.

24
The Death of Miles

Miles's death was horrible. Soldiers from the 126th New York[1] and from the 9th Vermont[2] were drafted to help carry the mortally wounded commander in a blanket to a spot near the Charlestown Pike, where an ambulance could reach him. The two Vermonters reported that as they bore him along toward Rigby's battery, which was still firing, Miles saw Rigby's battery colors still flying and exclaimed to his staff: "Why don't they haul down that God-damned flag? It has been the death of me."[3] At the hospital in Harper's Ferry it was concluded that nothing could be done for the man and he lingered on in excruciating pain for over a day, with his aide Binney holding his hand most of the time.[4]

The Friday New York *Herald* reported[5]—and Greeley's *Tribune* adopted the report next day[6]—that some time between Miles's wounding and death he had actually confessed to a treasonable intent to surrender the Ferry to his Southern friends. The *Herald*'s Frederick correspondent wrote:

> The men [Harper's Ferry parolees] who have arrived here [Frederick] look well and both officers and men are much chagrined at the unfortunate plight in which they find themselves, through no fault of their own. They are unanimous in the assertion that the surrender of Harper's Ferry was unnecessary. *It is currently reported that before his death he [Miles] acknowledged that his sympathies were with the South and that he had not defended this important post confided to his charge as he might and should have done.* (Emphasis added.)

That anyone should make such a gratuitous confession seems

quite improbable, and before the Harper's Ferry Commission Miles's aide Binney categorically denied that Miles had said any such thing:

Q. [by the Court]: Have you heard it stated that Colonel Miles, after he was wounded, said that he had always been in favor of the Southern Confederacy?

A. I know he never made such a statement; I never left his side, except for perhaps fifteen minutes at a time, after he fell until he died. I heard him remark several times previous to his being wounded, and after he was wounded, that he could not see where General McClellan was, or, if any attempt was to be made to succor us why it had not been done.[7]

. . . .

Q. You say you were with Colonel Miles from the time he was wounded until he died?

A. Yes, sir.

Q. Did his mind wander any during that time?

A. It did at times; at other times it was very clear.

Q. You heard everything he said?

A. Yes, sir.

Q. He uttered no treasonable expressions at all?

A. No, sir; and directly the reverse.[8]

A much amplified version of the gospel according to Binney may be found in the Baltimore *Sun:*

Through the kindness of Lieut. Benning [*sic*], who sat behind him, constantly holding his hand in his, I am permitted to copy from his memoranda some of the expressions which the dying Colonel uttered during the day while his mind was wandering. They are valuable, if for nothing more, as showing how cruel the insinuations which have constantly been thrown out against his loyalty: "Oh, where is General McClellan? Why don't he come forward and save me?" "Major [presumably McIlvaine], is our artillery at work?" "I have done my duty and can die like a soldier." "Don't let my staff leave me. Go on! Go on!" "I wish I could be in every place at once." "Stop them," referring to stragglers from their regiments.

In the latter part of the day his mind still continued to wander to the battlefield and he kept constantly cheering on his men calling them to stand where they are. Again he asked, "Oh, where is McClellan." "Captain, you are hard pressed but my orders are to hold on to the last—my ammunition is gone. Oh, where is our army." "Darn Colonel Ford. He has lost the heights. Oh, must I surrender?" "They made a target of me." "All right, all right. Give them every shell—every shell." "When we can do no more, we can do no more." "Five days cannonading heard in Baltimore and elsewhere and yet no assistance. Expresses a wish to see Gen. White. I am an old soldier. Gen. White will not forget me at headquarters." "I know, also, my staff, Mr. Binney, Mr. Hellman [Willmon] and Major McIlvaine also." "I can hear this." "General, go; oh why don't you go? Oh go, go, go, go on. Won't anybody go? Oh, go! my darling—go my darling." "My wife go." "receive [sic] me." "Come sign it." "McIlvaine be on then! be on! What a noble fellow." "Oh, Barney [sic], that key, the key; oh—"⁹

What, if any, significance to attach to these alleged dying declarations is a puzzling question. If they are supposed to prove that Miles did all he could to save Harper's Ferry while anxiously awaiting word from McClellan that relief was at hand, we now know that that could not have been true. Moreover, this purported transcript of a dying man's exclamations lacks the ring of authenticity. Both a psychiatrist and a psychologist who have read it over at the writer's request doubt its authenticity and so does the writer, a trial judge. In any event, it seems the kind of self-serving statement to which the law usually attaches little if any credit.

As for Binney: whether or not he was privy to any of Miles's plans to surrender Harper's Ferry, his credibility is nil. It has been noted previously that not only was his testimony before the Harper's Ferry Commission (largely in defense of Miles) replete with provable inaccuracies and inconsistencies, but shortly after the release of the commission's report Binney was "by direction of the President dismissed from the military service, with loss of all pay and allowances,: for absence without leave and attempting [in another matter] to practice a gross deception on the War Department."¹⁰ Accordingly, we cannot attach any real weight to the Baltimore *Sun*'s account of Binney's account of Miles's "dying words."

Following Miles's death on Tuesday afternoon (September 16) Binney, Willmon, and McIlvaine then escorted his rude

coffin to Baltimore, where, as after his fiasco at Bull Run, all
factions seemed to rally to Miles's defense. Wrote the New York
Tribune's Baltimore correspondent:

> The news from Harper's Ferry was received here [Baltimore]
> in various fashion last night. I thought I saw as many gleeful
> as long faces over it. At the place where wealthy Baltimore
> gets its evening news, there was much ignorance [*sic*]. "I told
> you so; I knew the tables would be turned!" "Now I can go to
> bed happy!" "Glory enough for me tonight?" "How *are* you,
> Stonewall Jackson?" and other exclamations and remarks
> could be heard on all sides. . . . *All expressed regret at the death of*
> *Col. Miles, who seemed to be a favorite with them—with everyone in*
> *the city, in fact.* (Emphasis added.)[11]

Years later the 126th New York's regimental history described
Baltimore's reaction to the parolees of that regiment about the
same time in this interesting passage:

> In passing through Baltimore they [the men of the 126th]
> had an opportunity to witness the divided feeling which
> characterized that city and the whole State of Maryland.
> Rebel sympathizers . . . put as much contempt into their faces
> as they were capable of showing, which was not a little.
> Others cheered them heartily, thus showing what spirit they
> were made of. *But what especially struck the paroled men was the*
> *solicitude of many professed Unionists to obtain from them an*
> *admission that Colonel Miles did his duty patriotically; that the*
> *surrender could not have been avoided.* As no such admission
> could be obtained from the soldiers, the questioners were a
> good deal chagrined and disappointed. Colonel Miles was in
> fact a Marylander and no doubt a Southerner at heart.
> (Emphasis added.)

From Baltimore the funeral procession moved slowly
through the green hills and dales of Baltimore County to the
peaceful little graveyard of "The Manor Church" (St. James's
Episcopal) near Miles's home in Sweet Air. There Dixon
Stansbury Miles was buried and there he lies today, beside his
wife, Sarah Briscoe Miles, and his infant son, John Steuart
Calhoun Miles.

25
An Official Verdict

In after years Stonewall Jackson's young aide, Kyd Douglas, felt impelled to defend the integrity of his fellow Marylander Miles against the ever-recurrent charge of treason:

> The memory of Colonel Miles has been harshly dealt with by his own people. He has been charged with cowardice and treachery at Harper's Ferry. He died with his face to the foe and should not be called a coward. Worse yet is the charge of treachery, for the crime is worse. It was said he had communicated with Jackson and had surrendered according to agreement. Such a charge is like stoning the dead. As closely as I was associated with General Jackson in this movement, I never had a suspicion of such an arrangement: no member of the staff ever heard of it; no one in our army believed it. Everything that Jackson did was inconsistent with it. Colonel Miles may not have been equal to the situation, perhaps was not, but he was no traitor. The surrender was a deep mortification to the Union; the charges against Miles could only make that greater.[1]

That Kyd Douglas could make such assertions in the face of all the damning evidence we have reviewed reflects principally two facts. (1) The Harper's Ferry Commission expressly noted its own reluctance (in what was necessarily a circumstantial case) to defame an old soldier who had ostensibly died in the service of his country.[2] Never so frankly expressed but of equal or greater importance, we can now see, was a decision by the Lincoln administration in the course of the Harper's Ferry inquiry to minimize the probability that Miles had deliberately thrown

Harper's Ferry to the enemy, lest such a finding tend to get McClellan off the hook on which Lincoln was now trying to hang him.

The attack on McClellan's competence through the Harper's Ferry Commission coincided exactly with the Lincoln administration's decision shortly after Antietam that McClellan must go. It was no accident that the report of the commission eventually appeared for the first time in the same newspaper issues which announced the president's removal of McClellan as commanding general of the Army of the Potomac. A brief review of events in Washington between the date of surrender (September 15, 1862) and the public appearance of the commission's report (November 10, 1862) leaves little doubt that Miles was a perhaps unintended but nevertheless real beneficiary of the administration's urgent need to justify its removal of the popular McClellan from power.

The news of Harper's Ferry's surrender must have reached the president sometime before Wednesday, September 17. On that day Secretary of the Treasury Chase noted in his diary:

> Went also to Gen. Halleck's. Found the President and Reverdy Johnson there; talked with a Union Captain who was at Harper's Ferry at the time of its surrender. *Says Maryland Heights were surrendered to the surprise of everyone;* that Miles was struck by a shell after the surrender of the post, just as he had put the white flag in the hands of an orderly; *that there was no necessity for the surrender and that the officers were very indignant.* (Emphasis added.)[3]

The following day (Thursday the Eighteenth) Navy Secretary Welles wrote in his diary:

> We have but few and foggy dispatches of any kind these troublesome days. Yesterday and day before there were conflicting accounts about Harper's Ferry, which, it is now admitted, was *thrown to the Rebels with scarcely a struggle.* (Emphasis added.)[4]

These two entries by key men around Lincoln reveal Washington's immediate recognition of need for an investigation into whether Harper's Ferry was really surrendered with "no necessity" and "thrown to the Rebels with scarcely a struggle." Significantly, however, the Chase entry already shows another influence at work. Reverdy Johnson, it will be recalled, was not only Maryland's leading Constitutional Democrat but Dixon Miles's personal lawyer during his Bull Run drunkenness trial and probably influential in securing him the command of Harper's Ferry. It would have been natural enough for Lincoln to have sent for Johnson to help him assess whether Miles had really sold out to the enemy.

It is even more likely, however, that Lincoln needed Johnson's advice on a delicate fact of political life: how would the same Marylanders who had been so offended by Miles's drunkenness charge likely react to an effort by the administration to make Dixon Miles out a traitor? In this connection one must remember that the president had already decided in his own mind that a Union victory at Antietam—the bloody battle being fought that very day—would quickly be followed by issuance of the momentous Emancipation Proclamation. This he had thus far been persuaded by his Cabinet to withhold, however, *principally on the ground that it could drive the four border states, including Maryland, hopelessly into the hands of the Confederacy.*[5] The effect which a post-mortem trial of Dixon Miles's loyalty might have on the key border state of Maryland at this particular time thus had to be a prime consideration in Abraham Lincoln's mind.

Nonetheless some kind of investigation was inevitable. On Monday, September 22, General White voluntarily asked for a court of inquiry into the causes of the week-old surrender of Harper's Ferry and its garrison,[6] and the following day[7] the Harper's Ferry Military Commission was convened for that purpose in Washington under the presidency of Major General David Hunter, a strongly abolitionist regular army officer who was personally close to Lincoln.[8] Testimony actually began on October 4[9] and continued almost daily until October 23.[10] There followed a delay of some ten days until November 3 when the commission's report was "issued"[11] and even then it did not reach the public prints until Monday, November 10, the same day that the public first learned of McClellan's dismissal.[12]

During this same period, relations between McClellan and the Lincoln administration, long bad, finally came completely apart.[13] Bitterly disappointed that McClellan had failed to exploit his "victory" at Antietam by pursuing and destroying Lee's army, Lincoln made a personal visit to the Army of the

Potomac on Wednesday, October 1, remaining several days to assess the situation.[14] Following Lincoln's return to Washington, on Monday, October 6, at the president's direction, Halleck peremptorily ordered McClellan to cross the Potomac River "now" and give battle to the enemy or drive him south.[15] Knowing McClellan's penchant for procrastination, it is doubtful that Lincoln really expected McClellan to obey this order. Realistically viewed, it was more in the nature of a record made to justify the inevitable removal when the time for it should arrive.

The order was, in fact, *not* obeyed for some three weeks.[16] When McClellan reported his cavalry horses worn out, Lincoln inquired with unaccustomed sarcasm just what McClellan's cavalry had been doing lately that would tire anybody's horses.[17] It was October 26 by the time the first Union division was across the river and November 2 by the time the last one crossed.[18] On November 5, Lincoln—rightly or wrongly—directed Halleck to relieve McClellan of his post.[19] On the same day Halleck issued the order,[20] and late on the night of November 7 the order was served on McClellan.[21] To the surprise of many, he made no effort to retain his command and civilian control of the army passed one of its most crucial tests.

Against this background of climaxing tension and of determination by the president, after his visit to McClellan on October 1, to end once and for all the power struggle between McClellan and the Lincoln administration, it is not surprising to observe a parallel change in the interest of the Harper's Ferry Commission during the same period.

Almost the only reference to McClellan during the first half of the proceedings was a brief mention by Miles's aide Binney on October 7, 1862, of indefinite rumors at Harper's Ferry that McClellan was coming north; of Cole's and Russell's offering to "open up communication" with McClellan; and of reports that these two cavalrymen reached McClellan—but never came back.[22] Russell did not appear until October 16, 1862, near the close of the government's case. He testified then that he had "no doubt whatsoever" about Franklin's ability to relieve Harper's Ferry on Monday if it had held out,[23] despite the need to fight his way through Pleasant Valley in order to do so.[24] General White, obviously concerned about the implication that Harper's Ferry had surrendered prematurely, or even needlessly, pressed hard to make Russell admit that various difficulties made Russell's confidence in Franklin's probable success highly speculative. However, Russell persisted:

> I think he [Franklin] could have whipped the enemy and reached Harper's Ferry both, before night.[25]

A list of subpoenaed witnesses, found in the surviving file of the Harper's Ferry Commission in the National Archives, apparently dates from just before October 16, when Russell testified. It reveals that in addition to Russell the government originally expected to call two more witnesses.*

One was Captain Cole, Miles's second messenger to McClellan, whose testimony we now know would have been that Miles was, in fact, fully advised the night before the surrender that McClellan's relieving army was at hand and that McClellan believed he could rescue the Harper's Ferry garrison if it would only hold out.

Whereas Russell's testimony, standing alone, could perhaps be used to blame McClellan for slowness in marching to the relief of Harper's Ferry as much as to blame Miles for a premature surrender, the tendency of the Cole testimony would have been all the other way. It would have established beyond cavil that Miles had acted the role of a traitor and thus that nothing McClellan could have done would likely have succeeded in the face of Miles's determination to "throw Harper's Ferry to the Rebels" (as Secretary Chase put it). *Incredible though it may seem, it is an indisputable fact that the judge advocate, after originally listing Cole, the key to the whole investigation, as his witness, at the last moment decided not to have Cole tell his story to the court of inquiry, apparently because it would have tended to clear McClellan.*

As if this were not enough to establish the administration's decision to use the Harper's Ferry Commission as a vehicle to get McClellan, a second piece of evidence found in the commission file is strongly confirmatory. On October 10, Colonel

---

*Of the twenty government witnesses listed, check-marks ("×"'s and "+"'s) appear in front of all names except Russell, Cole, and Smith. The latter two never did testify. All others had already testified before Russell did.

Cameron of the 65th Illinois wrote the judge advocate general (Holt):

> Major Bush of the 125th N.Y. or Major Smith of the 111th N.Y. can name the picket or officer in charge of it who passed the Confederate prisoners from Harper's Ferry to Enemy's lines.[26]

The file list of subpoenaed government witnesses, apparently written just before October 16, expressly included Smith, along with Russell and Cole, as government witnesses.[27] Like Cole, Smith was thereafter scratched by the judge advocate; he never testified.

It is true, of course, that a prosecutor may drop a witness for various reasons, such as the doubtful credibility of the witness or the cumulative nature of his proposed testimony. However, the nature of the testimony and the rank of the officer giving it in this case make such explanations unlikely. The obvious fact is that Smith's testimony would have tended to confirm Miles's treachery and thus to explain and excuse McClellan's failure to reach Harper's Ferry in time.

The flimsiness of the government's "case" against McClellan is amply demonstrated in two ways. Firstly, the only testimony even remotely relevant was given briefly by Halleck in the last days of the hearings (October 28–29).[28] He simply noted that McClellan's army had marched an average of only six miles a day on its way from Rockville (just outside Washington) to Frederick.[29] He neither mentioned nor explained such important factors as the disorganized state of the army after the recent debacle at Bull Run II or—critically significant—the fact that neither McClellan nor Halleck had known for sure until Lee's "lost order" came to hand at Frederick on Saturday the thirteenth whether Lee really intended to strike at Washington, Baltimore, Philadelphia, or elsewhere. Obviously McClellan had to be able to move in any of several directions whenever the Rebel goal became clearer and this must inevitably affect the speed of his movement.[30] All such sophistication was lost, however, in the simple effort to get McClellan.

Secondly, the commission plainly did not dare to call McClellan or any of his officers to explain the reasons for such phenomena as their six-miles-a-day progress northward through Maryland. In his final report McClellan wrote:

I have been greatly surprised that this [Harper's Ferry Commission], in its investigations, never called upon me, nor upon any officer of my staff, nor, so far as I know, upon any officer of the Army of the Potomac, able to give an intelligent statement of the movements of that army.[31]

We note incidentally the failure of the judge advocate to elicit from General Halleck while on the stand that—as Halleck later stated in his official report *after* McClellan's removal from command of the Army of the Potomac—Halleck's chief of staff (General Cullum) had expressly ordered Miles to confine his defense of Harper's Ferry principally to Maryland Heights.[32] It was this order that had made Miles such a liar when he kept telling his officers that Washington would not treat holding Maryland Heights as holding Harper's Ferry. For whatever reason, Halleck never testified on this subject. Equally interesting is a letter dated October 7, 1862, in the commission's file,[33] to the judge advocate from General White, asking for a subpoena to General Cullum to testify. *But Cullum never testified.* It is only against this complex politico-military background that one knowing the true facts can understand the Report of the Harper's Ferry Commission (which is appended hereto in its entirety).[34]

With marvelously evenhanded justice the commission incredibly placed the principal[35] blame for the Harper's Ferry debacle *equally* on Dixon Miles and George McClellan. Miles, the commission concluded, had acted with "incapacity amounting almost to imbecility."[36] However, while the commission recited certain of Miles's more bizarre actions and omissions to act, it declined to infer therefrom anything more than "criminal neglect."[37] As for McClellan, the Commission recited its single piece of "evidence" (Halleck's six-miles-a-day statistic) and concurred with the general in chief in the solemn conclusion that "General McClellan could, and should, have relieved and protected Harper's Ferry."[38]

From a pragmatic viewpoint the administration's ploy seems to have worked. Typical was the reaction of Greeley's New York *Tribune* in reporting simultaneously on McClellan's removal and the Harper's Ferry Commission's report:

There will be no complaint against this report of whitewashing. Its array of facts and its logical conclusions upon them are impregnable. The country will gratefully recognize the courage and just severity with which *the Commission, while awarding due censure to inferior officers, has declared that the shame of the surrender of Harper's Ferry rests chiefly on Gen. McClellan,* for if McClellan had moved with decent swiftness he would have raised the siege or would have taken the enemy in detail, with the Potomac dividing his forces. (Emphasis added.)[39]

It would be hard to conceive a greater travesty on justice than the official conclusion of the Harper's Ferry Commission that George McClellan must bear equal responsibility with Dixon Miles for the surrender of Harper's Ferry. For present purposes, however, the point to be made is simply that the Lincoln administration's transcendent need to discredit McClellan before dismissing him—and decision to that end to withhold key evidence from the Commission—seems to explain the otherwise puzzling question why the Harper's Ferry Commission found no more than "criminal neglect" and "incapacity amounting almost to imbecility" on Miles's part.

No finding of the military establishment, however, could shake the intuitive feelings of the Union men whom Miles had surrendered that they had been the victims of a deliberate intention to turn Harper's Ferry over to the Rebels. One has only to read the numerous regimental histories that appeared during the years after the war to realize how widespread was the belief—sometimes express, sometimes only implied—that Miles had done his own men in. Consider the following (emphasis added):

126th Regiment, New York Infantry (1869):

A post fortified by nature as few places are; furnished with all the munitions of war; and with 11,500 brave, earnest hearts to guard it, was *about to be yielded up with scarcely a struggle, by a miserable sympathizer with secession.*[40]

32nd Regiment, Ohio Infantry (1896):

. . .Want of judgment *or the basest treachery on the part of the commanding general* was the cause of the disgraceful surrender.[41]

7th Squadron, Rhode Island Cavalry (1865):

Colonel Miles, after a slight show of defense and *for reasons that his death will forever conceal,* decided to surrender to the investing foe.[42]

12th Regiment, National Guard, State of New York (1869):

They [the men of the 12th Regt.] seemed determined to rout the enemy and just when victory was within their reach *Colonel Miles raised the white flag and thus foiled the grand efforts of loyal troops.*[43]

Cole's Cavalry, Potomac Home Brigade (1895):

The rank and file thought they had been sold out and did not hestitate to give expression thereto. Colonel Miles was shot and killed and it was generally supposed by one of his own men. *If he was a traitor, he received his just deserts.*[44]

9th Regiment Vermont Infantry (1909):

[In the days before the siege] grumbling, bitter criticism of Miles and *growing distrust of his loyalty* were to be heard on all sides.
. . . .
As to his loyalty, *there was a universal distrust among the junior officers and men,* who judged both from what was done and left undone, by a commander in such an important crisis.
. . . .
God alone knows the truth of it and will reward him for his patriotism or *punish him for his treason.*[45]

115th Regiment, New York Infantry (1865):

Treason or cowardice in high places had already placed us at the mercy of the foe and it was now almost madness to resist.
. . . .
The rebels demanded the surrender of Harper's Ferry and the Union army; and General Miles, *the Benedict Arnold of modern days,* complied with the demand without hestitation.
. . . .
A dark cloud of sorrow hung over all hearts, while tears and threats of vengeance *against the traitor who sold us* were mingled freely together.[46]

The feelings of the men who were there at Harper's Ferry

cannot be disregarded. Their intuitive suspicions may not constitute proof of Miles's treason but they do constitute a finding
by one of nature's grand juries that there was enough ground
for suspicion to justify a full-dress trial of the question. Accordingly, we have heretofore presented the facts in as great
detail and as accurately as possible more than a century after
the events in question. What remains now is to marshal the key
evidence, much as a lawyer would sum up his case to a trial jury,
to show that Miles's men were not only *reasonable* but, in fact,
right in thus mistrusting their commander.

26

The Summing Up

Any inquiry into why Dixon Miles did the many strange things he did at Harper's Ferry might well begin with his penchant for alcohol and/or use of opium, both of which were well established in the course of his earlier (Bull Run) trial.

It might be sufficient on this point to note the almost total absence of any evidence of his drinking during the Harper's Ferry crisis. Of some forty-five witnesses the only ones who even suggested that alcohol was the culprit were (1) Captain Means of the Loudon County Rangers, who found Miles unreasonably unwilling to believe the Rebels were gathering at Leesburg just before the invasion (September 4, 1862) in the force Means reported, and (2) Colonel Downey of the 3rd Maryland (PHB), who told how Miles had bumbled and could not remember Colonel Ford's name when sending Downey over to Maryland Heights on the morning of Saturday the thirteenth. The same morning Miles unreasonably refused to believe that the two Rebel brigades reported on Maryland Heights by Lieutenant Pearce of the 32nd Ohio were any more than a few skirmishers, but Pearce never suggested in his testimony that he thought Miles was under the influence of alcohol.

Moreover, Miles's aide, Binney, affirmatively testified, for whatever Binney's testimony is worth, that Miles had given up drinking after his Bull Run fiasco, and at Harper's Ferry kept no liquor in his quarters. This, together with the striking absence of any testimony that Miles was drinking by *any* of the forty-two *other* witnesses (most of whom had necessarily had opportunity to observe Miles during the siege of Harper's

Ferry) would alone make untenable a drinking explanation of Miles's actions (except, possibly, for a binge on the night of Friday the twelfth).

The use of drugs is a somewhat different question. It might have been more difficult for his associates to recognize symptoms of drug abuse than the use of alcohol. Knowing that Miles had taken tincture of opium with this brandy during the Bull Run crisis, we cannot rule out the possibility that, deprived of alcohol, he resorted to drugs for the courage to face the overwhelming problems that suddenly and unexpectedly fell on him when Lee crossed the Potomac. Aside, however, from some references to his mental dullness/confusion,[1] there is absolutely no affirmative evidence to support a drug abuse theory.

In any event the real answer to a drug abuse theory, or neurasthenic theory, or any other explanation that turns on a breakdown of Miles's personality when confronted with suddenly overwhelming problems is this. Such a breakdown might well result in strange behavior, but such strangeness would not always tend to give a military advantage to the Rebels. In fact, however, virtually every strange thing that Miles did during the siege tended to *help the Rebel cause.* Because that was its constant tendency, the odds are heavy that that was also its purpose.

Thus the finding of the Harper's Ferry Commission that Miles was guilty of mere "criminal neglect" and "incapacity amounting almost to imbecility" missed the vital point. *His "neglects" and his "imbecilities" all ran in one direction and when viewed as a whole could not be explained other than by a deliberate purpose to see Harper's Ferry fall to the Rebels.* As Shakespeare put it in *Hamlet:* "though this be madness yet there's method in it." Examination of the most important decisions in question makes clear the method in Miles's madness.

1. The Battle of Maryland Heights

(a) It can be argued that Miles's out-and-out disobedience of an order by his department commander (Wool) to build a blockhouse atop Maryland Heights—even to the extent of sending home an engineer detailed for that specific purpose—was just the act of an eccentric field commander who thought he "knew better" than the commanding general. But note well that Miles's violation of this order could *only* help the Rebels—and did so.

(b) It can be argued that Miles's refusal to let Ford keep Potts's battery to control Solomon's Gap (the only practical rear entrance to Maryland Heights) was reasonably justified by Miles's need for artillery to protect Harper's Ferry against possible invasion from the west, but Miles had by then been told by the general in chief's chief of staff (Cullum) to "mainly confine his defense" to Maryland Heights, and putting a battery at Solomon's Gap had been recommended as imperative for that purpose by Ford and others. When the Rebel attack came, the lack of Union artillery at Solomon's Gap put the Rebels on Elk Ridge almost immediately and fathered a Union disaster.

(c) It can be argued that having made Bolivar Heights his main line of defense in his own mind, it was not unreasonable for Miles to assign Ford initially only a handful of infantry to defend Maryland Heights and then to deny Ford adequate reinforcements as the battle progressed. But this is totally inconsistent with his instruction from Cullum and his hour-old assurance to White that he would mainly confine his defense to that position. The assignment of Miles's greenest regiment (the 126th New York) to "reinforce" Ford; his diversion of another full regiment (115th New York) to guard McGrath's guns instead of reversing the Rebels' slight manpower advantage atop the Heights; and his countermand of the 65th Illinois's alert to go over to Maryland Heights two hours before Ford ordered the Heights evacuated, all combined to result in the loss of a key Union position, which, psychologically at least, set the stage for the ultimate surrender of Harper's Ferry.

(d) As for the possibility of reoccupying Maryland Heights on Sunday the fourteenth, under no circumstances can it be argued that Miles's refusal to let the infantry and artillery escape to the Heights was reasonable or even made in good faith. He constantly asserted that his orders were to "hold Harper's Ferry" and that this necessarily excluded the reoccupation of Maryland Heights. This was not just absurdly technical. It flew directly in the face of his instruction from Cullum in case he were surrounded by greatly superior forces to "mainly confine his defense" to Maryland Heights. In this respect Miles *had* to be a liar. The result was to ensure that the whole garrison would fall to Jackson.

2. The Battle of Bolivar Heights

(a) It is hard to see how Miles could reasonably have believed he could successfully defend all of the three-mile-long Bolivar Heights line with the limited number of troops available to him, particularly since he had to be aware of General Saxton's discovery only four months earlier, in the face of Jackson's attack from the West, that he (Saxton) must retire to the much shorter and more defensible Camp Hill line, just west of Harper's Ferry village. (Miles also had the benefit of a suggestion by White—not accepted, of course—for a last-minute, partial shortening of the Bolivar Heights line.) As Miles should have anticipated, the thinness of the Union line would prove to be a constant source of weakness for the garrison.

(b) It is hard to see how Miles could reasonably have refused expert engineering advice to clear all the woods on Bolivar Heights (his theory being that such woods served to mask what the garrison was doing there). Reasonable or not, however, his decision in fact enabled the Rebels to use the woods successfully to shelter their attack on the southernmost sector of Bolivar Heights on the afternoon of Sunday the fourteenth.

(c) It is hard to find even an arguable reason why Miles positioned almost all of the Union troops defending Bolivar Heights along the naturally defensible half which lies north of the Charlestown Pike (now I-340), leaving only one regiment (3rd Maryland [PHB]) with some help from one other regiment (9th Vermont), to guard the whole wild half that lies south of the pike. If Stonewall Jackson could see immediately the uselessness of attacking the northern sector of Bolivar Heights and concentrate all his effort on the relatively undefended southern sector of the line, it is hardly likely that Miles was any less aware of what area needed defending and what did not. The result of Miles's misallocation of resources was to facilitate Jackson's attack on the southern sector with no counterbalancing advantage for the northern sector, where Jackson never intended more than a feint.

(d) It is hard to conceive any possible justification for returning Rebel POWs through the sparsely defended southern sector of the Bolivar Heights line on Friday the twelfth and Saturday the thirteenth. If Stonewall Jackson did not already know of its poorly defended condition, he must thereby have been made aware. It was this sector which Jackson, in fact, made his primary target on Sunday the fourteenth. Miles could not have been unaware of the implications of what he was doing when, contrary to all regular practice, he sent the Rebel POWs home this way.

(e) It can be argued that in particular circumstances a reserve should be saved to retrieve a defeat, even though normally its preferred use is to exploit a success. Here, however, we are at a loss to find any such circumstances. General White's Sunday afternoon order bringing forward Miles's "reserve" (12th New York Militia) from its useless interior position to try to drive Pender's Rebels from Bull's Hill after Rigby's guns had reversed Pender's attack seems unquestionably sound. Right or wrong, moreover, Miles's order returning the 12th New York to inactivity on Camp Hill effectively ended the possibility of driving Pender from Bull's Hill, the favorable location from which Jackson would launch his assault next morning (Monday the fifteenth).

3. Unnecessary Retreat

Along with these major strategic and tactical decisions by Miles which somehow *always* redounded to the Rebels' benefit, we note a number of other decisions (either by Miles or someone he arranged to have take the responsibility) which tended to give ground to the Rebels without a clear necessity to do so.

(a) At the very start of the invasion, as the Rebels poured across the Potomac a few miles south of Harper's Ferry, Miles quickly pulled back his outposts under Colonels Banning and Maulsby at Point of Rocks and at Brunswick (then called Berlin), with no effort to harass the invaders, even though the Rebels then had no thought of attacking Harper's Ferry and, in fact, immediately marched off to Frederick.

(b) One of the clearest examples of Miles's affinity for premature sacrifice was his order to Captain Faithful in Frederick to destroy a large quantity of extremely valuable medical supplies rather than let them fall into Rebel hands. In this instance we know with certainty that such a sacrifice was uncalled for because Faithful simply paid no attention to Miles's order and had all the medicines safely shipped off to Baltimore (and several hundred hospitalized Union soldiers off to Gettysburg) before the Rebels ever reached Frederick.

(c) We do not really know what if any role Miles played in the unfortunate decision of Signal Officer Fortescue to abandon "the lookout" on Maryland Heights (so that McClellan had no way of communicating with Miles when the telegraph lines were cut on the critical day of Friday the twelfth) but it seems most unlikely that Fortescue would have left without Miles's consent (and possibly at Miles's instigation, if the next incident is any indication).

(d) On Friday the twelfth Miles carefully implanted in the minds of two key Union officers on Maryland Heights the idea that the Union defenders might fight but that in the end they would probably have to give up the Heights. (1) Ford's executive officer, Major Hewitt, was directed by Miles to plant a bundle of combustibles at the southeast corner of the mountain, to be set off to call for friendly artillery fire to replace an infantry defense atop Maryland Heights if the infantry defense should fail (a difficult and delicate operation under the most favorable circumstances), and (2) Captain McGrath, in command of the big naval guns and other Union artillery on the Heights, was told by Miles on the same day to "fight 'em, damn 'em, fight 'em"—but to be prepared to spike the cannon and throw them down the mountain if necessary. Hewitt's uneducated attempt to follow Miles's order resulted in chaos and disaster next day and the disappearance of McGrath's great Union guns downhill accomplished all that the Rebels could have wanted on Maryland Heights.

(e) We know (although only because of the fortuitous presence of Mrs. Elizabeth Brown in a room above) that at the very height of Saturday morning's battle for Maryland Heights, Miles was secretly telling Ford how his men "would have to fall back to the Ferry; they could not hold the Heights; the thing was impossible; the Rebel force was too strong." Yet only two hours later Miles was putting on an appearance of shock when first he saw the evacuees wending their way down the mountain: "God Almighty; what does that mean? They are coming down!" In light of all that Miles had done to make Ford surrender Maryland Heights, his dramatic reaction of "surprise" had to be feigned.

4. **Holding the Garrison Prisoner**

Just as Miles arranged for his troops to retreat from his outposts at every possible point, he constantly insisted that they stay put in the center of the Harper's Ferry complex, where they must become prisoners of the Rebels whenever a surrender could be effectuated.

(a) This strategy was clearly revealed in Miles's initial determination to prevent the Sunday night escape of his cavalry—which could have done little if any good by remaining in Harper's Ferry but which would have been a great prize for Stonewall Jackson.

(b) We have already seen how Miles absurdly—and with full consciousness of his untruth—repeatedly invoked Washington's order to hold Harper's Ferry to the last extremity as his reason for not retiring on Sunday night to the safety of Maryland Heights. His invocation of the same authority to prevent his troops from escaping from the whole Harper's Ferry complex may not have been subject to the same infirmity (i.e., Washington really did want him to continue to hold the Harper's Ferry complex so far as he knew). But he could not reasonably have attached such importance to Washington's "last extremity" policy on Sunday night, yet have attached *no* importance to it on Monday morning, when he surrendered in less than an hour to a force hardly larger than his own, before his artillery was out of antipersonnel ammunition and without even awaiting an enemy infantry assault.

Plainly, there are only two possible explanations for such an about-face. Miles's aide, Binney (whom President Lincoln would shortly cashier for practicing a " 'gross fraud' on the War Department") tried to convince the Harper's Ferry Commission that Miles suddenly became "a little flustered" that Monday morning.[2] But such a defense of Miles's strange actions and omissions fails, like all the other instances just reviewed, on the telltale fact that such actions and omissions *always* favored the Rebels. The second and only other possible explanation of Miles's about-face is that he knew perfectly well what he was doing and that his purpose was to make sure that as many of the Union garrison as possible would still be on hand for the surrender that Miles had long ago determined on in his own mind.

5. Concealment of Imminent Relief

To cap all this evidence of Miles's constant care to have Harper's Ferry fall to the Rebels, we have seen, finally, his incredible action on Sunday night concealing from his own men the crucial message from McClellan that relief was at hand. It can hardly be doubted that McClellan's promise of immediate relief (and with it the news that Franklin was probably already in Pleasant Valley) would have electrified a despairing garrison and inspired the brigade commanders' surrender council to fight to "the last extremity." That Miles had to understand this and intend the natural and probable consequences of his deliberate act of concealment seems just as clear. When he not only advanced to Monday morning the Monday night surrender deadline on which he had told McClellan to rely but deliberately withheld from his surrender council the vital news that McClellan apparently intended to meet Miles's original deadline, Dixon Miles branded himself a traitor.

6. Conspiracy?

That Miles was plainly determined to see Harper's Ferry fall to the Rebels and used every possible opportunity to achieve that goal does not, of course, *necessarily* mean that he did so in concert with the enemy. Not only, however, would some intercourse with the enemy seem likely in such a situation, but there is some circumstantial evidence that such may have been the case here.

Miles's private hour with Jackson's spy, Rouse, just before Lee was persuaded by Jackson to reverse his original plan to bypass Harper's Ferry on his way to Pennsylvania, seems suspicious. Suspicious, too, is Miles's unorthodox practice of returning Rebel POWs directly to Jackson each day as late as Sunday the fourteenth—a device by which Miles could easily have kept Jackson current on the progress and further needs of a conspiracy between them. Finally, there is the evidence that Jackson definitely anticipated (whether or not it was ever held) a secret meeting with Miles on Sunday the fourteenth to work out a twenty-four-hour truce to be followed by the garrison's surrender—at the very time Miles's messengers were carrying his assurance to McClellan that Harper's Ferry was safe for forty-eight hours. All this, however, is admittedly speculative and it would be foolish to assert that the evidence of conspiracy is of a calibre with the evidence of disloyalty.

9. Judgment

Whether Miles did what he did in concert with Stonewall Jackson is of little importance, however, in comparison with the finding required by all the evidence—old and new—that ten thousand angry Union soldiers had to be *right* in doubting Miles's loyalty to the union cause. He surrendered his post precipitately to a barely larger attacking force. He did so without even awaiting an infantry assault, although his artillery still had a quantity of anti-personnel shells available to meet such an attack. Even a musketry defense could have held the Rebels for some time. He obtained the assent of his senior officers to such a surrender by fraudulently concealing from them the crucial news that McClellan's relieving army was only hours away and that McClellan himself "felt confident he could relieve the place." In light of the mass of circumstantial evidence we have reviewed—from Miles's refusal to fortify and defend Maryland Heights to his countermand of White's order to exploit the only Union success on Sunday afternoon—a trial jury should find that Harper's Ferry was, as Gideon Welles put it, "thrown to the Rebels with scarcely a struggle" by a man the historian of the 115th New York not inaptly called the "Benedict Arnold" of the Civil War.

Appendix

Report of the Harper's Ferry Commission

WASHINGTON, D. C., *November 3, 1862.*

The Commission met pursuant to adjournment.

* * * * * * *

The Commission adopted a report, which accompanies this record, marked A, of the circumstances attending the evacuation of Winchester by General Julius White, which was signed by the president, Major-General Hunter, and attested by the judge-advocate.

The Commission then adopted a report in relation to the circumstances attending the evacuation of Maryland Heights and the surrender of Harper's Ferry, which was signed by the president and judge-advocate of the Commission, and accompanies this record.

Thereupon the Commission adjourned to meet again at 11 a.m. tomorrow.

D. HUNTER,
Major-General, President.

REPORT

The Commission, consisting of Maj. Gen. D. Hunter, U. S. Volunteers, president; Maj. Gen. G. Cadwalader, U. S. Volunteers; Brig. Gen. C. C. Augur, U. S. Volunteers; Capt. Donn

Source: U.S. War Department, *The War of the Rebellion: A Compilation of the Official Records of the Union and Confederate Armies,* 128 vols. (Washington, D.C.: G.P.O., 1880–1901, series I, vol. XIX, pt. 1, pp. 794–800.

Piatt, assistant adjutant general of Volunteers; Capt. F. Ball, jr., aide de camp, U. S. Army; Col. A. Holt, Judge-Advocate-General, called by the Government to investigate the conduct of certain officers connected with, and the circumstances attending, the abandonment of Maryland Heights and the surrender of Harper's Ferry, have the honor to report as follows:

On the 3d day of September, General White entered Harper's Ferry, with his command, from Winchester. The next day he was ordered to Martinsburg, to take command of the forces at that place. On the 12th of September he again returned to Harper's Ferry, where he remained until its surrender, without assuming command.

On the 7th of September, General McClellan (the larger portion of his command having preceded him) left Washington, under orders, issued some days previously, to drive the enemy from Maryland. He established that night his headquarters at Rockville, and from which place, on the 11th of September, he telegraphed to General Halleck to have Colonel Miles ordered to join him at once.

On the 5th of September, Col. Thomas H. Ford, of the Thirty-second Ohio, took command of the forces on Maryland Heights.

Forces were placed at Solomon's Gap and Sandy Hook. Those at Sandy Hook, being under Colonel Maulsby, retired, by order of Colonel Miles, to the eastern slope of Maryland Heights two or three days previous to their evacuation by Colonel Ford.

On the 11th of September the force at Solomon's Gap was driven in by the enemy. Colonel Ford called upon Colonel Miles for re-enforcements, and on Friday, the 12th of September, the Thirty-ninth and One hundred and twenty-sixth New York Regiments were sent him, and on the morning of the 13th he was further re-enforced by the One hundred and fifteenth New York and a portion of a Maryland regiment under Lieutenant-Colonel Downey.

Colonel Ford made requisition for axes and spades to enable him to construct defenses on the heights, but obtained none, and on the 12th, with twelve axes belonging to some Maryland regiment, being all he could obtain, a slight breastwork of trees was constructed near the crest of the heights, and in front of which for a short distance a slashing of timber was made.

The forces under Colonel Ford were stationed at various

points on Maryland Heights, the principal force being on the crest of the hill near the breastwork and lookout. Skirmishing commenced on Friday, the 12th, on the crest of the hill.

Early in the morning of the 13th the enemy made an attack on the crest of the hill, and, after a short engagement, the troops retired in some confusion to the breastwork, where they were rallied. About 9 o'clock a second attack was made, which the troops behind the breastwork resisted for a short time, and until Colonel Sherrill, of the One hundred and twenty-sixth New York, was wounded and carried off the field, when the entire One hundred and twenty-sixth Regiment, as some witnesses testify, with the exception of two companies, as Major Hewitt states, broke and fled in utter confusion. Both men and most of the officers fled together, no effort being made to rally the regiment except by Colonel Ford and Lieutenant Barras, acting adjutant, and some officers of other regiments, directed by Colonel Miles, who was then on the heights.

Soon after, the remaining forces at the breastwork fell back under a supposed order from Major Hewitt, who himself says that he gave no such order, but merely sent instructions to the captains of his own regiment that, if they were compelled to retire, to do so in good order. Orders were given by Colonel Ford for the troops to return to their position, and they advanced some distance up the heights, but did not regain the breastwork.

That morning Colonel Miles was on Maryland Heights for some hours, consulting with Colonel Ford. He left between 11 and 12 o'clock without directly ordering Colonel Ford to evacuate the heights, but instructing him, in case he was compelled to do so, to spike his guns and throw the heavy siege guns down the mountain. About 2 o'clock, perhaps a little later, by order of Colonel Ford, the heights were abandoned, the guns being spiked according to instructions.

On Sunday, Colonel D'Utassy sent over to the Maryland Heights four companies, under Major Wood, who brought off without opposition four brass 12-pounders, two of which were imperfectly spiked, and also a wagon-load of ammunition.

General White, on his return to Harper's Ferry on the 12th of September, suggested to Colonel Miles the propriety of contracting his lines on Bolivar Heights so as to make a better defense; but Colonel Miles adhered to his original line of defense, stating that he was determined to make his stand on

Bolivar Heights. General White also urged the importance of holding Maryland Heights, even should it require the taking the entire force over there from Harper's Ferry. Colonel Miles, under his orders to hold Harper's Ferry to the last extremity, while admitting the importance of Maryland Heights, seemed to regard them as applying to the town of Harper's Ferry, and held that to leave Harper's Ferry even to go on Maryland Heights would be disobeying his instructions.

General McClellan established his headquarters at Frederick City on the morning of the 13th of September.

On the night of the 13th, after the evacuation of Maryland Heights, Colonel Miles directed Captain (now Major) Russell, of the Maryland cavalry, to take with him a few men and endeavor to get through the enemy's lines and reach some of our forces, General McClellan if possible, and to report the condition of Harper's Ferry; that it could not hold out more than forty-eight hours unless re-enforced, and to urge the sending of re-enforcements. Captain Russell reached General McClellan's headquarters at Frederick at 9 a.m. on Sunday, the 14th of September, and reported as directed by Colonel Miles. Immediately upon his arrival, General McClellan sent off a messenger, as Captain Russell understood, to General Franklin. At 10 a.m. Captain Russell left for General Franklin's command, with a communication to General Franklin from General McClellan. He reached General Franklin about 3 o'clock that afternoon, and found him engaged with the enemy at Crampton's Gap. The enemy was driven from the gap, and the next morning, the 15th, General Franklin passed through the gap, advancing about a mile, and, finding the enemy drawn up in line of battle in his front, drew his own forces up in line of battle. While there stationed, the cannonading in the direction of Harper's Ferry, which had been heard very distinctly all the morning, Harper's Ferry being about 7 miles distant, suddenly ceased; whereupon General Franklin sent word to General McClellan of the probable surrender of Harper's Ferry by Colonel Miles, and did not deem it necessary to proceed farther in that direction.

The battle of South Mountain was fought on Sunday, the 14th, and on the same day, during the afternoon, the enemy at Harper's Ferry attacked the extreme left of the line on Bolivar Heights, but, after some time, were repulsed by the troops under the command of General White. On Sunday night the cavalry at Harper's Ferry made their escape, under Colonel Davis, of the Twelfth Illinois Cavalry,* by permission of Colonel Miles, and reached Greencastle, Pa., the next morning, capturing on their way an ammunition train belonging to General Longstreet, consisting of some 50 or 60 wagons.

The Commission regard this escape of cavalry as being worthy of great commendation to the officers conducting the same.

Several of the infantry officers desired permission to cut their way out at the same time the cavalry made their escape, but Colonel Miles refused, upon the ground that he had been ordered to hold Harper's Ferry to the last extremity.

On the morning of the 15th the enemy opened their batteries from several points, seven to nine, as estimated by different witnesses, directing their attack principally upon our batteries on the left of Bolivar Heights.

The attack commenced at daybreak; about 7 o'clock Colonel Miles represented to General White that it would be necessary to surrender. General White suggested that the brigade commanders be called together, which was done. Colonel Miles stated that the ammunition for the batteries was exhausted, and he had about made up his mind to surrender. That was finally agreed to by all present, and General White was sent to arrange articles of capitulation. The white flag was raised by order of Colonel Miles, but the enemy did not cease firing for some half or three-quarters of an hour after. Colonel Miles was mortally wounded after the white flag was raised. The surrender was agreed upon about 8 a.m. on Monday, the 15th of September.

The following was the testimony of officers commanding batteries:

At the time of the surrender, Captain Von Sehlen had some ammunition; could not tell what amount, but mostly shrapnel; had lost about 100 rounds on Saturday, the 13th, by the explosion of a limber, caused by one of the enemy's shells.

Captain Rigby had expended, during the siege of Harper's Ferry, about 600 rounds, being all that he had with the exception of canister.

Captain Potts had expended about 1,000 rounds, being all that he had with the exception of canister.

---

*Col. B. F. Davis, Eighth New York Cavalry, was the officer meant, and he was brevetted for this service.

Captain Graham had but two guns of his battery under his immediate command on the morning of the surrender; had probably 100 rounds of all kinds, but no long-time fuses.

Captain Phillips had expended all his ammunition except some 40 rounds of canister and some long-range shells, too large for his guns.

Captain McGrath's battery had been spiked and left on Maryland Heights on Saturday.

It appears that during the siege, and shortly previous, Colonel Miles paroled several Confederate prisoners and permitted them to pass through our lines. During the week previous to the evacuation of Maryland Heights, a Lieutenant Rouse, of the Twelfth Virginia Cavalry, who had been engaged in a raid upon a train from Harper's Ferry to Winchester a short time before, was captured and brought into Harper's Ferry. He escaped while on the way to the hospital, by pretending to be sick, but was retaken. He was paroled, but returned in command of some rebel cavalry on the morning of the surrender. The attention of General A. P. Hill was called to the fact that Lieutenant Rouse was a paroled prisoner, but no attention was paid to it. Lieutenant Rouse himself, on being spoken to about it, laughed at the idea of observing his parole.

On Saturday, the day of the attack upon and evacuation of Maryland Heights, Colonel Miles directed that 16 Confederate prisoners be permitted to pass through our lines to rejoin the rebel army at Winchester. Other cases are testified to, but the above-named are of the most importance.

Of the subordinate officers referred to in this case, with the exception of Col. Thomas H. Ford, the Commission finds nothing in their conduct that calls for censure. On the contrary, General Julius White merits its approbation. He appears from the evidence to have acted with decided capability and courage.

In this connection the Commission calls attention to the disgraceful behavior of the One hundred and twenty-sixth New York Infantry, and recommend that Major Baird, for his bad conduct, as shown by the evidence, should be dismissed the service. Some of the officers of this regiment, Lieutenant Barras, acting adjutant, and others, not known by name to the Commission, behaved gallantly, and should be commended.

COL. THOMAS H. FORD

In the case of Colonel Ford, charged with improper conduct in abandoning Maryland Heights, the Commission, after a careful hearing of the evidence produced by the Government, and that relied on by the defense, and a due consideration of the arguments offered by counsel, finds:

That on the 5th of September Colonel Ford was placed in command of Maryland Heights by Colonel Miles; that Colonel Ford, finding the position unprepared by fortifications, earnestly urged Colonel Miles to furnish him means by which the heights could be made tenable for the small force under his command should a heavy one be brought against him. These reasonable demands were, from some cause unknown to the Commission, not responded to by the officer in command of Harper's Ferry; that subsequently, when the enemy appeared in heavy force, Colonel Ford frequently and earnestly called upon Colonel Miles for more troops, representing that he could not hold the heights unless re-enforced; that these demands were feebly, or not at all, complied with; that, as late as the morning of the 13th of September, Colonel Ford sent two written demands to Colonel Miles for re-enforcements, and saying that, with the troops then under his command, he could not hold the heights, and, unless relieved or otherwise ordered, he would have to abandon them; that, as late as 11 o'clock a.m. of the 13th, a few hours previous to the abandonment of this position, Colonel Miles said to Colonel Ford that he (Colonel Ford) could not have another man, and must do the best he could; and, if unable to defend the place, he must spike the guns, throw them down the hill, and withdraw to Harper's Ferry in good order.

The Commission is, then, satisfied that Colonel Ford was given a discretionary power to abandon the heights or not, as his better judgment might dictate, with the men and means then under his command; and it is believed from the evidence, circumstantial and direct, that the result did not, to any great extent, surprise, nor in any way displease, the officer in command at Harper's Ferry.

But this conclusion, so much relied upon by the defense, forces the Commission to consider the fact: Did Colonel Ford, under the discretionary power thus vested in him, make a proper defense of the heights, and hold them, as he should have done, until driven off by the enemy?

The evidence shows conclusively that the force upon the heights was not well managed; that the point most pressed was weakly defended as to numbers, and, after the wounding of the gallant colonel of the One hundred and twenty-sixth New York

Infantry, it was left without a competent officer in command, Colonel Ford, himself, not appearing nor designating any one who might have restored order and encouraged the men. That the abandonment of the heights was premature is clearly proven. Our forces were not driven from the field, as full time was given to spike the guns and throw the heavier ones down the precipice, and retreat in good order to Harper's Ferry. The loss in killed and wounded does not indicate a desperate conflict, and the opinion of officers sustaining that abandonment is weakened by the fact that the next day a force returning to the heights found them unoccupied, and brought away, unmolested, four abandoned guns and a quantity of ammunition.

In so grave a case as this, with such disgraceful consequences, the Commission cannot permit an officer to shield himself behind the fact that he did as well as he could, if in so doing he exhibits a lack of military capacity. It is clear to the Commission that Colonel Ford should not have been placed in command on Maryland Heights; that he conducted, the defense without ability, and abandoned his position without sufficient cause, and has shown throughout such a lack of military capacity as to disqualify him, in the estimation of this Commission, for a command in the service.

COL. D. S. MILES.

The Commission has approached a consideration of this officer's conduct, in connection with the surrender of Harper's Ferry, with extreme reluctance. An officer who cannot appear before any earthly tribunal to answer to explain charges gravely affecting his character, who has met his death at the hands of the enemy, even upon the spot he disgracefully surrendered, is entitled to the tenderest care and most careful investigation. These this Commission has accorded Colonel Miles, and, in giving an opinion, only repeats what runs through our nine hundred pages of evidence, strangely unanimous upon the fact that Colonel Miles' incapacity, amounting to almost imbecility, led to the shameful surrender of this important post.

Early as the 15th of August he disobeys orders of Major-General Wool to fortify Maryland Heights. When it is attacked by the enemy, its naturally strong positions are unimproved, and, from his criminal neglect, to use the mildest term, the large force of the enemy is almost upon an equality with the few men he throws out for their protection.

He seemed to have understood and admitted to his officers

that Maryland Heights was the key to the position, and yet he placed Colonel Ford in command with a feeble force; made no effort to strengthen him by fortifications, although, between the 5th and the 13th of September, there was ample time to do so; and to Colonel Ford's repeated demands for means to intrench and re-enforcements to strengthen the position, he made either inadequate return or no response at all. He gave Colonel Ford discretionary power as to when he should abandon the heights, the fact of the abandonment having, it seems, been determined in his own mind, for, when the unhappy event really occurred, his only exclamations were to the effect that he feared Colonel Ford had given them up too soon. This, too, when he must have known that the abandonment of Maryland Heights was the surrender of Harper's Ferry. This leaving the key of the position to the keeping of Colonel Ford, with discretionary power, after the arrival of the capable and courageous officer who had waived his rank to serve wherever ordered, is one of the more striking facts illustrating the utter incapacity of Colonel Miles.

Immediately previous to and pending the siege of Harper's Ferry he paroled rebel prisoners, and permits, indeed, sends them to the enemy's headquarters. This, too, when he should have known that the lack of ammunition, the bad conduct of some of our troops, the entire absence of fortifications, and the abandonment of Maryland Heights were important facts they could, and undoubtedly did, communicate to the enemy. Sixteen of these prisoners were paroled on the 12th, and a pass given them in the handwriting of Colonel Miles, and some of them left as late as the 14th; while a rebel officer, by the name of Rouse, after an escape, is retaken, and subsequently has a private interview with Colonel Miles, is paroled, and after the surrender appears at the head of his men, among the first to enter Harper's Ferry.

It is not necessary to accumulate instances from the mass of evidence that throughout scarcely affords one fact in contradiction to what each one establishes, that Colonel Miles was unfit to conduct so important a defense as that of Harper's Ferry.

This Commission would not have dwelt upon this painful subject were it not for the fact that the officer who placed this incapable in command should share in the responsibility, and in the opinion of the Commission Major-General Wool is guilty to this extent of a grave disaster, and should be censured for his conduct.

The Commission has remarked freely on the conduct of Colonel Miles, an old officer, killed in one of the battles of our country, and it cannot, from any motives of delicacy, refrain from censuring those in high command when it thinks such censure deserved. The General-in-Chief has testified that General McClellan, after having received orders to repel the enemy invading the State of Maryland, marched only 6 miles per day on an average when pursuing the invading enemy. The General-in-Chief also testifies that, in his opinion, General McClellan could, and should, have relieved and protected Harper's Ferry, and in this opinion the Commission fully concur.

The evidence thus introduced confirms the Commission in the opinion that Harper's Ferry, as well as Maryland Heights, was prematurely surrendered. The garrison should have been satisfied that relief, however long delayed, would come at last, and that 1,000 men killed in Harper's Ferry would have made a small loss had the post been secured, and probably save 2,000 at Antietam. How important was this defense we can now appreciate. Of the 97,000 composing at that time the whole of Lee's army, more than one-third were attacking Harper's Ferry, and of this the main body was in Virginia. By reference to the evidence, it will be seen that at the moment Colonel Ford abandoned Maryland Heights his little army was in reality relieved by Generals Franklin's and Sumner's corps at Crampton's Gap, within 7 miles of his position, and that after the surrender of Harper's Ferry no time was given to parole prisoners even, before 20,000 troops were hurried from Virginia, and the entire force went off on the double-quick to relieve Lee, who was being attacked at Antietam. Had the garrison been slower to surrender or the Army of the Potomac swifter to march, the enemy would have been forced to raise the siege or have been taken in detail, with the Potomac dividing his forces.

D. HUNTER,
Major-General, President.

J. HOLT,
    Judge-Advocate-General.

Bibliography

Ambrose, Stephen E. *Halleck: Lincoln's Chief of Staff.* Baton Rouge, La.: Louisiana State University Press, 1962.

Ansley, Norman. "The United States Secret Service: An Administrative History." *Journal of Criminal Law, Criminology and Police Science* 47 (May-June 1956).

Barnes, J. K., Surgeon General. *Medical and Surgical History of the War of the Rebellion.* Baltimore, Md.: 1870.

Bartlett, John Russell. *Personal Narrative of Exploration and Incidents in Texas, New Mexico, California, Sonora and Chihuahua* . . . 2 vols. London: G. Routledge & Co., 1854; New York: D. Appleton & Co., 1856; Chicago: Rio Grande Press, 1965.

Barton, William Eleazar. *The Life of Clara Barton.* Boston/New York: Houghton Mifflin Co., 1922.

Baucr, Karl Jack. *The Mexican War, 1846–1848.* New York: Macmillan, 1972.

Beals, Carleton. *Brass Knuckle Crusade (The Great Know-Nothing Conspiracy: 1820–1860).* New York: Hastings House, 1960.

Bell, Thomas. *At Harper's Ferry, Va., September 14, 1862. How the Cavalry Escaped out of the Toils* [*sic*]. Brooklyn, N.Y.: 1900. [Pamphlet found in U.S.A.A.M.H.R.C., Carlisle Barracks, Pa., Civil War Repository.]

Benet, Stephen Vincent. *A Treatise on Military Law and the Practice of Courts Martial.* New York: D. Van Nostrand, 1862, 1868.

Blackford, William Willis. *War Years with Jeb Stuart.* New York: C. Scribner's Sons, 1945.

Brown, Joseph Willard. *The Signal Corps, U.S.A. in the War of the Rebellion.* Boston: U.S. Veteran Signal Corps Assn., 1896; New York: Arno Press, 1974.

Bushong, Millard Kessler. *A History of Jefferson County, West Virginia.* Charles Town, W. Va.: Jefferson Publishing Co., 1941.

Caldwell, James FitzJames. *The History of a Brigade of South Carolinians Known First as "Gregg's Brigade" and Subsequently as "McGowan's Brigade."* Philadelphia: King & Baird, Printers, 1866.

Campbell, James Havelock. *McClellan.* New York: Neale Publishing Co., 1916.

Canan, H.V. "Confederate Military Intelligence." *Maryland Historical Magazine* 59 (March 1964): 35, 37.

Carman, Ezra Ayers. *History of the Civil War, Maryland Campaign, September, 1862.* [Unpublished, in Manuscript Division, Library of Congress.]

Catton, Bruce. *Mr. Lincoln's Army.* New York: Doubleday & Co., 1951; New York: Pocket Books, Inc., 1964.

Chase, Salmon P. "Diary of Salmon P. Chase." In *Annual Report of the American Historical Association for the Year 1902.* 2 vols. Washington, D.C.: Government Printing Office, 1903.

Clark, C. B. "Politics in Maryland during the Civil War." *Maryland Historical Magazine* 38 (1943): 243; 39 (1944): 149.

Clark, James. H. *The Iron Hearted Regiment: Being an Account of the Battles, Marches and Gallant Deeds Performed by the 115th Regiment, N.Y. Volunteers.* Albany, N.Y.: J. Munsell, 1865.

Colegrove, S. "The Finding of Lee's Lost Order." In *Battles and Leaders of the Civil War.* 4 vols. New York: The Century Co., 1887; New York: Thomas Yoseloff, 1956. 2: 603.

Corliss, Augustus W. "History of the Seventh Squadron, Rhode Island Cavalry." State of Rhode Island, *Adjutant General's Report,* 1865.

Crozier, Emmett. *Yankee Reporters: 1861–65.* New York: Oxford University Press, 1956.

Cullum, George Washington. *Biographical Register of Officers and Cadets, U.S. Military Academy.* 6 vols. Boston: Houghton Mifflin Co., 1891.

Dickert, D. Augustus. *History of Kershaw's Brigade.* Newberry, S.C.: E.H. Aull Co., 1899; Dayton, Ohio: William Stanley Hoole, Press of Morningside Bookshop, 1976.

Douglas, Henry Kyd. *I Rode with Stonewall,* Chapel Hill, N.C.: University of North Carolina Press, 1940; Greenwich, Conn.: Fawcett Publications, Inc., 1965.

Dowley, Morris Francis. *History and Honorary Roll of the 12th Regiment, Infantry, N.G.S.N.Y.* New York: T. Farrell & Son, 1869.

Early, Jubal Anderson. *Jubal A. Early: Autobiographical Sketch and Narrative of the War between the States, with Notes by R. H. Early.* Philadelphia and London: J.B. Lippincott Co., 1912.

Eisenschiml, Otto. *The Celebrated Case of Fitz John Porter, an American Dreyfus Affair.* Indianapolis and New York: Bobbs-Merrill Co., Inc., 1950.

Forbes, J. G. *Report on the Trial of Brig. Gen. William Hull, Commanding the Northwestern Army of the United States, by a Court-Martial Held at Albany on Monday, 3rd January 1814 and Succeeding Days.* New York: Eastburn, Kirk & Co., 1814.

Franklin, William B. "Notes on Crampton's Gap and Antietam." In *Battles and Leaders of the Civil War.* 4 vols. New York: The Century Co., 1887; New York: Thomas Yoseloff, 1956. 2: 591.

Freeman, Douglas Southall. *Robert E. Lee.* 4 vols. London: C. Scribner's Sons, 1934–35, 1937.

Freeman, Douglas Southall. *Lee's Lieutenants.* 4 vols. New York: C. Scribner's Sons, 1942–44, 1946.

Graham, Albert Adams. *History of Richland County, Ohio.* Mansfield, Ohio: A. A. Graham & Co., 1880.

Greeley, Horace. *The American Conflict.* 2 vols. Hartford, Conn.: O. D. Case & Co., 1864–66: Chicago: G. and C. W. Sherwood, 1864–66; New York: Negro Universities Press, 1969.

Hall, Florence Howe. *The Story of the Battle Hymn of the Republic.* Freeport, N.Y.: Books for Libraries Press, 1971.

Hawkins, Archibald. *The Life and Times of Hon. Elijah Stansbury, an "Old Defender" and Ex-Mayor of Baltimore.* Baltimore, Md.: J. Murphy & Co., Printer, 1874.

Hays, Ebenezer Z. *History of the Thirty-Second Regiment (Ohio Veteran Volunteer Infantry).* Columbus, Ohio: Cott & Evans, printer, 1896.

Hotchkiss, Jed. *Make Me a Map of the Valley: The Civil War Journal of Stonewall Jackson's Topographer.* Edited by Archie P. McDonald. Dallas, Tex.: Southern Methodist University Press, 1973.

Howe, Henry. *Historical Collections of Ohio.* 3 vols. Cincinnati, Ohio: Derby, Bradley & Co., 1847. 2 vols. Columbus, Ohio: H. Howe & Son, 1889–91.

Howe, Julia Ward. *Reminiscences, 1819–1899.* Boston and New York. Houghton, Mifflin Co., 1899; New York: Negro Universities Press, 1969.

Hungerford, Edward. *The Story of the Baltimore and Ohio Railroad (1827–1927).* 2 vols. New York and London: G. P. Putnam's Sons, 1928.

Johnson, Robert Underwood, and Buel, Clarence Clough. *Battles and Leaders of the Civil War.* 4 vols. New York: The Century Co., 1887; New York: Thomas Yoseloff, 1956.

Johnston, Christopher. "The Stansbury Family." *Maryland Historical Magazine* 9 (1914): 72.

Larson, Robert W. *New Mexico's Quest for Statehood, 1846–1912.* Albuquerque, N.M.: University of New Mexico Press, 1968.

Longstreet, James. *From Manassas to Appomattox.* Philadelphia: J. B. Lippincott Co., 1896.

Longstreet, James. "The Invasion of Maryland." In *Battles and Leaders of the Civil War.* 4 vols. New York: The Century Co., 1887; New York: Thomas Yoseloff, 1956. 2: 663.

Loudon County Civil War Centennial Commission. *Loudon County and the Civil War.* Leesburg, Va.: Potomac Press, 1961.

Luff, W. M. "March of the Cavalry from Harper's Ferry, September 14, 1862." In *Military Essays and Recollections*, vol. 2. Chicago: M.O.L.L.U.S. (Illinois Commandery), 1894.

Manakee, H. R. *Maryland in the Civil War*. Baltimore, Md.: Maryland Historical Society, 1961.

Marine, William Matthew. *The British Invasion of Maryland, 1812–1815*. Baltimore, Md.: Society of the War of 1812, 1913; Baltimore, Md.: Genealogical Publishing Co., 1977.

Maryland House of Delegates. *Report of the Committee on Federal Relations in Regard to Calling of a Sovereign Convention*. Frederick, Md.: State of Maryland, 1861.

McClellan, George Brinton. *Report on the Organization and Campaigns of the Army of the Potomac*. New York: Sheldon & Co., 1864.

McClellan, George Brinton. *McClellan's Own Story*. New York: C. L. Webster & Co., 1886.

McClellan, George Brinton. *The McClellan Papers*. Microfilm, 82 Reels, Manuscript Collection, Library of Congress.

McDonald, William N. *A History of the Laurel Brigade, Originally Ashby's Cavalry*. Baltimore, Md.: Mrs. Kate S. McDonald, 1907; Arlington, Va.: R. W. Beatty, 1969.

Moore, Frank, ed. *The Rebellion Record: A Diary of American Events*. 12 vols. Volumes 1–6, New York: Putnam, 1861–63; volumes 7–12, New York: Van Nostrand, 1864–68; volumes 1–12, New York: Arno Press, 1977.

Murfin, James V. *The Gleam of Bayonets*. [Introduction by J. I. Richardson.] New York and London: Thomas Yoseloff, 1965; New York: Bonanza Books, 1968.

Newcomer, Christopher Armour. *Cole's Cavalry or Three Years in the Saddle in the Shenandoah Valley*. Freeport, N.Y.: Books for Libraries Press, 1970 (Reprint of 1895 ed.).

Nichols, William H. "The Siege and Capture of Harper's Ferry." In *Personal Narratives of Events in the War of the Rebellion*. Series 4, no. 2, Providence, R.I.: The Rhode Island Soldiers and Sailors Society, 1889.

Norton, Henry King. *Deeds of Daring or History of the 8th New York Volunteer Cavalry*. Norwich, N.Y.: Chenango Printing House, 1889.

Pettengill, Samuel B. *The College Cavaliers*. Chicago: H. McAllaster & Company, 1883.

Pfanz, Harry W. *Harper's Ferry Troop Movement Maps, 1862*, U.S. Department of the Interior, National Park Service [Available from U.S. Commerce Department, National Technical Information Service, 5285 Port Royal Road, Springfield, Virginia, 22151], 1976.

Phisterer, Federick. *New York in the War of the Rebellion*. 6 vols. Albany, N.Y.: Weed, Parsons & Company, 1890; Albany, N.Y.: J. B. Lyon Company, 1912.

Pierce, Bessie Louise. *A History of Chicago (1847–1871)*. 3 vols. New

York and London: Alfred A. Knopf, 1937; Chicago: University of Chicago Press, 1975.

Poague, William Thomas. *Gunner with Stonewall.* Jackson, Tenn.: McCowat-Mercer Press, 1957.

Reeling, Viola Crouch. *Evanston, Its Land and Its People.* Evanston, Ill.: Daughters of the American Revolution, Ft. Dearborn Chapter, 1928.

Reid, Whitelaw. *Ohio in the War.* 2 vols. Cincinnati, Ohio, and New York: Wilstach & Baldwin, 1868.

Ripley, Edward Hastings. *Vermont General.* EWdited by Otto Eisenschiml. New York: Devin-Adair Company, 1960.

Ripley, E. H. "Memories of the Ninth Vermont at the Tragedy of Harper's Ferry." In *Personal Recollections of the War of the Rebellion,* vol. 4. M.O.L.L.U.S. (New York Commandery), 1909.

Rosebloom, Eugene H., and Weisenburger, Francis P. *A History of Ohio.* Columbus, Ohio: The Ohio State Archeological and Historical Society, 1953.

Rosebloom, Eugene H. "Salmon P. Chase and the Know Nothings." *Mississippi Valley Historical Review* 25 (1938): 349.

Seward, William Henry. *William Henry Seward: An Autobiography.* Edited by Frederick William Seward. 3 vols. New York: Derby & Miller, 1891.

Shaara, Michael. *The Killer Angels.* New York: David McKay Company, 1974.

Sherman, John. *Recollections of Forty Years in the House, Senate and Cabinet.* 2 vols. Chicago: The Werner Company, 1895; New York: Greenwood Press, 1968.

Smith, Justin Harvey. *The War with Mexico.* 2 vols. New York: The Macmillan Company, 1919.

Smith, William A. "Stonewall Jackson's Intentions at Harper's Ferry." *The Century Magazine* 38 (1889) [New Series, vol. 16]: 310.

Steiner, Bernard Christian. *Life of Reverdy Johnson.* Baltimore, Md.: The Norman Remington Company, 1914; New York: Russell & Russell, 1970.

Strother, David Hunter. *A Virginia Yankee in the Civil War: The Diaries of David Hunter Strother.* Edited by C. D. Eby. Chapel Hill, N.C.: University of North Carolina Press, 1961.

Tanner, R. G. *Stonewall in the Valley,* Garden City, N. Y.: Doubleday & Company, 1976.

Taylor, Walter H. *Four Years with General Lee.* Edited by J. I. Robertson. Bloomington, Ind.: Indiana University Press, 1962; New York: Bonanza Books.

Thomas, Lately. *Sam Ward, King of the Lobby.* Boston: Houghton Mifflin Company, 1965.

Thompson, Benjamin W. *Recollections of War Times.* [Unpublished memoir, now in Civil War Times Illustrated Collection, U.S.A.M.H.R.C., Carlisle Barracks, Pennsylvania.]

Thompson, James Henry. *The History of the County of Highland in the State of Ohio.* Hillsboro, Ohio: Hillsboro *Gazette,* 1893.

Trimble, Allen. *Autobiography and Correspondence of Allen Trimble.* [reprint from Old Northwest Genealogical Society, "Genealogy of Trimble"] Columbus, Ohio: 1909.

Tuttle, Mary McArthur. "William Allen Trimble, United States Senator from Ohio." *Ohio Archaeological and Historical Quarterly* 14 (1905):225.

U. S. Army, *Telegrams Received by Maj. Gen. H. W. Halleck While General in Chief and Chief of Staff.* 5 vols. Washington: War Department Printing Office, 1877.

U.S. Army, *Telegrams sent by Maj. Gen. H. W. Halleck While General in Chief and Chief of Staff.* 4 vols. Washington: War Department Printing Office, 1877.

U.S. Congress, 36 Cong., 1 Sess., House of Representatives, Exec. Doc. 2. *Message from the President of the United States, etc.* (including Report of the Secretary of War for 1859–1860).

U.S. Congress, 37 Cong., 2 Sess., Senate Doc. 7, *Message of the President of the United States, etc.* (including copies of the charges, testimony and findings in the court of inquiry concerning Colonel Dixon S. Miles's behavior at the Battle of Bull Run I).

U.S. Congress, 37 Cong., 3 Sess. *Report of the Joint Committee on the Conduct of the War.* vol. 3. 1863.

U.S. National Archives, Washington, D. C. [The records of the *National Archives* are a basic source of material for almost any research concerning the Civil War. Its military and pension records (Record Group 79) are the usual source of information about the background, military record and/or subsequent history (civilian as well as military) of individual soldiers referred to here. Of particular interest for the present study is File KK311 in Record Group 153, which contains the original transcript and some exhibits in the proceedings before the Harper's Ferry Commission and the Winchester Commission.]

U.S. War Department. *The War of the Rebellion: A Compilation of the Official Records of the Union and Confederate Armies.* 128 vols. Washington, D. C.: Government Printing Office, 1880–1901. *Referred to in all notes here as "WR/OR."* [Nearly all references here are to part I of volume XIX, series I, which contains the transcript of all testimony before the Harper's Ferry Commission, as well as most relevant Confederate battle reports.]

Vanity Fair Album. series 12, no. 214. London: Vanity Fair, 1880.

Walker, John G. "Jackson's Capture of Harper's Ferry." In *Battles and Leaders of the Civil War.* 4 vols. New York: The Century Co., 1887; New York: Thomas Yoseloff, 1956. 2:604.

Waring, George E. "The Garibaldi Guard." In *The First Book of the Authors Club (Liber Scriptorum).* New York: The Authors' Club (De Vinne Press), 1893.

Welles, Gideon. *Diary of Gideon Welles (1861–1864),* vol. 1. Edited by John T. Morse. Boston and New York: Houghton Mifflin Company, 1911.

Wellman, Manly Wade. *Harper's Ferry, Prize of War.* Charlotte, N.C.: McNally of Charlotte, 1960.

White, Julius. "The Capitulation of Harper's Ferry." In *Battles and Leaders of the Civil War.* 4 vols. New York: The Century Co., 1887; New York, Thomas Yoseloff, 1956. 2:612.

Willard, Frances Elizabeth. *The Story of Evanston, a Classic Town.* Chicago: Woman's Temperance Publishing Assn., 1892.

Willson, Arabella M. [Stuart]. *Disaster, Struggle, Triumph: The Adventures of 1000 "Boys in Blue."* Albany, N.Y.: Argus Co., 1870.

Wilmer, L. Allison; Jarrett, J. H.: and Vernon. George W. F. *History and Roster of Maryland Volunteers, War of 1861–1865.* 2 vols. Baltimore, Md.: Press of Guggenheimer, Weill & Co., 1898.

Wilson, James Grant. *Biographical Sketches of Illinois Officers Engaged in the War Against the Rebellion of 1861.* Chicago: J. Barnet, 1862, 1863.

Wittke, Carl Frederick. *History of the State of Ohio.* 6 vols. Columbus, Ohio: Ohio State Archaeological and Historical Society, 1941–44.

Wood, W. B., and Edmonds, Major. *Military History of the Civil War (1861–1865).* [Original London publication entitled *The Civil War in the United States, 1861–1865.*] New York: Jack Brussel, 1959.

Wooster, R. A. "The Membership of the Maryland Legislature of 1861." *Maryland Historical Magazine* 56 (1961):94.

Notes

Chapter 1. Overview

1. W. B. Wood and Major Edmonds, *Military History of the Civil War, 1861–1865* (New York: Jack Brussel, 1959), chap. 11, last frame. The raw statistic for the Union in McClellan's official report was 87,164 but from that a deduction of 20% is necessary to make this "present for duty" statistic comparable to Rebel reports of their own strength, which were limited to "number of muskets in line of battle."

2. J. V. Murfin, *The Gleam of Bayonets;* in Introduction by J. I. Robertson. (New York and London: Thomas Yoseloff, 1965; New York: Bonanza Books, 1968).

3. See Appendix (Report of the Harper's Ferry Commission).

Chapter 2. Miles's Military Career

1. Miles and his wife Sarah (Briscoe) are buried alongside his father, Captain Aquila Miles, and wife Elizabeth (Stansbury), and her brother, Dixon Stansbury, and wife Sophia (Levy) in the cemetery of old St. James Episcopal Church, sometimes called "The Manor Church," in Baltimore County near the Harford County line. Miles's mother died in 1805 and his father in 1808.

2. Christopher Johnston, "Stansbury Family," *Maryland Historical Magazine* 9 (1914): 72.

3. Ibid., pp. 86–87, and W. M. Marine, *The British Invasion of Maryland, 1812–1815.* (Baltimore, Md.: Society of the War of 1812, 1913; Baltimore, Md.: Genealogical Publishing Co., 1977), p. 447.

4. See West Point application papers of Major Dixon Stansbury's own son, Madison Smith Stansbury, and letter therein from U.S. Representative Peter Little to Secretary of War Peter Porter dated February 7, 1829 (National Archives, Record group 94).

5. Hull was eventually convicted of cowardice but completely cleared of the treason charge. See J. G. Forbes, *Report on the Trial of Brig. Gen. William Hull Commanding the Northwestern Army of the United States, by a Court-Martial Held at Albany on Monday, 3rd January 1814 and Succeeding Days (1814)* (New York: Eastburn, Kirk & Co., 1814).

6. Census and probate records of Harford County, Maryland, reveal an Aquila Miles heading a household there in 1790, 1800, and 1810, and dying in 1818, leaving another Aquila among his sons. Obviously neither of these could be the captain, who died in 1808. The 1790 Census records reveal only one other Aquila Miles in any of the thirteen original states. This was the individual referred to in the text. Some connection between the Maryland Aquila Miles, the South Carolina Aquila Miles and Captain Aquila Miles seems likely in view of the unusual nature of the name, but no connection is established.

7. See West Point application papers of Dixon S. Miles in Record Group 94, National Archives.

8. Ibid., letter of Smith and Little to Calhoun dated March 18, 1818. In similar correspondence several years later, when Dixon Stansbury was seeking an Academy appointment for his own son, Senator Smith again described the Stansburys as "a most respectable family" (Smith to Calhoun, February 5, 1825), and again as "highly respectable citizens of Baltimore County" (Smith, Little, and Barney to Barbour, January 15, 1826). See West Point application papers of Madison Smith Stansbury in National Archives, Record Group 94.

9. Ibid., Little to Porter, February 7, 1829.

10. G. W. Cullum, *Biographical Register of Officers and Cadets, U.S. Military Academy,* 6 vols. (Boston: Houghton, Mifflin Co., 1891), 1:334.

11. This and subsequent data on Miles's West Point career are taken from a memorandum of April 25, 1972, prepared for the then superintendent, General W. A. Knowlton, by S. P. Tozeski, Chief of the U.S.M.A. Archives, a copy of which is in the writer's possession.

12. Cullum, *Biographical Register of Officers and Cadets, U.S.M.A.,* 1: 334–35.

13. See Sarah Ann Miles's application for widow's army pension dated November 4, 1862, in National Archives, Record Group 94. Interestingly, a Philip P. Briscoe married a Harriet Ann Miles in the same church on October 25, 1827.

14. Sarah Ann Miles's 1862 pension application (see preceding note) and her 1874 claim for an increase therein were both witnessed by one "Mary Briscoe" who swore to "intimate" acquaintance over a 40-year period. Machett's nineteenth-century Baltimore directories identify a "Mrs. Mary Briscoe" (more often "Mary H. Briscoe") as running boardinghouses at various locations in that city between 1824 and 1891. The 1865–66 Machett Baltimore Directory locates "Mary H. Briscoe" at 45 Saratoga St. The files of the Union secret police in the National Archives contain a letter dated May 15, 1865, from "Mary H. Briscoe, Baltimore, Corner of Saratoga and St. Paul Sts.," seeking for her brother, whom she knows to be "confined in prison for no just cause," a "fair investigation," and an early trial at which he "will be allowed to have witnesses from his own county." National Archives, Record Group 94, File 4015, Turner-Baker Papers.

15. Wealthy, slave-owning planter-lawyer, James T. Briscoe was a delegate from prosecessionist Calvert County in the 1861 Maryland House of Representatives. R. A. Wooster, "The Membership of Maryland Legislature of 1861," *Maryland Historical Magazine* 56 (1961): 100. He was a signatory, along with such other southern sympathizers as S. Teacle Wallis, of a call for a state secession convention. See Maryland House of Delegates, "Report of the Committee on Federal Relations in Regard to Calling of a Sovereign Convention" (May 9, 1861). He procured passage of a bill giving control of the state's arms to secessionist groups. Baltimore *Republican,* June 21, 1861, p. 2, col. 1. He was one of the men who reorganized the defunct Maryland Democratic Party in 1864. C. B. Clark, "Politics in Maryland During the Civil War," *Maryland Historical Magazine* 39 (1944): 149.

16. Cullum, *Biographical Register of Officers and Cadets, U.S.M.A.,* 1: 334.

17. Baltimore *American,* December 12, 1835 (See Hayward File, Maryland Historical Society, Baltimore, Maryland).

18. Cullum, *Biographical Register of Officers and Cadets, U.S.M.A.,* 1: 335.

19. Affidavits of M. B. Trezenanch and John S. Toof dated February 18, 1888, in Mexican War widow's pension file for May Miles O'Bannon (File #6166, Cert. #4710), Record Group 94, National Archives.

20. U.S. War Department, *The War of the Rebellion: A Compilation of the Official Records of the Union and Confederate Armies,* 128 vols. (Washington, D.C.: Government Printing Office, 1880–1901) [Referred to in all footnotes hereafter as "WR/OR."], series I, vol. XVII, pt. II, page 638. O'Bannon was also chief quartermaster for Brig. Gen. J. K. Jackson in the Army of the Mississippi in September 1862. WR/OR, series I, vol. XVI, pt. II, p. 849. This was plainly the source of an erroneous rumor

occasionally encountered to the effect that O'Bannon was with General T. J. (Stonewall) Jackson when O'Bannon's fathe-in-law (i.e., Miles) surrendered Harper's Ferry to T. J. Jackson.

21. WR/OR, series I, vol. XXV, pt. II, p. 665.

22. The source of the middle name "Steuart" is not established. It may refer to the wealthy Steuart family of Baltimore which produced General George Hume Steuart (born 1828). Like Miles a West Pointer, Steuart defected to the Confederacy in 1861 and quickly gained command of the First Maryland Infantry, Confederate States of America. H. R. Manakee, *Maryland in the Civil War* (1961), pp. 53, 133, 152.

23. Headstone in St. James Episcopal Church Cemetery near Sweet Air in Baltimore County.

24. Cullum, *Biographical Register of Officers and Cadets, U.S.M.A.*, 1: 335.

25. Machett's 1840 Baltimore Directory, p. 256, lists "Capt. Dixon Miles" as resident at 85 E. Lombard St.

26. Dr. Miles contributed various reports on operations performed at James Hospital in Baltimore during 1863–64 for Surgeon General Barnes's *Medical and Surgical History of the War of the Rebellion* Baltimore: 1870. A Masonic symbol and the inscription "To Our Beloved Brother" mark his 1878 gravestone in St. James Episcopal Church Cemetery, near Sweet Air in Baltimore County.

27. Dr. Miles appeared for the first time at the Harper's Ferry hearings on October 13, 1862, immediately after the first evidence strongly suggestive of treason. WR/OR, series I, vol. XIX, pt. I, p. 664.

28. Cullum, *Biographical Register of Officers and Cadets, U.S.M.A.*, 1: 335.

29. Baltimore *American*, November 7, 1921 ("Seventy Five Years Ago").

30. Cullum, *Biographical Register of Officers and Cadets, U.S.M.A.*, 1: 335. That this was not a routine award is indicated by General Taylor's underscoring of Miles's name (along with four others, including Lieut. Braxton Bragg and Capt. Joseph K. F. Mansfield), to be promoted even if the brevet nominations list were found to be too long. National Archives, Record Group 94, Microfilm M-567, Roll 328, 298 AGO 1846.

31. K. Jack Bauer, *The Mexican War, 1846–1848* (New York: Macmillan: 1972), 87–88.

32. Ibid., p. 87; Justin Harvey Smith, *The War with Mexico*, 2 vols. (New York: The Macmillan Company, 1919), 1: 210.

33. Bauer, *The Mexican War, 1846–1848*, p. 93.

34. Ibid., p. 94.

35. Smith, *The War with Mexico* 1: 245.

36. Bauer, *The Mexican War, 1846–1848*, p. 97.

37. Ibid.

38. Ibid.

39. Ibid.

40. Ibid.

41. Ibid., p. 101.

42. Baltimore *American* (no date), Hayward File, Maryland Historical Society.

43. Cullum, *Biographical Register of Officers and Cadets, U.S.M.A.*, 1: 335.

44. Baltimore *American*, May 19, 1847, Hayward File, Maryland Historical Society.

45. National Archives, Record Group 94, Microfilm M-567, 497M SGO 1847.

46. Baltimore *American*, July 12, 1847, Dielman File, Maryland Historical Society.

47. National Archives, Record Group 94, Microfilm M-567, Roll 363, 455T (including 6 10W SGO, 1847).

48. Cullum, *Biographical Register of Officers and Cadets, U.S.M.A.*, 1: 335.

49. Bauer, *The Mexican War, 1846–1848*, p. 335.

50. Ibid.

51. Cullum, *Biographical Register of Officers and Cadets, U.S.M.A.*, 1: 335.

52. Archibald Hawkins, *The Life and Times of Hon. Elijah Stansbury, an "Old Defender" and Ex-Mayor of Baltimore* (Baltimore, Md.: J. Murphy & Co., 1874), pp. 155, 161.

53. *Report of the Secretary of War for 1852*, p. 3: "The efforts of our department have been principally directed to the defense of our frontiers and those of Mexico from the Indian tribes within our borders. For this purpose, out of about 11,000 officers and men borne on the rolls of the army, about 8,000 are employed in the defense of Texas, New Mexico, California and Oregon or of emigrants destined to the two last."

54. Robert W. Larson, *New Mexico's Quest for Statehood, 1846–1912* (Albuquerque, N.M.: University of New Mexico Press, 1968), p. 79.

55. Cullum, *Biographical Register of Officers and Cadets, U.S.M.A.*, 1: 335.

56. *Secretary of War's Report for 1852*, p. 60.

57. John Russell Bartlett, *Personal Narrative of Explorations and Incidents in Texas, New Mexico, California, Sonora and Chihuahua . . .* , 2 vols. (London: G. Routledge, 1854; New York: D. Appleton, 1856; Chicago: Rio Grande Press, 1965), 2: 392–94.

58. On his way to New Mexico, at St. Louis on June 12, 1851, Miles wrote to the Commissioner of Pensions, asking that a bounty-land certificate of eligibility be sent to his wife in Baltimore. Miles to J. L. Heath, June 12, 1851, National Archives, Record Group 94. Miles's youngest son, Alexander Briscoe Miles, was born on September 17, 1851, and his youngest daughter, Sarah Ann Miles (Marrian), was born on April 21, 1850. Widow's Army Pension Application of Sarah Ann Miles, November 4, 1862, National Archives, Record Group 94.

59. May O'Bannon's *Declaration of Widow for Pension—Mexican War*, February 17, 1888, Cert. no. 4710, File no. 6166, National Archives, Record Group 94.

60. WR/OR, series I, vol. XVII, part II, p. 638.

61. 37th Cong., 2nd sess., Sen. Doc. no. 7, *Message of the President of the United States* (furnishing copies of the charges, testimony, and findings in the Court of Inquiry re Col. Dixon S. Miles's behavior at the Battle of Bull Run I), p. 8.

62. Ibid., p. 55.

63. Ibid.

64. National Archives, Record Group 94, M617, Roll 366 (Dec. 1855 post returns for Ft. Fillmore, N.M.).

65. Larson, *New Mexico's Quest for Statehood, 1846–1912*, p. 79.

66. Ibid.

67. Letter from Gov. W. C. Lane to Col. Miles, U.S.A. Commanding, March 19, 1853, in *Report of Inspector General Joseph K. F. Mansfield for 1851–53*, Acc. 5209, in Manuscript Division, Library of Congress.

68. Larson, *New Mexico's Quest for Statehood*, pp. 81–82.

69. G. W. Cullum, *Biographical Register of Officers and Cadets, U.S.M.A.*, 1: 335.

70. Ibid. The northern column was commanded by Colonel Robert Loring, who would become a top Confederate commander during the Civil War.

71. *Secretary of War's Report for 1857*, Senate Exec. Doc. #11, 35th Cong., 1st sess., 2: 137 (Miles to Bonneville, July 13, 1857).

72. Ibid.

73. Ibid.

74. Ibid.

75. Ibid.

76. U.S. Archives Record, Group 393, Military Department of New Mexico, Letters Sent 10: 239–40 (Garland to Thomas, August 1, 1858).

77. Ibid., 10: 277 (Bonneville to Thomas, October 19, 1858).

78. Ibid., 10: 240 (Garland to Bonneville, August 7, 1858).

79. Ibid.

80. Ibid.

81. Ibid., 10: 256 (Nichols to Miles, September 9, 1858).

82. Ibid., 10: 260 (Bonneville to Thomas, September 20, 1858).

83. Ibid.

84. Ibid., 10: 256 (Nichols to Miles, September 9, 1858).

85. Ibid., 10: 261 (Bonneville to Miles, September 23, 1858).

86. Ibid., 10: 277 (Bonneville to Thomas, October 19, 1858).

87. Ibid., 10: 261 (Bonneville to Miles, September 23, 1858).

88. Ibid.

89. Ibid.

90. Ibid.

91. Ibid.

92. Ibid., 10: 263 (Bonneville to Miles, September 26, 1858).

93. Ibid.

94. Ibid., 10: 261 (Bonneville to Miles, 9/23/58).

95. Ibid. (Bonneville to Miles, 9/23/58).

96. *Secretary of War's Report for 1858*, 2: 329 (Nichols to Miles, October 14, 1858).

97. Ibid., 2: 310 (Miles to Bonneville, September 22, 1858).

98. Ibid.

99. Ibid., 2: 312.

100. Letter from D. S. Miles to G. W. Cullum, dated August 27, 1859, summarizing his experience in New Mexico, now in Cullum File, AOG, U.S. Military Academy Archives.

101. *Secretary of War's Report for 1858*, 2: 311 (Miles to Bonneville, September 22, 1858).

102. Ibid., 2: 316–17 (Bonneville to Miles, September 26, 1858).

103. Cullum, *Biographical Register of Officers and Cadets, U.S.M.A.*, 1: 335.

104. 36th Congress, 1st sess., House of Representatives, Executive documents, *Message from the President of the United States to the Two Houses of Congress at the Commencement of the Thirty-Sixth Congress*, including the Report of the Secretary of War for 1859–60, Table A ("Organization of the Regular Army of the U.S., July 1, 1859"), 2: 592–93.

105. Letter from D. S. Miles to G. W. Cullum, dated August 27, 1859, summarizing his experience in New Mexico; now in Cullum File, AOG, U.S. Military Academy Archives.

106. Cullum, *Biographical Register of Officers and Cadets, U.S.M.A.*, 1: 335.

107. 36th Congress, 1st sess., House of Representatives, Executive Documents, *Message from the President of the United States to the Two Houses of Congress at the Commencement of the Thirty-Sixth Congress*, including the Report of the Secretary of War for 1859–1860, Table A ("Organization of the Regular Army of U.S., July 1, 1859"), 2: 592–93.

Chapter 3. Fiasco at Bull Run

1. U.S. War Department, *The War of the Rebellion: A Compilation of the Official Records of the Union and Confederate Armies* (Washington, D.C.: Government Printing Office, 1880 to 1901), series I, vol. I, pp. 676–77. (This series is referred to hereafter as "WR/OR.")

2. Hq, Dept. of Pennsylvania, Special Order no. 66, June 10, 1861.

3. Ibid.

4. Baltimore *Republican*, June 20, 1861, p. 3.

5. Ibid.

6. The editorial itself has not been located but its tenor is clearly inferable from correspondence about it written by Miles to one Asbury Jarrett of Baltimore, dated June 27, 1861, and July 2, 1861, and a letter to the editor of the *American* referring to material in these letters, signed by "Legion" and almost certainly written by Jarrett, all now in the possession of the Maryland Historical Society in Baltimore.

7. Senator Miles, a farmer with twenty-seven slaves and total assets of $44,500, was quite typical of the Maryland Senate in 1861. Only three of the twenty-one members owned no slaves. See R. A. Wooster, "The Membership of the Maryland Legislature of

1861," *Maryland History Magazine,* Baltimore Md.: Maryland Historical Society, 56 (1961): 99.

8. Handwritten letters from Miles to his friend Asbury Jarrett dated June 27 and July 2, 1861, together with a letter inferably written by Jarrett to the Baltimore *American* "a few days" later are available in the files of the Maryland Historical Society in Baltimore, Md.

9. For a good description of the takeover of Maryland by the Federal Government during May and June of 1861, see Harold R. Manakee, *Maryland in the Civil War* (Baltimore, Md.: Genealogical Publishing Co., 1961, pp. 47–61.

10. New York *Herald,* July 1, 1861, p. 2.

11. New York *Herald,* September 14, 1862, p. 1, col. 1.

12. Miles's letter of July 2, 1861, to Asbury Jarrett, now in the Maryland Historical Society files (see n. 6 above), acknowledges his acquaintance with Simon Cameron, then secretary of war. Moreover, Miles was always close to his old West Point classmate, Lorenzo Thomas, long-time adjutant general of the Army. *Dictionary of American Biography,* s.v. "Thomas, Lorenzo."

13. Hq, Dept. of Northeastern Virginia, Special Order #26, 7/6/61. See WR/OR, series I, vol. LI, pt. I, supp., p. 411; See also Hq, Dept. of Northeastern Virginia, General Order #13, 7/8/61, in ibid., pp. 413–14.

14. Hq, Dept. of Northeastern Virginia, J. B. Fry, AAG to Col. D. S. Miles, WR/OR, series I, vol. LI, part I, supp., p. 419.

15. In New York, an early edition of the Monday *Herald* headlined "A Great Battle: Brilliant Union Victory." The lead paragraph began: "I am en route to Washington with details of a great battle. We have carried the day. The rebels accepted battle in strength but are totally routed."

16. Richardson's battle report is reprinted in Frank Moore, ed., *The Rebellion Record* (New York: Putnam, 1860–61). 3: 11.

17. Ibid., pp. 11–13. Miles's version is found at pp. 31–33 of the same volume.

18. Ibid., p. 12 (Richardson) and p. 32 (Miles).

19. U.S. Senate, 37th Cong., 2nd sess., Ex. Doc. #7 (Transcript of Proceedings before Court of Inquiry), pp. 6–7.

20. Ibid., p. 29.

21. Special Order #44, Hq, Dept. of Northeastern Virginia, 7/25/61. See WR/OR, series I, vol. LI, pt. I, p. 425.

22. Moore, *Rebellion Record* (Docs.), 2: 12–13.

23. Washington *Star,* August 1, 1861, reprinted in *Rebellion Record,* 3: 441.

24. Miles's demand and McDowell's endorsement on the file jacket are found in File NN (Index no. 498), Record Group 153, National Archives.

25. A complete record of this proceeding was furnished by President Lincoln to Congress on demand and was printed as Ex. Doc. #7, U.S. Senate, 37th Cong., 2nd sess. (12/26/61).

26. Ibid., p. 56.

27. Ibid., pp. 3–4.

28. Ibid., p. 7.

29. Ibid., p. 9.

30. Ibid., p. 11.

31. Ibid., p. 13. Accord as to the two hats in testimony of Dr. Todd (p. 18). See also Emmett Crozier, *Yankee Reporters: 1861–65* (New York: Oxford University Press, 1956), p. 103: "The [*Tribune*] correspondent found Colonel Miles in high spirits [before the tide of battle turned against the North]. Two hats were perched on his head, one inside the other, and he was capering about foolishly before a group of officers." However, it appears that wearing two hats may not have been unusual for Miles. An officer of the 39th N.Y. Inf. later wrote: "He [Miles] habitually wore two hats. . . . It may have been a cool headgear but it had not a commanding presence." G. E. Waring. "The Garibaldi

Guard," in *The First Book of the Authors' Club (Liber Scriptorum)* [New York: The Authors' Club *(De Vinne Press)* 1893], pp. 572–73.

32. 37th Cong., 2nd sess., U.S. Senate, Ex. Doc. #7 (Transcript of Proceedings before Court of Inquiry), p. 24.

33. Ibid., p. 25.

34. Ibid., p. 28.

35. Ibid., pp. 23–24.

36. Ibid., pp. 47–48.

37. Waring, "The Garibaldi Guard," pp. 468–575.

38. 37th Cong., 2nd sess., U.S. Senate, Ex. Doc. #7 (Transcript of proceedings before Court of Inquiry), p. 29.

39. Ibid., p. 18.

40. Ibid., p. 38.

41. Ibid., pp. 28–39.

42. Ibid., p. 38.

43. Ibid., p. 51.

44. Bernard C. Steiner, *Life of Reverdy Johnson* (Baltimore, Md.: The Norman Remington Co., 1914), p. iii.

45. Ibid., p. 34.

46. Ibid., pp. 37–38.

47. Ibid., p. 67, n. 10.

48. Ibid., pp. 43–44. See also p. 41 (abolitionists referred to as a "body of frenzied or knavish citizens").

49. Ibid., p. 40.

50. Ibid., p. 40, n. 47.

51. Ibid., p. 46.

52. Ibid., p. 44.

53. Ibid., p. 51. See also Johnson's argument, reprinted in Moore, *Rebellion Record* (Docs.), 2: 185.

54. Steiner, *Life of Reverdy Johnson*, pp. 58–59.

55. Ibid., p. 59.

56. Ibid., pp. 64–65.

57. See, for example, a letter from Fannie (Mrs. Jefferson) Davis to Johnson dated July 19, 1866, hoping for good news that Johnson had been able to obtain her husband's release from Fortress Monroe while awaiting his treason trial. See also letter from General Lee to Johnson dated January 27, 1866, thanking him for his Supreme Court argument on the subject of the test oath and also requesting advice on a probate matter (both letters now found among the Reverdy Johnson Papers in the Manuscript Division of the Library of Congress).

58. Steiner, *Life of Reverdy Johnson*, p. 39.

59. Ibid., pp. 54–55. Most notable was his defense of one of McClellan's corps commanders, Major General Fitz John Porter, who was charged with deliberately failing to come to the aid of General John Pope at Bull Run II. Otto Eisenschiml, *The Celebrated Case of Fitz John Porter: An American Dreyfus Affair* (Indianapolis and New York: The Bobbs-Merrill Co., Inc., 1950), p. 14.

60. The loss to McClellan's new army-in-the-making of having top line officers like Franklin and Richardson (by now a Brigadier General) again tied up at court-martial hearings for days on end seems a reasonable practical basis for the failure of the court to order a court-martial. Admittedly, however, the language used by the court of inquiry in its opinion was poorly chosen.

61. Moore, *Rebellion Record*, 4: 2 (Diary) January 1, 1862.

62. Steiner, *Life of Reverdy Johnson*, p. 56.

63. Baltimore *American*, February 8, 1862, reprinted in Moore, *Rebellion Record*, 4:26 (Diary).

64. Baltimore *American*, February 8, 1862.

65. Ibid.

66. Ibid.

67. Ibid.

68. Just a month later (on March 5, 1862) the legislature elected Johnson to the U.S. Senate by a vote of 56 to 28. Steiner, *Life of Reverdy Johnson*, p. 57.

Chapter 4. The Command of Harper's Ferry

1. The other two lifelines were the Pennsylvania Railroad, which Lee's Maryland Campaign was designed to sever by destroying the great railroad bridge at Harrisburg, and the New York Central Railroad, whose path lay so far to the north that it was never threatened by the Confederacy.

2. Special Order #66, par. 20, Hq, Army of the Potomac, March 8, 1862. The original assignment was only to command "the Brigade charged with guarding the line of the Washington Branch Railway [of the B & O]" but four days later, the above was amended by Special Order #72, par. 1, same Hq, to include within the limits of the command assigned to Colonel Miles "the portion of the Baltimore & Ohio Railroad between Harper's Ferry and Baltimore. Colonel Miles' Headquarters will be at the Relay House." Then on March 29, 1862, by Special Order #95, par. 9 of the same Hq, Miles was assigned, in addition to his earlier jurisdiction, the duty of protecting the lines of the Baltimore & Ohio Railway "from Baltimore to the Western limits of the Department of the Potomac" and was directed to establish his Headquarters "for the present" at Harper's Ferry. All orders are found in vol. 1, Special Orders, Army of the Potomac (1862), in the National Archives, Record Group 94.

3. Horace Greeley, *The American Conflict,* 2 vols. (Hartford, Conn.: O. D. Case & Co., 1864–1866; Chicago: G. and C. W. Sherwood, 1864–66; New York: Negro Universities, 1969), 2: 202: "As to General McClellan, his most glaring fault in the premises would seem to have been his designation [March 29] of Colonel Miles, after his shameful behavior at Bull Run, to the command of a post so important as Harper's Ferry."

4. Johnson was elected U.S. Senator from Maryland just three days before Miles's first order to take command of the Railroad Brigade. Bernard C. Steiner, *Life of Reverdy Johnson* (Baltimore, Md.: The Norman Remington Co., 1914; New York: Russell & Russell, 1970), p. 57.

5. Edward Hungerford, *The Story of the Baltimore & Ohio Railroad (1827–1927),* 2 vols. (New York and London: G. P. Putnam's Sons, 1928), 1: 350–51.

6. W. B. Wood and Major Edmonds, *Military History of the Civil War (1861–1865)* reprinted ed., 1959, chap. 9, "Jackson's Valley Campaign": "History affords few instances of a small force producing such great results as followed from Jackson's Valley Campaign. . . . The Confederate Generals played upon the fears of the Washington politicians and by so doing paralysed the plan of [the Peninsular] Campaign of [McClellan]."

7. Ibid.

8. The official record of Saxton's defense of Harper's Ferry is found in his Report to the Secretary of War, reprinted as Document no. 52 in Frank Moore, ed., *Rebellion Record* (New York: Putnam, 1862), 6: 159–60 (cited hereafter as "Saxton Report"). Certain details are taken from the papers supporting Saxton's award of the Medal of Honor in 1893. See particularly affidavits of Capt. James G. Thorndyke (Saxton's aide) dated April 14, 1893, and April 22, 1893 in Medal of Honor File, Record Group 94, National Archives (cited hereafter as "Thorndyke affidavits").

9. Ibid. Thorndyke affidavits.

10. Saxton Report.

11. Ibid.

12. Ibid.

13. Ibid.

14. Wood and Edmonds, *Military History of the Civil War.* Chapt. 9, Frame 10.

15. Thorndyke affidavit.

16. G. W. Cullum, *Biographical Register of Officers and Graduates of the U.S. Military Academy,* supp., vol. 4 (1901), p. 76 (Cullum #1424).

17. Saxton Report.

18. *Encyclopedia Americana* (1953), s.v. "Wool, John Ellis."

19. U.S. War Department, *The War of the Rebellion. A Compilation of the Official Records of the Union and Confederate Armies,* 128 vols. (Washington, D.C.: G.P.O. 1880–1901) [hereafter "WR/OR"], series I, vol. XIX, pt. I, p. 792.

20. General Order #28, Hq, 8th Army Corps, August 28, 1862, now found in National Archives, Record Group 49, Orders and Special Orders, Middle Dept., vol. 306 (1862).

21. Re arrests on mere suspicion of disloyalty, see letter from Wool to Halleck dated September 13, 1862, enclosing General Order #30, Hq, Middle Dept., September 1, 1862, both found in WR/OR, series I, vol. XIX, pt. II, pp. 286–87. Re the loyalty oath, see C. B. Clark, "Politics in Maryland During the Civil War," *Maryland History Magazine* 38 (June 1943): 243.

22. Even in New York the strong unionists mistrusted Wool. The files of the Union Secret Police contain a report from a New York source dated January 31, 1963, which uses this language: "It is consequently of the greatest importance to be prepared for any emergency and to have *instead of old Wool a decidedly loyal commander of this District* and, of course, troops under him which can be used with trust in suppressing the riots which will soon come" (emphasis added). Letter from Dr. E. J. Koch to "Colonel Olcott, Special Commissioner of the War Department," dated January 31, 1863, found as Item 2117 of the Turner-Baker Papers in National Archives, Record Group 94.

23. *New York Times,* September 1, 1862, p. 1.

24. See N. 59, Chapt. 3 above.

Chapter 5. Invasion

1. *U.S. War Department, The War of the Rebellion. A Compilation of the Official Records of the Union and Confederate Armies,* 128 vols. (Washington, D.C. G.P.O.: 1880–1901) [hereafter "WR/OR"], series I, vol. XIV, pt. II, pp. 590–91.

2. Ibid., p. 592.

3. Ibid., pp. 601–2.

4. See, for example, *New York Times,* September 9, 1862, p. 1. col. 3.

5. *New York Times,* September 6, 1862, p. 1.

6. Civil War Centennial Commission, County of Loudon, Commonwealth of Virginia, *Loudon County and the Civil War* (1961), p. 41.

7. WR/OR, series I, vol. XIX, pt. I, p. 754.

8. Ibid., p. 755.

9. Ibid., p. 180.

10. Ibid., p. 755.

11. Ibid.

12. The testimony of Colonel Stephen W. Downey that when sending Downey up Maryland Heights on the morning of Saturday, September 13, 1862, Miles could not remember the name of his commander on the Heights might also suggest intoxication, although Downey himself did not use the word *drunkenness,* stating merely that Miles was "not in a condition to command" and "not competent to command." Ibid., pp. 621–22.

13. Ibid., p. 755.

14. Ibid., p. 180. The same wire did report, however, that an unnamed Leesburg man had reported enemy infantry (but no artillery) passing through all day.

15. WR/OR, series I, vol XIX, pt. I, p. 755. White's Ford, which is no longer used or even accessible, was about three miles upriver from the present White's Ferry (then known as Conrad's Ferry). A more southerly crossing, at Edwards Ferry, was apparently used for cavalry headed for Poolesville as part of their screening mission.

16. Ibid.

17. Ibid.

18. Ibid.

19. WR/OR, series I, vol. XIX, pt. II, p. 180.

20. Ibid., pp. 180–81.

21. Ibid. The unauthorized retreat of "an Ohio regiment" from Noland's Ferry "without firing a gun" was also reported by Union observers on nearby Sugar Loaf Mountain, in a dispatch next morning. See WR/OR, series I, vol. XIX. pt. II, pp. 184–85.

22. WR/OR, series I, vol. XIX, pt. I, p. 522.

23. Ibid., p. 520.

24. Ibid., p. 755.

25. Ibid.

26. Ibid.

27. Ibid.

28. WR/OR, series I, vol. XIX, pt. I, supp., p. 790.

29. Ibid.

30. Wool had sent one of his own staff, Colonel Cram, to look over the situation at Point of Rocks. Cram initially (and inexplicably) reported that "all [was] quiet there." WR/OR, series I, vol. XIX, pt. I, p. 523. By noon of the fifth, however, Cram was reporting "reason to believe that 30,000 rebels crossed at the mouth of the Monocacy River last night." WR/OR, series I, vol. XIX, pt. II, pp. 188 89. (He also reported a rumor that two brigades of Rebels were now in Charlestown, "8 miles from Harper's Ferry".) Whether Miles and Cram were together or communicated with each other during the morning of the fifth does not appear from the records.

31. WR/OR, series I, vol. XIX, pt. I, p. 522.

32. WR/OR, series I, vol. XIX, pt. II, p. 188.

33. Ibid., pp. 188–89.

34. Wool testified before the Harper's Ferry Commission that when sending the above message he (Wool) assumed that Miles had completed a blockhouse which Wool in August had ordered built on the crest of Maryland Heights to protect the heavy guns on its forward slope against attack from the rear, as, in fact, occurred. Miles had simply refused to build the blockhouse but Wool was not yet aware of that fact. WR/OR, series I, vol. XIX, pt. I, p. 791. See also p. 519.

35. Ibid.

36. WR/OR, series I, vol. XIX, pt. II, pp. 208–9.

37. The *retrospective* "journal" kept by Miles's aide, Lt. Henry Martin Binney, is in demonstrable error, particularly as to dates, so often that it cannot be considered reliable.

38. For what it is worth, Binney described the Banning retreat on Saturday, September 6, as follows:

Colonel Banning, Eighty-seventh Ohio, with his two howitzers, falls back to Berlin and shells the rebels' advance guard, and on the opposite side of the Potomac. Colonel Banning again retreats before superior numbers to Knoxville. . . . Scouts and refugees report the enemy in large force, and advancing toward Knoxville. They advance toward Banning's position, who shells their advance and retires back to Sandy Hook and forms a junction with Colonel Maulsby's Maryland regiment. Colonel Miles . . . sends an engine and platform car to Berlin and recovers the limber to howitzer, equipment and ammunition left by Banning at Berlin. (WR/OR, series I, vol. XIX, pt. I, p. 534)

39. Ibid.

40. WR/OR, series I, vol. XIX, pt. I, supp., p. 795.
41. Ibid., pp. 794–95.
42. WR/OR, series I, vol. LI, pt. II, pp. 136–37.
43. Ibid.
44. Ibid.

Chapter 6.   Miles vs. White

1. For White's life generally, see obituary in Chicago *Herald*, May 13, 1890, p. 2. He eventually became a Union major general in the war and was active in veterans' politics after the war. In 1871 he was elected president of the first board of commissioners for Cook County and in 1872 was appointed U.S. minister to Argentina by President Grant.

2. James Grant Wilson, *Biographical Sketches of Illinois Officers Engaged in the War against the Rebellion of 1861* (Chicago: J. Barnet, 1863), p. 77.

3. *Smith & DuMoulin's Chicago City Directory* (1859–60), p. 416.

4. V. C. Reeling, *Evanston, Its Land and Its People* (Evanston, Ill.: Daughters of the American Revolution, Ft. Dearborn Chapter, 1928), p. 259.

5. B. L. Pierce, *A History of Chicago, (1848–1871)*, 3 vols., (New York and London: Alfred A. Knopf, 1937; Chicago: University of Chicago Press, 1975), 2: 253, n. 27.

6. Frances Willard, *The Story of Evanston: A Classic Town*, (Chicago: Woman's Christian Temperance Publishing Assn., 1892), p. 176.

7. Wilson, *Biographical Sketches of Illinois Officers Engaged in the War against the Rebellion*, p. 77.

8. Ibid.

10. Chicago *Herald*, May 13, 1890, p. 2, col. 5.

11. E. H. Ripley, *Vermont General*, ed. Otto Eisenschiml (New York: Devin-Adair Company, 1960), p. 11.

12. S. B. Pettengill, *The College Cavaliers* (Chicago: H. McAllaster & Company, 1883), p. 51.

13. Ibid., p. 52.

14. Recited in the official report of a special military commission convened to investigate the conduct of General White and the circumstances attending the evacuation of Winchester, Virginia, on 9/2/62 (commonly known as the Winchester Commission). White was completely exonerated. National Archives, Record Group 153, Winchester Court of Inquiry (File KK311).

15. U.S. War Department, *The Way of the Rebellion: A Compilation of the Official Records of the Union and Confederate Armies*, 128 vols. (Washington, D.C.: G.P.O., 1880–1901) [hereafter "WR/OR"], series I, vol. XIX, pt. I, p. 532.

16. WR/OR, series I, vol. XIX, pt. II, p. 174.

17. WR/OR, series I, vol. XIX, pt. I, p. 792.

18. Ibid.

19. In the absence of time-stamps on these wires we have sequenced them in the same order they were presented to the Harper's Ferry Commission by Wool. See WR/OR, series I, vol. XIX, pt. I, p. 790.

20. Ibid., p. 754.

21. WR/OR, series I, vol. XIX, pt. II, p. 180.

22. Ibid., p. 182.

23. Ibid., pp. 521, 790.

24. WR/OR, series I, vol. XIX, pt. I, p. 522; also pt. II, p. 181.

25. Ibid., pt. II, p. 181. (Wool sent Miles a *separate* wire advising of White's assignment to Martinsburg. Ibid., pt. I, p. 522.)

26. Ibid., pt. II, p. 181.

27. The published copy is dated September 6 (WR/OR, series I, vol. XIX, pt. II, p. 198), whereas the handwritten copy in the file of the Harper's Ferry Commission is dated September 5.

28. WR/OR, series I, vol. XIX, pt. II, p. 199.

29. Ibid., p. 218.

30. Ibid.

31. WR/OR, series I, vol. XIX, pt. I, p. 787.

32. Ibid., p. 757.

33. Ibid., p. 534.

Chapter 7.   The Union Right: D'Utassy's 1st Brigade

1. U.S. War Department, *The War of the Rebellion: A Compilation of the Official Records of the Union and Confederate Armies,* 128 vols. (Washington, D.C.: G.P.O. 1880–1901) [hereafter "WR/OR"], series I, vol. XIX, pt. I, p. 34. Cameron's 65th Illinois Infantry, and Phillips's Light Artillery were added to the 1st Brigade when they came in later with White on Friday, September 12, from Martinsburg.

2. U.S. Senate, 37th Cong., 2nd sess., Ex. Doc. no. 7 (Transcript of Proceedings Before Court of Inquiry), pp. 47–48.

3. The formation and early history of the Garibaldi Guard are described quite entertainingly by its first major, G. E. Waring, in "The Garibaldi Guard," in *The First Book of the Authors' Club (Liber Scriptorum)* [New York: The Authors' Club (DeVinne Press), 1893], pp. 568–75.

4. Ibid., pp. 570–71.

5. Ibid., p. 570.

6. Ibid.

7. Ibid., p. 568.

8. Ibid., p. 569.

9. *In re White,* TR 40 (Cumulative TR 70), 10/18/62, National Archives, Record Group 153, Winchester Court of Inquiry (File KK311).

10. WR/OR, series I, vol. XIX, pt. I, p. 552.

11. Waring, "The Garibaldi Guard," p. 572.

12. Letter from H. S. Olcott to P. H. Watson, assistant secretary of war, 1/9/63, now in National Archives, Record Group 94, Turner-Baker Papers, File #2117. The War Department's "Secret Service" was a different organization from the present Treasury Department "Secret Service," which was not organized until 1865. Norman Ansley, "The United States Secret Service: An Administrative History," *Journal of Criminal Law, Criminology and Police Science* 47 (May–June 1956).

13. Ibid.

14. War Department, Adjutant General's Office, General Orders #159, dated Washington, May 29, 1863. Copy found in the Manuscript Division of the Library of Congress.

15. Ibid., pp. 1, 2, 11.

16. Ibid., pp. 2, 3, 4, 5, 6, 12.

17. Ibid., p. 13.

18. "Statement of Facts" prepared by D'Utassy for presentation to President Lincoln on March 25, 1864, found in National Archives, Record Group 94, Turner-Baker Papers, File #2117.

Chapter 8.   The Union Left: Trimble's 2nd Brigade

1. U.S. War Department, *The War of the Rebellion: A Compilation of the Official Records of the Union and Confederate Armies,* 128 vols. Washington, D.C.: G.P.O., 1880–1901) [hereafter "WR/OR"], series I, vol. XIX, pt. I, p. 533.

2. Mary M. Tuttle, "William Allen Trimble, U.S. Senator from Ohio." *Ohio Archaeological and Historical Quarterly* 14 (1905): 236.

3. Allen Trimble, *Autobiography and Correspondence of Allen Trimble* (reprint from "Genealogy of Trimble," Columbus, Ohio: Old Northwest Genealogical Society, 1909), p. 2.

4. Ibid., p. 233.

5. Ibid., pp. 83–85, 237; and Mary M. Tuttle, "William Allen Trimble, U.S. Senator from Ohio." *Ohio Archeological and Historical Quarterly,* 1905, pp. 225, 226, 231.

6. E. H. Rosebloom and F. P. Weisenburger, *A History of Ohio* (Columbus, Ohio: Ohio State Archeological and Historical Society, 1953), p. 381.

7. Henry Howe, *Historical Collections of Ohio,* 3 vols. (Cincinnati, Ohio: Derby, Bradley & Co., 1847; 2 vols., Columbus, Ohio: H. Howe & Son 1889–91).

8. Trimble, *Autobiography of Allen Trimble,* pp. 226–27.

9. Ibid., p. 225. For the career of Carey A. Trimble, a member of the U.S. House of Representatives from 1859 to 1863, see *Biographical Directory of American Congress (1774–1961),* s.v. "Trimble."

10. Ibid., pp. 234, 239.

11. J. H. Thompson, *The History of the County of Highland in the State of Ohio* (Hillsboro, Ohio: Hillsboro *Gazette,* 1878), p. 34.

12. WR/OR, series I, vol. XIX, pt. I, pp. 741–49, 756.

13. Ibid., p. 746.

14. Ibid.

15. Ibid., p. 743.

16. Trimble, *Autobiography of Allen Trimble,* p. 239.

17. WR/OR, series I, vol. XIX, pt. I, p. 743.

18. Ibid.

19. Ibid.

20. Ibid., pp. 535, 743.

21. Ibid., p. 756.

22. Ibid.

23. E. H. Ripley, *Vermont General,* ed. Otto Eisenschiml (New York: Devin-Adair Company, 1960), pp. 27–28.

Chapter 9.   Maryland Heights: Ford's 3rd Brigade

1. U.S. War Department, *The War of the Rebellion: A Compilation of the Official Records of the Union and Confederate Armies,* 128 vols. (Washington, D.C.: G.P.O., 1880–1901) [hereafter "WR/OR"], series I, vol. XIX, pt. I, p. 533.

2. Ibid.

3. Ibid.

4. See Appendix.

5. A. A. Graham, *History of Richland County (Ohio)* [Mansfield, Ohio: A. A. Graham & Co., 1880], p. 703.

6. Ibid.

7. Ibid.

8. Carl Wittke, *History of the State of Ohio,* 6 vols. (Columbus, Ohio: Ohio State Archeological and Historical Society, 1941–44), 4: 55.

9. Ibid.

10. Graham, *History of Richland County (Ohio)*, p. 703.
11. Ibid., p. 381.
12. Ibid., p. 703.
13. Ibid., p. 380.
14. John Sherman, *Recollections of Forty Years in the House, Senate and Cabinet*, 2 vols. (Chicago: The Werner Co., 1895; New York: Greenwood Press, 1968), 1: 103.
15. Graham, *History of Richland County (Ohio)*, p. 380.
16. Ibid., p. 381.
17. See generally Carlton Beals, *Brass Knuckle Crusade (The Great Know-Nothing Conspiracy: 1802–1860)* New York: Hastings House, 1960. The name came from a reputed instruction to members that when questioned about the organization they were to reply simply: "I know nothing." However, the "know-nothing" name also captured the anti-intellectual spirit of the movement.
18. Wittke, *History of the State of Ohio*, 4: 302.
19. A local historian, perhaps a little overenthusiastically, described the speech as follows:

As a specimen of crushing repartee, nothing in the English language excels it. Pitt, in his palmiest days, never made more brilliant points in the same speech than did Governor Ford in that speech. It was an occasion that called out fully his peculiar powers. (Graham, *History of Richland County [Ohio]*, p. 380)

21. Wittke, *History of the State of Ohio*, 4: 303–5.
22. Allen Trimble, *Autobiography and Correspondence of Allen Trimble* (reprint from "Genealogy of Trimble" [Columbus, Ohio: Old Northwest Genealogical Society, 1909]), pp. 226–27.
23. E. H. Rosebloom, "Salmon P. Chase and the Know Nothings," *Mississippi Valley Historical Review* 25 (1938): 349.
24. American Historical Association, *Annual Report for the Year 1902* (1903), 2: 278–79.
25. Rosebloom, "Salmon P. Chase and the Know Nothings," p. 349.
26. Ibid.
27. Ibid.
28. Graham, *History of Richland County (Ohio)*, pp. 324–25.
29. Ibid.
30. Years later a skeptical pension examiner wrote: "The claimant [Dr. Hewitt] is a man of good standing and so popular as a man, that I believe each witness I examined was to some extent biased in his favor." Letter from Charles T. Forbes, Special Examiner, to John C. Black, Commissioner of Pensions, dated March 24, 1886, now in Hewitt's pension file in the National Archives, Record Group 94.
31. Graham, *History of Richland County (Ohio)*, p. 326.
32. Whitelaw Reid, *Ohio in the War*, 2 vols. (Cincinnati, Ohio, and New York: Wilstach & Baldwin, 1868), p. 213.
33. Ibid.
34. Ibid.
35. Ibid., p. 214.
36. Ford's personnel file in the National Archives, Record Group 79, shows Ford to have been "absent with leave at Wheeling, Va." during March and April 1862 and "absent on sick leave in Ohio" during May and June 1862. The July–August leave record is missing.
37. WR/OR, series I, vol. XIX, pt. I, p. 576.
38. Handwritten instructions from Ford to Chase (by this time secretary of the treasury) as to the arguments to be made to President Lincoln for a reversal of Ford's dismissal, which had been recommended by the Harper's Ferry Commission. Found in the Harper's Ferry Commission file in the National Archives, Record Group 153, File KK311.

Chapter 10.   The Strategic Importance of Maryland Heights

1. U.S. War Department, *The War of the Rebellion: A Compilation of the Official Records of the Union and Confederate Armies,* 128 vols. (Washington, D.C.: G.P.O., 1880–1901) [hereafter "WR/OR"], series I, vol. XIX, pt. I, p. 533.

2. Jackson to Lee, May 7, 1861, WR/OR, series I, vol. II, p. 814.

3. "In your preparation for the defense of your position [Harper's Ferry], it is considered advisable not to intrude upon the soil of Maryland, unless compelled by the necessities of war." Ibid., p. 822.

4. M. W. Wellman, *Harper's Ferry, Prize of War* (Charlotte, N.C.: McNally of Charlotte, 1960), pp. 37–38.

5. Frank Moore, ed., *Rebellion Record,* 12 vols. Volumes 1–6, New York: Putnam, 1861–63; Volumes 7–12, New York: Van Nostrand, 1864–68; Volumes 1–12, New York: Arno Press, 1977, 6: 159–60.

6. Ibid.

7. W. B. Wood, and Major Edmonds, *Military History of the Civil War (1861–1865),* [Globe Lithographing Co., 1959], Chapter 9, 10th frame.

8. WR/OR, series I, vol. XIX, pt. I, pp. 691–92.

9. Ibid.

10. Ibid.

11. Ibid., p. 691.

12. Ibid., pp. 519, 791.

13. Hq, 8th Army Corps, Special Order #77, par. VII; reprinted in WR/OR, series I, vol. XIX, pt. I, p. 789.

14. That Rodgers reached Harper's Ferry before September 6 is deducible from a scroll order by Miles dated September 6, 1862, found in Rodgers's military personnel file, purporting to appoint Rodgers "Inspector-General" of Miles's new "Division" at Harper's Ferry. National Archives, Record Group 79.

15. WR/OR, series I, vol. XIX, pt. I, pp. 791, 793.

16. Ibid., p. 793.

17. Ibid., p. 535.

18. Ibid., p. 793.

19. The wires were cut at 10:00 A.M. on Saturday the sixth. WR/OR, series I, vol. XIX, pt. II, pp. 208–9. See also pt. I, p. 520. Indirect communications through Wheeling, West Virginia, remained open until Friday, September 12. WR/OR, series I, vol. XIX, pt. II, p. 270.

20. G. B. McClellan, *McClellan's Own Story* (New York: C. L. Webster & Co., 1886), pp. 549–50.

21. Seward did not return to Washington from a visit to New York until September 3, 1862, and spent that evening with the president. W. H. Seward, *Autobiography of William H. Seward,* 3 vols. (New York: Derby & Miller, 1891), 3: 127. McClellan left Washington for Rockville on the afternoon of September 7, 1862. G. B. McClellan, *Report on the Organization and Campaigns of the Army of the Potomac* (New York: Sheldon & Co. 1864), p. 347.

22. McClellan, *McClellan's Own Story,* p. 550.

23. Ibid.

24. WR/OR, series I, vol. LI, pt. I, p. 4.

25. S. E. Ambrose, *Halleck: Lincoln's Chief of Staff* (Baton Rouge, La.: Louisiana State University Press, 1962), pp. 82–83 ("one of the more penetrating insights of the war").

26. McClellan, *McClellan's Own Story,* p. 550.

27. WR/OR, series I, vol. XIX, pt. I, p. 793.

28. Ibid.

29. S. B. Pettengill, *The College Cavaliers* (Chicago: H. McAllaster & Co., 1883), pp. 51–52.

30. WR/OR, series I, vol. XIX, pt. I, p. 768.

31. Halleck's testimony was largely concerned with demonstrating the slowness and incompetence of *McClellan* in order to justify the upcoming dismissal of McClellan as the top Union field commander. See chapter 25 below.

32. Moore, *Rebellion Record,* 6: 220.

33. See letter from White to Holt (judge advocate) dated October 7, 1862, in Harper's Ferry Commission file in National Archives, Record Group 153, File KK311.

34. WR/OR, series I, vol. XIX, pt. I, p. 533.

35. WR/OR, series I, vol. XIX, pt. I, pp. 789, 791, 793.

36. Letter from Maj. John A. Steiner to Col. Thos. H. Ford, dated November 21, 1862, found in the file of the Harper's Ferry Commission, National Archives, Record Group 153, File KK311.

37. Ibid.

38. Ibid.

39. WR/OR, series I, vol. XIX, pt. I, pp. 656 (Potts) and 706, 710 (Pearce).

40. Ibid., pp. 656, 706.

41. Ibid., p. 710.

42. Letter from Maj. John A. Steiner to Col. Thos. H. Ford, dated November 21, 1962, found in the file of the Harper's Ferry Commission, National Archives, Record Group 153, File KK 311.

43. WR/OR, series I, vol. XIX, pt. I, pp. 706–7, 710–11.

44. *New York Times,* September 8, 1862, p. 1, col. 3. The same dispatch appeared simultaneously in the Baltimore *Republican,* September 8, 1862, p. 2.

Chapter 11.   Camp Hill: Ward's 4th Brigade

1. U.S. War Department, *The War of the Rebellion: A Compilation of the Official Records of the Union and Confederate Armies,* 128 vols. (Washington, D.C.: G.P.O., 1880–1901) [hereafter "WR/OR"], series I, vol. XIX, pt. I, p. 533.

2. Frank Moore, ed., *Rebellion Record,* (New York: Putnam, 1862), 6: 159–60 (Saxton Report to Secretary of War).

3. Colonel Trimble testified that Miles told him from the first that he proposed to defend the Bolivar Heights line, despite suggestions by Trimble and others that it was too long a line for the number of troops available. WR/OR, series I, vol. XIX, pt. I, p. 743.

4. The time of the 12th New York Militia had already expired (August 27, 1862) and that of the 87th Ohio was almost up. There had already been a lot of jockeying over whether these men ought to stay on at Harper's Ferry for the duration of the invasion. Wool, in Baltimore, was determined they should stay: "Surely your regiment will not desire to leave at the present, when their general asks them to remain a few days. . . . They would be branded as cowards." WR/OR, series I, vol. XIX, pt. II, p. 181. A deliberate decision to keep these militiamen out of the front lines could have resulted from agreement with them or simply a feeling by Miles that discretion was the better part of valor. But this is all speculation. The regimental history takes full credit for the regiment's volunteering to stay at Harper's Ferry till October 15 "instead of returning to New York, as did other regiments." M. Francis Dowley, *History and Honorary Roll of the 12th Regiment, Infantry, NGSNY* (New York: T. Farrell & Son, 1869), p. 18.

5. Lately Thomas, *Sam Ward: "King of the Lobby"* (Boston: Houghton Mifflin & Co., 1965), p. 6.

6. Ibid.

7. Ibid.

8. Ibid., p. 7.

9. Ibid., p. 27.

10. Ibid., p. 7.

11. Ibid., p. 289.

12. *Vanity Fair,* 12th Series, "Men of the Day, No. 214" January 10, 1880.

13. Thomas, *Sam Ward: "King of the Lobby,"* p. 285.

14. Ibid., pp. 284–308.

15. See *Dictionary of American Biography* (1932), s.v. "Howe, Julia Ward."

16. Ibid.

17. Julia Ward Howe, *Reminiscences 1819–1899* (Boston and New York: Houghton Mifflin Co., 1899; New York: Negro Universities Press, 1969), p. 255.

18. Ibid., pp. 253–54.

19. Ibid., p. 255.

20. Ibid., p. 256.

21. Ibid., p. 269.

22. Florence Howe Hall, *The Story of the Battle Hymn of the Republic* (Freeport, N.Y.: Books for Libraries Press, 1971), pp. 59–60.

23. Howe, *Reminiscences, 1819–1899,* pp. 274–75.

24. Dowley, *History and Honorary Roll Call of the 12th Regiment, Infantry, NGSNY* appendices: "Brig. Gen. William G. Ward" and "Col. John Ward."

25. Ibid.

26. Ibid.

Chapter 12.   All Quiet at Harper's Ferry

1. U.S. War Department, *The War of the Rebellion: A Compilation of the Official Records of the Union and Confederate Armies,* 128 vols. (Washington, D.C.: G.P.O., 1880–1901) [hereafter "WR/OR"], series I, vol. XIX, pt. I, p. 545. See also *New York Times,* September 12, 1862, p. 1, col. 3, and September 13, 1862, p. 1, col. 4.

2. WR/OR, series I, vol. XIX, pt. I, p. 522, and pt. II, p. 188.

3. Ibid., pt. I, supp., p. 795.

4. Ibid., p. 794.

5. Ibid., p. 791.

6. Ibid., pt. II, p. 204.

7. Ibid., p. 207.

8. Ibid.

9. E. H. Ripley, *Vermont General,* ed. Otto Eisenschiml (New York: Devin-Adair Company, 1960), p. 24.

10. WR/OR, series I, vol. XIX, pt. II, pp. 590–91.

11. *New York Times,* September 9, 1862, p. 1 (reprinted from Baltimore *American,* September 8, 1862).

12. The worried wires between Lincoln and his Western field commanders attempting to pin down Bragg's whereabouts are found in WR/OR, series I, vol. XVI, pt. II, pp. 207, 495, 496, 497, and 500.

13. *New York Times,* September 13, 1862, p. 1.

14. WR/OR, series I, vol. XIX, pt. I, pp. 517–18.

15. Ibid. See also *New York Times,* September 13, 1862, p. 1, cols. 3–4.

16. *New York Times,* September 13, 1862, p. 1, cols. 3–4.

17. WR/OR, series I, vol. LI, pt. I, supp., p. 798.

18. WR/OR, series I, vol. XIX, pt. I, supp., p. 798.

19. Ibid., pt. II, p. 205.

20. Ibid.

21. WR/OR, series I, vol. XIX, pt. II, p. 206.

22. Ibid., p. 206.

23. Ibid.

24. Ibid., pt. I, p. 791.

25. Wool to White, September 8, 1862, WR/OR, series I, vol. XIX, pt. I, p. 520 (second wire).

26. Ibid. (third wire).

27. Miles to Halleck, September 9, 1862, WR/OR, series I, vol. XIX, pt. I, p. 757.

28. Washington *Evening Star,* September 13, 1862, p. 2, col. 2 (from Baltimore *American* "of this morning").

29. Miles to Halleck, September 9, 1862, National Archives, Record Group 153, Harper's Ferry Court of Inquiry File (KK 311).

30. Miles to White, September 10, 1862, WR/OR, series I, vol. 51, pt. I, supp., p. 812.

31. WR/OR, series I, vol. XIX, pt. I, p. 536 (Binney's retrospective "journal," reporting that Davis's 8th New York Cavalry "saw no enemy during a reconnaisance toward Winchester on Wednesday the 10th").

32. *New York Times,* September 19, 1862, p. 4.

33. Ibid.

34. *New York Times,* September 11, 1862, p. 1.

35. Ibid. See also a contemporaneous optimistic wire to the New York *Herald* from young Capt. John Ward, brother of fourth brigade commander Col. William Ward: "All is quiet in this locality. We have seen nothing of the rebels up to the present time and are prepared for them whenever they choose to make our acquaintance. We have thrown up excellent earthworks in front [of Camp Hill]. Our supplies reach us by Cumberland. The [12th New York] regiment is spunky and its return home is uncertain." New York *Herald,* September 10, 1862, p. 1.

Chapter 13.   The Rebel Game Plan Changes

1. U.S. War Department, *The War of the Rebellion: A Compilation of the Official Records of the Union and Confederate Armies,* 128 vols. (Washington, D.C.: G.P.O., 1880–1901) [hereafter "WR/OR"], series I, vol. XIX, pt. II, pp. 590–91.

2. Ibid., pp. 591–92.

3. Ibid.

4. Ibid., pp. 593–94.

5. Ibid.

6. James Longstreet, "The Invasion of Maryland," in *Battles and Leaders of the Civil War,* 4 vols. (New York: The Century Co., 1887; New York: Thomas Yoseloff, 1956), 2: 663. Longstreet later fixed the date of this conversation as having occurred on Sunday, September 7. James Longstreet, *From Manassas to Appomattox* (Philadelphia: JB Lippincott Co., 1896), pp. 201–2. But Lee reached Frederick on the sixth. This and the general pattern of events leads us to adopt Longstreet's first recollection (i.e., that this conversation occurred on the sixth).

7. Longstreet, "The Invasion of Maryland," p. 663.

8. See, for example, the 1975 Pulitzer Prize winner, *The Killer Angels,* by Michael Shaara, stressing Longstreet's instinctive penchant for the defense at Gettysburg.

9. Longstreet, "The Invasion of Maryland," p. 663.

10. Ibid., Cf. Longstreet's wording in his autobiography, *From Manassas to Appomattox,* pp. 201–2: "As the subject was not continued, I supposed it was a mere expression of passing thought. . . ."

11. The name *scout* was widely used during the Civil War as a euphemism for *spy.* See, for example, S. B. Pettengill, *The College Cavaliers* (Chicago: H. McAllaster & Co., 1883), p. 47, describing General White's guide, Tom Noakes, as "a spy, euphemistically called a confidential scout." "Among the better known spies with the [Rebel] armies were . . . Jackson's Col. Turner Ashby. . . ." H. V. Canan, "Confederate Military Intelligence," *Maryland Historical Magazine* 59 (March 1964): 37. Ashby had been killed three months earlier during Jackson's Valley Campaign, but "Ashby's Cavalry" was now the "Laurel Brigade," of which Rouse's Company B of the 12th Virginia Cavalry was a

part. W. N. McDonald, *A History of the Laurel Brigade, Originally Ashby's Cavalry* (Baltimore: Mrs. Kate McDonald, 1907; Arlington, Va.: R. W. Beatty Ltd., 1969), p. 68.

12. WR/OR, series I, vol. XIX, pt. II, pp. 737–38.

13. Ibid.

14. Ibid.

15. Ibid. The mere fact that Miles chose to "interrogate" Rouse *personally* is probably not, standing alone, a suspicious circumstance. "It had been customary in past wars for commanders to handle intelligence matters and the tendency to personalize military intelligence was carried into the Civil War. While some officers allowed their Provost Marshals to handle aspects of it, commanders were usually their own intelligence officers." Canan, "Confederate Military Intelligence," p. 35.

16. Ibid.

17. WR/OR, series I, vol. XIX, pt. II, pp. 737–38.

18. Cf. McClellan's confirmation of the usual practice a month later: "By direction of the Commanding General all paroled rebel prisoners to be returned to the enemy's lines, whether wounded or otherwise, *will not be permitted to pass our lines to the front.* All such prisoners will be sent to Frederick, Maryland; thence, via Baltimore, to Fort Monroe, for return within their own lines" (emphasis added). McClellan to Halleck, September 7, 1862, U.S. Army, *Telegrams Received by Maj. Gen. H. W. Halleck While General in Chief and Chief of Staff* (1877), p. 158.

19. Millard K. Bushong, *A History of Jefferson County, West Virginia* (Charles Town, W. Va.: Jefferson Pub. Co. 1941), p. 144; McDonald, *A History of the Laurel Brigade, Originally Ashby's Cavalry* p. 31.

20. Longstreet, "The Invasion of Maryland," p. 663.

21. Ibid.

22. Ibid. Longstreet's account of the same episode in his autobiography, *From Manassas to Appomattox,* p. 202, is substantially similar.

23. John G. Walker, "Jackson's Capture of Harper's Ferry," in *Battles and Leaders of the Civil War,* 4 vols. (New York: The Century Co. 1887; New York: Thomas Yoseloff, 1956), 2: 604.

24. Ibid.

25. Ibid.

26. Ibid., p. 605.

27. Ibid.

28. Ibid.

29. Ibid.

30. Ibid.

31. Ibid., p. 606.

32. Lee to Davis, September 12, 1862, WR/OR, series I, vol. XIX, pt. II, pp. 604–5.

33. *Supra,* pp. 119–20.

34. That Lee was getting Baltimore papers on the day of publication is indicated, for example, by Lee's dispatch to Davis from Leesburg, Virginia, on Thursday, September 5, which refers to a story in the Baltimore *Sun* "of this morning." WR/OR, series I, vol. XIX, pt. II, p. 592.

35. E. Z. Hays, *History of the Thirty-Second Regiment (Ohio Veteran Volunteer Infantry)* (Columbus, Ohio: Cott & Evans, 1896), p. 33.

36. WR/OR, series I, vol. XIX, pt. II, pp. 601–2.

37. D. H. Strother, *A Virginia Yankee in the Civil War: The Diaries of David Hunter Strother,* ed. C. D. Eby (Chapel Hill, N.C.: University of North Carolina Press, 1961), p. 106.

38. WR/OR, series I, vol. XIX, pt. II, pp. 603–4.

39. Ibid.

40. Ibid.

41. Ibid.

42. Ibid.

43. D. S. Freeman, *Robert E. Lee,* 4 vols. (London: Charles Scribner's Sons, 1934, 1935, 1937), 2: 365.

44. To the same effect, see Lee's letter to Davis of September 12, 1862, explaining his change of plans. WR/OR, series I, vol. XIX, pt. II, pp. 604–5.

45. WR/OR, series I, vol. XIX, pt. I, p. 852. (Quoted with apparent approval by D. S. Freeman in *Lee's Lieutenants,* 4 vols. (New York: Charles Scribner's Sons, 1942–44, 1946), 2: 185, n. 4. See also a war correspondent's view in *New York Times,* September 8, 1862, p. 1, col. 3: "Should [the Rebels attack the Union batteries in the rear] . . . and capture the guns [on Maryland Heights] Harper's Ferry below will be entirely at their mercy."

46. WR/OR, series I, vol. XIX, pt. I, p. 953.

47. James V. Murfin, *The Gleam of Bayonets* (New York and London: Thomas Yoseloff, 1965), p. 336.

48. "It was while Jackson was leaving Frederick that 96-year-old Barbara Fritchie allegedly defied 'Stonewall' by displaying an American flag from her house on Patrick Street—an incident immortalized in verse by poet John Greenleaf Whittier. After exhaustively studying the supposed incident, C. M. and W. R. Quinn in the *Maryland Historical Magazine* for September 1942 concluded that it must be classed as tradition." Harold R. Manakee, *Maryland in the Civil War* (Baltimore, Md.: Maryland Historical Society, 1961), p. 17 n.

Chapter 14.   Envelopment

1. H. Kyd Douglas, *I Rode with Stonewall* (Greenwich, Conn.): Fawcett Publications 1965), pp. 153–54.

2. Downey had been commissioned a full colonel but neither he nor anyone else at Harper's Ferry knew it. He later achieved passing notoriety as Wyoming's territorial delegate to Congress by introducing into the 46th Congress a bill (with the Apostle's Creed as preamble) appropriating funds to decorate the Capitol dome with paintings of the life of Christ. He achieved more lasting fame back home in Wyoming as legislative "father" of the University of Wyoming, whence graduated a majority of his twelve children, including daughter Evangeline, mother of the present writer.

3. U.S. War Department, *The War of the Rebellion: A Compilation of the Official Records of the Union and Confederate Armies,* 128 vols. (Washington, D.C.: G.P.O., 1880–1901) [hereafter "WR/OR"], series I, vol. XIX, pt. I, p. 621.

4. Wool to White, September 8, 1862, WR/OR, series I, vol. XIX, pt. I, p. 520. See also Miles to Ford, September 9, 1862, WR/OR, series I, vol. LI, pt. I, supp., p. 804, and Miles to White, September 10, 1862, ibid., p. 812.

5. Miles to White, September 9, 1862, WR/OR, series I, vol. LI, pt. I, supp., p. 804.

6. The text's summary of the Boonsboro incident is reconstructed from Binney's retrospective "journal" (WR/OR, series I, vol. XIX, pt. I, pp. 535–36) and Kyd Douglas's memoirs, *I Rode with Stonewall,* pp. 153–54.

7. WR/OR, series I, vol. XIX, pt. II, p. 249 (White to Wool) and WR/OR, series I, vol. L, pt. I, supp., p. 812 (White to Miles), both dated September 10, 1862.

8. WR/OR, series I, vol. XIX, pt. II, p. 249.

9. The words "to Rohrersville" and the time (9:00 P.M.) do *not* appear in the handwritten copy found among the records of the Harper's Ferry Commission but *are* found in the copies of General Halleck's received wires, now in the Library of Congress.

10. Miles to Halleck, September 11, 1862, found in Harper's Ferry Court of Inquiry File, National Archives, Record Group 153-KK311.

11. WR/OR, series I, vol. XIX, pt. I, p. 622.

12. Ibid.

13. WR/OR, series I, vol. LI, pt. I, supp., p. 820.

14. Ibid.

15. D. H. Strother, *A Virginia Yankee in the Civil War,* ed. C. D. Eby (Chapel Hill, N.C.: University of North Carolina Press, 1961), p. 106.

16. WR/OR, series I, vol. XIX, pt. II, p. 270.

17. WR/OR, series I, vol. XIX, pt. 1, p. 953 (Jackson's Official Report).

18. WR/OR, series I, vol. LI, pt. I, supp., p. 819. See also WR/OR, series I, vol. XIX, pt. I, p. 636.

19. WR/OR, series I, vol. LI, pt. I, supp., p. 820.

20. WR/OR, series I, vol. XIX, pt. I, pp. 852–53.

21. Ibid., p. 691.

22. The 8,000 figure adopts the estimate of J. V. Murfin in *The Gleam of Bayonets* at p. 135, which may be high. The postwar estimate of Lee's adjutant is equivalent to about 6400. See W. H. Taylor, *Four Years with General Lee,* ed. J. I. Robertson (Bloomington, Ind.: Indiana University Press, 1962; New York: Bonanza Books) p. 273.

23. WR/OR, series I, vol. XIX, pt. I, pp. 691, 852–53, 862.

24. Ibid., p. 707.

25. WR/OR, series I, vol. LI, pt. I, supp., p. 819.

Chapter 15.   Maryland Heights: Friday

1. U.S. War Department, *The War of the Rebellion: A Compilation of the Official Records of the Union and Confederate Armies,* 128 vols. (Washington, D.C.: G.P.O., 1880–1901) [hereafter WR/OR], series I, vol. XIX, pt. I, p. 853.

2. Ibid.

3. Ibid.

4. The east slope of Elk Ridge is so steep that it would not be possible to scale it in the face of almost any opposition.

5. WR/OR, series I, vol. XIX, pt. I, p. 853.

6. Ibid.

7. Ibid., pp. 862–63.

8. Ibid., pp. 860–61. Kershaw had 1041 officers and men; Barksdale had 960.

9. D. S. Freeman, *Lee's Lieutenants,* 4 vols. (New York: Charles Scribner's Sons, 1942–44, 1946), 2: 187, n. 14.

10. The 7th Squadron of Rhode Island cavalry was made up in substantial part of Dartmouth and Norwich University students on their summer vacation. S. B. Pettengill, *The College Cavaliers* (Chicago: H. McAllaster,1883) chap. 1. They were withdrawn from Maryland Heights by order of Colonel Miles early in the engagement, for what reason does not appear. WR/OR, series I, vol. XIX, pt. I, p. 544.

11. E. H. Ripley, "Memories of the Ninth Vermont at the Tragedy of Harper's Ferry, Sept. 15, 1862," in *Personal Recollections of the War of the Rebellion,* M.O.L.L.U.S. (New York Commandery), 1909, 4: 137.

12. D. A. Dickert, *History of Kershaw's Brigade* (Newberry, S.C.: E. H. Aull Co., 1899; Dayton, Ohio, William Stanley Hoole Press, 1976), p. 148.

13. WR/OR, series I, vol. XIX, pt. I, p. 542.

14. Ibid., p. 601.

15. Ibid.

16. Ibid.

17. Ibid.

18. Ibid.

19. Ibid., p. 709.

20. Ibid., p. 545.

21. Ibid., p. 863.

22. Ibid., pp. 570, 672.

23. Ibid., p. 614.

24. Cf. Pettengill, *The College Cavaliers* (Chicago: H. McAllaster & Co., 1883), p. 62 ("25 feet high"); and WR/OR, series I, vol. XIX, p. 77 ("probably 15 feet high").

25. WR/OR, series I, vol. XIX, pt. I, pp. 567, 702, 704.

26. Ibid., p. 863.

27. *Biographical Directory of the American Congress 1774–1961*, p. 1594.

28. A. M. Willson, *Disaster, Struggle, Triumph: The Adventures of 1,000 "Boys in Blue"* (Albany, N.Y., Argus Co. 1870), p. 57.

29. WR/OR, series I, vol. XIX, pt. I, p. 727.

30. Ibid., p. 607.

31. Ibid., pp. 543, 566.

32. Ibid., pp. 673, 707.

33. Ibid., p. 567.

34. Ibid., p. 853.

35. Ibid. Cobb did not occupy Sandy Hook until Saturday afternoon. Ibid., p. 854.

36. W. H. Nichols, "The Siege and Capture of Harper's Ferry by the Confederates," in *Personal Narratives of Events in the War of the Rebellion* (Providence, R.I.: Soldiers & Sailors Society, 1889), 4: 2: 22.

37. Ibid.

38. WR/OR, series I, vol. XIX, pt. I. pp. 566–67.

39. Ibid.

40. Ibid.

41. Ibid.

42. Ibid., pp. 568–68.

43. National Archives, Record Group 79, service and pension files of Eugene McGrath and widow Ann Kierman McGrath. The prewar New York City directories (Doggett's 1850–51 and Trow's 1859) show him to have been a bootmaker with shop adjoining his home at 559 Hudson Street.

44. WR/OR, series I, vol. XIX, pt. I, p. 693.

45. Frank Moore, ed., *The Rebellion Record*, 12 vols. Volumes 1–6, New York: Putnam, 1861–63; Volumes 7–12, New York: Van Nostrand, 1864–68; Volumes 1–12, New York: Arno Press, 1977, 6: 160.

46. Julius White, "The Capitulation of Harper's Ferry," in R. U. Johnson and C. C. Buel, *Battles and Leaders of the Civil War*, 4 vols. (New York: The Century Co. 1887; New York: Thomas Yoseloff, 1956), 2: 612.

47. E. H. Ripley, *Vermont General*, ed. Otto Eisenschiml (New York: Devin-Adair Co., 1960), p. 26: "The brigade is quite a reinforcement for us," Ripley wrote home.

48. WR/OR, series I, vol. XIX, pt. I, p. 746.

49. Ibid., p. 746.

50. Ibid., p. 596.

51. Ibid.

52. Ibid., p. 568.

53. Ibid.

54. Ibid., p. 596.

55. Ibid., p. 727.

56. Ibid., pp. 568, 772.

57. Ibid., p. 568.

58. Ibid. Another witness estimated that it was after midnight and probably nearer 1:00 A.M. by the time Hewitt returned to his troops on the hill. Ibid., p. 772.

59. Ibid., pp. 763–64.

60. Ibid., p. 764. Powell was right. Jackson bivouacked at Opequon Creek on Friday evening and did not reach Halltown, in sight of Bolivar Heights, until early afternoon of Saturday the 13th. H. Kyd Douglas, *I Rode with Stonewall* (Chapel Hill, N.C.: University of North Carolina Press, 1940. Greenwich, Conn.: Fawcett Publications, Inc., 1965), p. 157.

61. WR/OR, series I, vol. LI, pt. I, supp., p. 819.

62. *New York Times*, September 14, 1862, p. 1.

63. WR/OR, series I, vol. XIX, pt. I, p. 520, and pt. II, pp. 208–9.

64. 37th Cong., 3rd sess., *Report of the Joint Committee on the Conduct of the War* (1863), 3: 483.

65. 37th Cong., 3rd sess., *Report of the Joint Committee on the Conduct of the War* (1863), 3: 483.

66. Ibid.

67. WR/OR, series I, vol. XIX, pt. I, p. 521. (Wool promptly "consented" to the transfer. Ibid., p. 521.)

68. 37th Cong., 3rd sess., *Report of the Joint Committee On The Conduct of the War* (1863), 3: 483.

69. Ibid., p. 484.

70. J. W. Brown, *The Signal Corps, U.S.A., in the War of the Rebellion* (Boston: U.S. Veteran Signal Corps Assn., 1896; New York: Arno Press, 1974), p. 228.

71. Ibid. It was the operators of this chain of signal stations who, in order to avoid the tedium of relaying a host of insignificant matters in their daily sundown reports, originated the famous phrase "All quiet on the Potomac." Ibid., pp. 228–29.

72. National Archives, Record Group 79, military service and pension files of Captain Louis R. Fortescue and widow, Mildred H.E. Fortescue.

73. Brown, *The Signal Corps, U.S.A., in the War of the Rebellion,* p. 227.

74. WR/OR, series I, vol. LI, pt. I, p. 119.

75. Ibid., pp. 823–24.

76. Ibid., pp. 824–25.

77. See "Memorandum of Paroled Prisoners," in Harper's Ferry Court of Inquiry File, National Archives, Record Group 153 (KK 311).

78. See individual signed paroles in Harper's Ferry Court of Inquiry File, National Archives, Record Group 153 (KK 311).

Chapter 16. Maryland Heights: Saturday Morning

1. E.g., New York *Daily Tribune*, September 18, 1862, p. 8, col. 2: "The abandonment of the key to the whole position certainly requires the most careful investigation. . . . The evacuation received the merited condemnation of officers and men. Everyone saw that the way for the Rebels was now open; the door locked, it is true, but the key hung outside."

2. U.S. War Department, *The War of the Rebellion: A Compilation of the Official Records of the Union and Confederate Armies,* 128 vols. (Washington, D.C.: G.P.O., 1880–1901) [hereafter "WR/OR"], series I, vol. XIX, pt. I, p. 863.

3. Ibid., pp. 543, 672.

4. Ibid., pp. 570, 672.

5. Ibid., p. 702.

6. Ibid., pp. 567, 704; cf. p. 709.

7. W. H. Nichols, "The Siege and Capture of Harper's Ferry," in *Personal Narratives of Events in the War of the Rebellion* (Providence, R.I.: Soldiers and Sailors Historical Society, 1889), 4: 2: 19, 21.

8. WR/OR, series I, vol. XIX, pt. I, p. 863.

9. Ibid., p. 601 (Hildebrandt) and p. 727 (Russell).

10. Ibid., p. 561.

11. Ibid., p. 860.

12. Ibid., p. 863.

13. Ibid., p. 583.

14. Arabella M. Willson, *Disaster, Struggle, Triumph: The Adventures of 1,000 "Boys in Blue"* (Albany, N.Y.: Argus Co., 1870), pp. 58–59.

15. WR/OR, series I, vol. XIX, pt. I, p. 672.

16. Ibid., p. 602.

17. Ibid., p. 727.

18. The adjutant told of taking the men out to practice loading their pieces in the moonlight Thursday night when they learned they would be going up on the Heights next day. WR/OR, series I, vol. XIX, pt. I, p. 675.

19. The 126th's commanding officer, Colonel Eliakim Sherrill, was a much respected politician (former congressman and state senator) but had only limited military experience (as a militiaman). Willson, *Disaster, Struggle, Triumph*, p. 19. He told his brigadier (Trimble) "that he knew nothing about military . . . that he was just in the field and green, but if there was to be fighting, he was ready to go." WR/OR, series I, vol. XIX, pt. I, p. 672. As for the other officers, the adjutant testified later that "a great many of the officers—most all the officers—were inexperienced. I do not think there was proper management on the hill. . . ." Ibid., p. 675.

20. Willson, *Disaster, Struggle, Triumph*, p. 19.

21. Ibid., p. 25.

22. WR/OR, series I, vol. XIX, pt. I, p. 707: Interestingly, this was not the only time Miles referred erroneously to an expectation of enemy attack from the direction of Rohrersville. On September 10, 1862, his wire to Halleck announcing discovery of Lee's column at Boonsboro read: "Enemy reported advancing from Boonesborough to Rohrersville. He may intend to pass on to Maryland Heights or the Potomac at Antietam Creek. Troops in position and ready." (The words "to Rohrersville" appear only on Halleck's received copy in the Library of Congress; *not* on the Harper's Ferry Commission's conformed copy in the National Archives, Record Group 153-KK311.) Miles's Wednesday report of a rebel column moving from Boonsboro to Rohrersville was as wrong as Miles's Saturday morning expectation of an attack on the plateau of the Rohrersville Road. The significance, if any, of Miles's preoccupation with the possibility of attack from Rohrersville is not, however, presently comprehensible.

23. WR/OR, series I, vol. XIX, pt. I, p. 615.

24. Ibid., p. 707.

25. It will be recalled that Miles's physician testified that Miles was on brandy and opium during the Battle of Bull Run I and for several days previously. 37 Cong., 2nd sess., U.S. Senate, Exec. Doc. no. 7, Transcript of Proceedings before Court of Inquiry, pp. 38–39.

26. Insofar as Miles's aide, Binney, can be trusted, he testified: "Since I have been with him, in February last, I have never known him to use intoxicating drink in any shape, kind or form. . . . I never saw him under the influence of liquor and never saw any liquors about his quarters, and I knew all his rooms." WR/OR, series I, vol. XIX, pt. I, p. 761. More significant is the absence of testimony by *any* of the several dozen Harper's Ferry Commission witnesses except Downey (quoted in text) and Means (ibid., p. 755) suggesting or even implying that Miles was under the influence of alcohol during the siege. It seems almost impossible that Miles could have concealed drinking to that extent. (There remains, however, a possibility that he was taking opium.)

27. WR/OR, series I, vol. XIX, pt. I, pp. 621–22.

28. Downey's 3rd Maryland (Potomac Home Brigade) was raised in the hilly western part of Maryland between October 1861 and May 1862 by Downey's mentor and future law partner, ex-Governor and now Congressman Francis Thomas. This regiment, while organized primarily to help defend the B & O Railroad and C & O Canal, had seen actual fighting during Jackson's Valley Campaign (at Franklin, Virginia, on May 12, 1862; Wardensville, Virginia, on May 29, 1862; and Moorefield, Virginia, on June 29, 1862). L. A. Wilmer, J. H. Jarrett, and G.W.F. Vernon, *History and Roster of Maryland Volunteers, War of 1861–5*, 2 vols. (Baltimore, Md.: Press of Guggenheimer, Weill & Co., 1898), 1: 569–70. Downey, who had served as General Frémont's aide, had five horses shot out from under him at the Battle of Cross Keys on June 8, 1862. Letter from S. W. Downey to J. H. Barney, dated October 10, 1901, a copy of which is in the present writer's possession.

29. WR/OR, series I, vol. XIX, pt. I, pp. 549, 625.

30. Ibid., p. 625.
31. Ibid., p. 549.
32. Ibid., p. 632.
33. Ibid., p. 746.
34. Ibid.
35. Ibid., p. 560.
36. Ibid., pp. 565–66.
37. Ibid., p. 563.
38. Ibid., p. 775.
39. WR/Or, series I, vol. XIX, pt. I, p. 525. The full text reads: "Brigr. Genl. White, with a magnanimity equal to his valor, proffers to the undersigned, commanding officer of this post, his services, and those of the troops he brought with him, for its defense in its present necessity. This act of high-toned chivalric generosity, of which there are but few precedents in our army, overwhelms me with the deepest gratitude. I cheerfully accept the invaluable assistance of the gallant General and will assign his brave troops to important positions. It is hereby ordered: wherever present, during the siege of this post, the troops will obey implicitly and with alacrity, all orders given by General White."
40. Ibid., p. 863.
41. Ibid.
42. Ibid.
43. Ibid.
44. Ibid., pp. 863, 867.
45. Ibid., p. 867.
46. Ibid., p. 863.
47. Ibid., pp. 863, 868.
48. Ibid.
49. Ibid., p. 868.
50. Ibid.
51. Ibid., p. 863.
52. Ibid., p. 863.
53. Ibid., p. 571.
54. Ibid., pp. 570–71, 733–35, 772.
55. Ibid., p. 728.
56. Ibid., p. 571; Willson, Disaster, Struggle, Triumph, p. 61.
57. WR/OR, series I, vol. XIX, pt. I, p. 735.
58. Ibid., p. 733.
59. The Union sources speak of Kershaw's attack on the Union *left* flank as well as Barksdale's attack on the Union *right* flank. We know from the Rebel sources (ibid., pp. 867–68) that their Colonel Nance did have a plan to flank the Union left but that it never was put into effect because Kershaw's approval was not obtained in time. What the Union troops saw was apparently just considerable Rebel activity on their (the Union) left flank which they perhaps prematurely assumed was going to grow into a flank attack.
60. Ibid., p. 728.
61. Ibid., p. 614.
62. See note 59, above.
63. Willson, Disaster, Struggle, Triumph, pp. 60–61.
64. Ibid., pp. 61–62.
65. Ibid., p. 62 (quoting letter to author from Lieutenant S. F. Lincoln of the 126th New York).
66. WR/OR, series I, vol. XIX, pt. I, p. 571.
67. Ibid., pp. 733–34.
68. Ibid., pp. 614 (Downey) and 728 (Russell). See also Willson, Disaster, Struggle, Triumph, p. 68.

69. WR/OR, series I, vol. XIX, pt. I, p. 771.
70. See chap. 15.
71. WR/OR, series I, vol. XIX, pt. I, p. 566.
72. Ibid., pp. 568–69.
73. Ibid., p. 566.
74. Ibid., p. 571.
75. Ibid., p. 733.
76. Ibid., p. 734.
77. Willson, *Disaster, Struggle, Triumph*, p. 72. See also p. 68 thereof quoting Phillips as writing the author that "a 2d Lieutenant, who told me he was acting for Colonel Ford, ordered me to withdraw my Regiment in good order, and place them on the first level in the woods beyond the lookout *as McGrath's Battery was going to shell the rebels*" (emphasis added).
78. WR/OR, series I, vol. XIX, pt. I, p. 771.
79. Ibid., p. 617 (Downey: "When they once got through Solomon's Gap they had an equal advantage of us and when they once got this side of the lookout they had every advantage.")
80. Ibid., p. 614.
81. Ibid., p. 867.
82. W. H. Nichols, "The Siege and Capture of Harper's Ferry," p. 21.
83. WR/OR, series I, vol. XIX, pt. I, p. 608.
84. Ibid., p. 568.

Chapter 17.   Maryland Heights: Saturday Afternoon

1. U.S. Department of War, *The War of the Rebellion: A Compilation of the Official Records of the Union and Confederate Armies*, 128 vols. (Washington, D.C.: G.P.O., 1880–1901) [hereafter "WR/OR"], series I, vol. XIX, pt. I, p. 690.
2. Ibid., p. 695.
3. Ibid., p. 707.
4. Ibid., pp. 615–16.
5. Ibid., p. 616.
6. Ibid.
7. Ibid., p. 601.
8. Ibid., pp. 536, 580.
9. Ibid., p. 603.
10. Ibid., p. 711.
11. Ibid., p. 761.
12. Ibid., p. 645.
13. Ibid.
14. Ibid.
15. Ibid.
16. Ibid.
17. Ibid.
18. Ibid.
19. Ibid.
20. Ibid., p. 582.
21. Ibid.
22. Ibid., p. 625.
23. Ibid. McGrath was anxious to have four companies of infantry to protect his battery from potential counter-battery fire from a knob extending out a quarter miles from his position. Ibid., p. 695.
24. Ibid., p. 627.

25. Ibid.

26. Sammon later referred to "some slight skirmishes in front of us." He also testified that five of his men were wounded on Maryland Heights. However, it appears that these five men were probably members of two companies of the 115th sent over with the 39th New York the previous day. Ibid., p. 601. See WR/OR, series I, vol. XIX, pt. I, pp. 601, 625.

27. Ibid., p. 772.

28. Ibid., p. 773.

29. Ibid., pp. 860–61. Barksdale had 960; Kershaw had 1041.

30. Ibid., p. 549.

31. Ibid., pp. 615, 617, 619, 620 (Downey); p. 729 (Russell).

32. Whether Ford's headquarters were located in the Unsell house is not entirely certain, but such was the conclusion of National Park Service historian Arthur L. Sullivan, according to a memorandum to Regional Director, Region 5 from Acting Superintendent, Harper's Ferry, dated December 26, 1961, concerning "Historical Base Map—September 1862." The Unsell (or Unseld) farm, Sullivan concluded, was the only old house on the west slope of Maryland Heights located about 200–300 yards from the known location of the naval battery (the known description of Ford's headquarters).

33. WR/OR, series I, vol. XIX, pt. II, p. 582. Note Mrs. Brown's recollection that she heard Ford "ordering men to leave." (Ibid., p. 711.)

34. Undated memorandum (one page) from Ford to Secretary Chase, explaining the presentation he desired to be made to President Lincoln concerning his (Ford's) petition to be restored to his rank and position as commander of the 32nd Ohio; found in National Archives, Record Group 153, Harper's Ferry Court of Inquiry File (KK 311).

35. WR/OR, series I, vol. XIX, pt. I, p. 582.

36. Ibid., p. 693.

37. Ibid., p. 582.

38. Ibid., p. 595.

39. National Archives, Record Group 79, Service and Pension Records of Capt. Charles J. Brown and wife Elizabeth Brown.

40. Ibid.

41. WR/OR, series I, vol. XIX, pt. 1, p. 719.

42. Ibid., p. 719.

43. Ibid., p. 741. Confirmation of Mrs. Brown's version came from Major Steiner of the 1st Maryland (PHB): "I just came in at the moment when you [Ford] were complaining of the breaking of certain troops that were on the mountain. Colonel Miles was about leaving. Says he, 'Colonel Ford, then do the best you can; spike your guns and throw them down the mountain.'" WR/OR, series I, vol. XIX, pt. I, p. 703.

44. Ibid., p. 719.

45. Ibid.

46. Ibid., p. 693.

47. Ibid., p. 582.

48. Ibid., p. 719.

49. Ibid., p. 749.

50. A Scotch highlander immigrant, Dan Cameron was an active Douglas Democrat and newspaper publisher in Chicago. J. G. Wilson, *Biographical Sketches of Illinois Officers Engaged in the War against the Rebellion of 1861* (Chicago: J. Barnet, 1862, 1863), pp. 28–29.

51. WR/OR, series I, vol. XIX, pt. I, pp. 631–32.

52. Ibid., p. 631.

53. Ibid., p. 635.

54. H. Kyd Douglas, *I Rode with Stonewall* (Chapel Hill, N.C.: University of North

Carolina Press, 1940; Greenwich, Conn.: Fawcett Publications, Inc. 1965), p. 157 ("early in the afternoon").

55. WR/OR, series I, vol. XIX, pt. I, p. 634.

56. Ibid., p. 634.

57. Ibid., p. 635.

58. Ibid.

59. Cameron himself had "no doubt whatever" that Harper's Ferry might have been held by throwing the entire Union force upon Maryland Heights at this time. See WR/OR, series I, vol. XIX, pt. I, pp. 631, 637.

60. Ibid., p. 772.

61. Ibid., p. 615.

62. Ibid.

63. Ibid.

64. Ibid., p. 621.

65. Ibid.

66. Ibid., p. 620.

67. Ibid., p. 729.

68. Ibid., p. 774.

69. Ibid., p. 707. See also Major Hewitt's testimony at ibid., p. 571, which may refer to Crumbecker's afternoon report but was apparently relied on by Hewitt in his testimony as justifying his *morning* order to retreat from the breastworks.

70. Ibid., p. 546.

71. Ibid., p. 580.

72. Ibid., p. 546.

73. Ibid., pp. 693–94.

74. Ibid., p. 699.

75. Ibid., pp. 693–94, 698–99.

76. Ibid., pp. 594–95.

77. Ibid., pp. 537–79.

78. Boston *Journal,* September 30, 1862, Editorial page, col. 5. That Binney had no illusion that he was a Captain appears from a slightly later petition for promotion found in his military personnel file, now in the National Archives, Record Group 79.

79. War Department, Adjutant General's Office, Special Order #420, December 20, 1862.

80. WR/OR, series I, vol. XIX, pt. 1, pp. 714–15.

81. Ibid.

82. Ibid., p. 594.

83. Fairness requires one to note that Miles not only denied to a *Tribune* reporter having given the order to evacuate Maryland Heights but added that the evacuation was "in direct opposition" to his orders. New York *Daily Tribune,* September 18, 1862, p. 8. We cannot, however, attribute any weight to this self-serving statement to the press for the purpose of determining the truth.

84. Ibid., p. 619.

85. Ibid., p. 576. See also J. H. Clark, *The Iron Hearted Regiment* (Albany, N.Y.: J. Munsell 1865), pp. 12–13: "As the Union troops were marching down the steep sides of the mountain and the flashing of bayonets lit up the scene, I was lying on Bolivar Heights suffering from the effects of poison eaten in rebel cake. Just then General [*sic*] Miles and staff rode up and were looking very attentively toward the scene of conflict. Suddenly the General started as though thunderstruck and exclaimed: 'They are all abandoning the heights!' and he dashed down the hill like a madman, to learn the cause."

86. A noncom in Downey's 3rd Maryland (PHB) many years later wrote that "when the regiment was marching through the Ferry Col. Downey met Col. Miles and demanded to know why Maryland Heights was evacuated. After some angry words Col. Downey said: 'Miles, you are a ——— traitor or coward for this.' " (Undated letter from

"J. H. Berry" [Barney], 1st Sgt. of Co. B, to editor, *National Tribune*, a copy of which is now in the possession of Dr. Barbara Mullens Moorman of Gloucester, Virginia.) However, when Barney years later wrote Downey, asking him to confirm the "coward or traitor" accusation, Downey could not remember using that language to Miles, although he stopped short of a denial. (Letter dated October 10, 1901 from S. W. Downey to J. H. Barney, a copy of which is in the present writer's possession.)

87. New York *Daily Tribune*, September 18, 1862, p. 8.

88. WR/OR, series I, vol. XIX, pt. I, p. 628.

Chapter 18.   Strange Interlude

1. U.S. War Department, *The War of the Rebellion: A Compilation of the Official Records of the Union and Confederate Armies*, 128 vols. (Washington, D.C.: G.P.O. 1880–1901) [hereafter WR/OR], series I, vol. XIX, pt. II, p. 221 (McClellan to Porter, September 9, 1862): "The army is tonight well posted to act in any direction the moment the enemy develops his movements."

2. Ibid., p. 254. McClellan messaged Halleck on September 11, 1862: "At the time this army moved from Washington, it was not known what the intentions of the rebels were in placing their forces on this side of the Potomac. It might have been a feint to draw away our troops from Washington . . . or it might have been supposed to be precisely what they are now doing. . . . This uncertainty, in my judgment exists no more."

3. Ibid., p. 269 (McClellan to Governor Curtin of Pennsylvania, 1:15 P.M., September 11, 1862, and Curtin to McClellan, 8:00 P.M., September 11, 1862).

4. WR/OR, series I, vol. LI, pt. I, supp., p. 816 (Marcy to Franklin, September 11, 1862).

5. WR/OR, series I, vol. LI, pt. I, supp., p. 822 (Marcy to Franklin, September 12, 1862): ". . . march at daylight tomorrow [from Urbana] to Buckeystown."

6. Ibid. (". . . and there await further orders, ready to move either to Frederick or Harper's Ferry, as may prove necessary.")

7. U.S. Congress, 37th Cong., 3rd Sess., House of Representatives, *Report of the Joint Committee on the Conduct of the War* (1863), p. 483 (Halleck to Miles, September 12, 1862, and McClellan to Halleck, September 12, 1862). See also General Wool's testimony, and another copy of the same message in WR/OR, series I, vol. XIX, pt. I, p. 521.

8. U.S. Congress, 37th Cong., 2nd Sess., Senate, Exec. Doc. no. 7, *Proceedings of a Court of Inquiry in the Case of Colonel D. S. Miles, 2nd Infantry* (1861), p. 2.

9. "By direction of the President of the United States . . . the Sixth Army Corps is temporarily attached to the Third, under Major General Heintzelman. Major Generals Fitz John Porter and William B. Franklin and Brig. Genl. Charles Griffin are relieved of their respective commands until the charges against them can be investigated by a court of inquiry." WR/OR, series I, vol. XIX, pt. II, p. 188.

10. Ibid., pp. 189–90.

11. S. Colegrove, "The Finding of Lee's Lost Order," in R. U. Johnson and C. C. Buel, *Battles and Leaders of the Civil War*, 4 vols. (New York: The Century Co., 1887; New York: Thomas Yoseloff, 1956), 2: 603.

12. Ibid. See also WR/OR, series I, vol. XIX, pt. I, p. 785.

13. WR/OR, series I, vol. LI, pt. I, supp., p. 829.

14. As early as 10:00 A.M. on Friday the twelfth McClellan had messaged Halleck: "I feel perfectly confident that the enemy has abandoned Frederick, moving in two directions, viz., on the Hagerstown and Harper's Ferry Roads." WR/OR, series I, vol. XIX, pt. II, pp. 270–71.

15. WR/OR, series I, vol. XIX, pt. I, pp. 45–46; for portion originally omitted see vol. LI, pt. I, pp. 826–27.

16. Ibid., vol. XIX, pt. I, p. 45.

17. Ibid., p. 46.

18. WR/OR, series I, vol. LI, pt. I, p. 829.

19. McClellan's preliminary draft was more definite as to his coming morning movement, here simply called "early" but originally scheduled "at 2."

20. McClellan's original draft said that unless Miles made a stout resistance "we shall be too late"; this was toned down to "may" in the final text. See scroll draft of McClellan to Halleck, 11:00 P.M., September 13, 1862, in Library of Congress, Manuscript Collection, McClellan Papers, microfilm reel 31 (of 82).

21. WR/OR, series I, vol. XIX, pt. I, pp. 785–86.

22. Franklin to McClellan, 10:00 P.M., September 13, 1862, Library of Congress, Manuscript Division, McClellan papers, reel 31 (microfilm).

23. After the war Lee wrote: "When they [the orders] were issued [on September 9] I supposed there would have been time for accomplishment and for the army to have reunited before Genl. McClellan could cross the South Mountains." J. V. Murfin, *The Gleam of Bayonets* (New York and London: Thomas Yoseloff, 1965; New York: Bonanza Books, 1968), p. 338.

24. Ibid.

25. Ibid., pp. 332–33, 338.

26. WR/OR, series I, vol. XIX, pt. II, p. 607.

27. Murfin, *The Gleam of Bayonets*, p. 338, quoting a postwar letter of Lee: "[Jackson] was *by verbal instructions* placed in command of the expedition" (emphasis added). D. S. Freeman, in *Lee's Lieutenants*, 4 vols. (London: Charles Scribner's Sons, 1942–44, 1946), 2: 162, thought that Jackson's ultimate command followed simply from his rank, although "the actual capture of the Ferry was to be the task of Lafayette McLaws, who was to seize Maryland Heights."

28. *New York Times*, September 8, 1862, p. 1, col. 3: "On Maryland Heights, opposite the village, we have several hundred pounders which guard the country for miles around."

29. WR/OR, series I, vol. XIX, pt. I, pp. 665–68.

30. Ibid., pt. 2, p. 607.

31. Douglas, *I Rode with Stonewall*, p. 159.

32. Walker, J. G., "Jackson's Capture of Harper's Ferry," in R. V. Johnson and C. C. Buel, *Battles and Leaders of the Civil War*, 4 vols. (New York, The Century Co., 1887; New York: Thomas Yoseloff, 1956), 2: 610.

33. Ibid., p. 609.

34. WR/OR, series I, vol. XIX, pt. II, p. 607.

35. Ibid.

36. Jed Hotchkiss, *Make Me a Map of the Valley: The Civil War Journal of Stonewall Jackson's Topographer*, ed. Archie P. McDonald (Dallas, Tex.: Southern Methodist University Press, 1973), p. xv.

37. Ibid., p. 81.

38. Ibid.

39. For the exchange of messages between Jackson, Walker, and McLaws on this subject during Sunday the fourteenth, see the report of Rebel Signal Officer J. L. Bartlett, WR/OR, series I, vol. XIX, pt. I, pp. 958–59.

40. *Hillmon* v. *New York Life Insurance Co.*, 145 U.S. 285 (1892).

41. WR/OR, series I, vol. XIX, pt. I, p. 632.

Chapter 19.   Messages to McClellan

1. U.S. War Department, *The War of the Rebellion: A Compilation of the Official Records of the Union and Confederate Armies*, 128 vols. (Washington, D.C.: G.P.O., 1880–1901) [hereafter "WR/OR"], series I, vol. XIX, pt. I, pp. 720, 729.

2. Ibid., p. 720.

3. Ibid., p. 528. See also E. H. Ripley, "Memories of the Ninth Vermont at the Tragedy of Harper's Ferry, Sept. 15, 1862", in *Personal Recollections of the War of the Rebellion.* (New York: M.O.L.L.U.S., New York Commandery, 1909), 4: 153.

4. WR/OR, series I, vol. XIX, pt. 1, p. 720.

5. Ibid.

6. U.S. Congress, 37th Cong., 3rd sess., House of Representatives, *Report of the Joint Committee on the Conduct of the War* (1863), p. 486.

7. S. P. Chase, "Diary of Salmon P. Chase," in *Annual Report of the American Historical Association for the Year 1902,* 2 vols. (Washington, D.C.: G.P.O., 1903), 2: 81.

8. WR/OR, series I, vol. XIX, pt. I, p. 721.

9. Ibid.

10. Ibid.

11. See, for example, Murfin, *The Gleam of Bayonets*, pp. 154–55, and H. W. Pfanz, *Special History Report, Troop Movement Maps, 1862*, Harper's Ferry National Historical Park, Maryland-W. Virginia, 1976, pp. 33–34.

12. C. A. Newcomer, *Cole's Cavalry; or, Three Years in the Saddle in the Shenandoah* (Freeport, N.Y.: Books for Libraries Press, 1970), pp. 44–45.

13. Scroll list of "Witnesses summoned to appear before the Military Commission now in session in Washington, D.C." found in National Archives, Record Group 153, Harper's Ferry Court of Inquiry File (KK 311).

14. Newcomer, *Cole's Cavalry*, pp. 44–45.

15. WR/OR, series I, vol. XIX, pt. I, p. 46.

Chapter 20.   Bolivar Heights: Sunday Afternoon

1. U.S. War Department, *The War of the Rebellion: A Compilation of the Official Records of the Union and Confederate Armies,* 128 vols. (Washington, D.C.: G.P.O., 1880–1901) [hereafter "WR/OR"], series I, vol. XIX, pt. I, p. 958.

2. Ibid.

3. Ibid.

4. J. G. Walker, "Jackson's Capture of Harper's Ferry," in R. U. Johnson and C. C. Buel, *Battles and Leaders of the Civil War,* 4 vols. (New York: The Century Co., 1887; New York: Thomas Yoseloff, 1956), 2: 609.

5. Jackson had just put his chief lieutenant, Major General A. P. Hill, under arrest for being a half hour late in obeying an order. H. K. Douglas, *I Rode with Stonewall* (Chapel Hill, N.C.: University of North Carolina Press, 1940; Greenwich, Conn.: Fawcett Publications, Inc., 1965), pp. 147–48, 158.

6. WR/OR, series I, vol. XIX, pt. I, p. 958.

7. Walker, "Jackson's Capture of Harper's Ferry," p. 609.

8. Ibid., p. 610.

9. WR/OR, series I, vol. XIX, pt. I, pp. 560, 742.

10. *New York Times,* September 18, 1862, p. 1.

11. WR/OR, series I, vol. XIX, pt. 1, p. 538.

12. Ibid., p. 549. Aside from the 126th New York and the 32nd Ohio, whose losses were largely on Maryland Heights on Saturday, total Union casualties for the entire siege and capture of Harper's Ferry were 21 killed and 73 wounded.

13. S. B. Pettenghill, *The College Cavaliers* (Chicago: H. McAllaster & Company 1883), pp. 73–74.

14. A. M. Willson, *Disaster, Struggle, Triumph: The Adventures of 1,000 "Boys in Blue"* (Albany, N.Y.: Argus Co., 1870), p. 79.

15. Luff, "March Of The Cavalry From Harper's Ferry, September 14, 1862," 2: 37.

16. WR/OR, series I, vol. XIX, pt. I, pp. 538, 547, 585, 591, 654, 664.

17. E. H. Ripley, *Vermont General,* ed. Otto Eisenschiml (New York: Devin-Adair Company, 1960), p. 30.

18. WR/OR, series I, vol. XIX, pt. I, p. 630.

19. Ibid., pp. 538, 585, 655.

20. Ibid., pp. 538, 585.

21. Ibid., p. 630.

22. Ibid., p. 657.

23. Ibid., p. 630.

24. Ibid., pp. 652, 654, 684.

25. Ibid., pp. 523, 528, 531.

26. Colonel Trimble testified that Miles "told me from the first that [the summit of Bolivar Heights] was to be the line." Ibid., p. 243.

27. Ibid., p. 527.

28. The definitive work on troop positions at Harper's Ferry has been published only recently by Dr. Harry W. Pfanz, Chief Historian of the National Park Service: *Special History Report, Troop Movement Maps, 1862,* Harper's Ferry National Historical Park, Maryland-W. Virginia 1976, pp. 73, 83. It is available from the U.S. Department of Commerce, National Technical Information Service, 5285 Port Royal Road, Springfield, Virginia, 22151.

29. WR/OR, series I, vol. XIX, pt. I, pp. 519, 791.

30. Willson, *Disaster, Struggle, Triumph,* pp. 78–79: "On the morning of the 14th the [Rebel] signalling was continuing and [Rebel] batteries were seen to be planted. And our troops were entirely unprotected and shelterless. Seeing this the 9th Vermont, the 126th New York and Captain Potts' battery set to work at about half past ten in the morning and constructed a rude work of logs and earth, stuffing in tents, clothing, army blankets, anything that would break the force of a ball; and dug a sort of trench or line of rifle pits. But for this precaution, which seems to have been taken without orders from the superior authorities, many more would have perished. . . ."

31. WR/OR, series I, vol. XIX, pt. I, p. 742. Before Downey arrived from Kearneysville on Friday the 12th, Stannard's 9th Vermont was placed in position to occupy the ground. Ibid., p. 741.

32. WR/OR, series I, vol. XIX, pt. 1, p. 743.

33. Ibid., p. 764.

34. Ibid., pp. 606–7.

35. Ibid.

36. Ibid.

37. Ibid.

38. Ibid.

39. Ibid., p. 738 (Rouse released a week before the siege).

40. Ibid., p. 800 (". . . and some of them [the Rebel parolees] left as late as the 14th").

41. See file of duplicate passes for parolees in National Archives, Record Group 153, Harper's Ferry Court of Inquiry File (KK 311).

42. Ibid., p. 633.

43. Willson, *Disaster, Struggle, Triumph,* p. 99.

44. WR/OR, series I, vol. XIX, pt. I, p. 633. ("They went right to the headquarters of the enemy, doubtless, charged with all the information that anybody could have.")

45. Ibid., p. 954.

46. Ibid.

47. Ibid.

48. Ibid.

49. Ibid., p. 980.

50. Ibid., p. 1000.

51. Ibid.

52. Ibid., pp. 980, 1004.

53. Ibid., p. 742.

54. Ibid., pp. 742, 747. Downey, too, was trying to find Miles. He sent eight or ten messengers to hunt him up but without success. Ibid., p. 622.

55. Ibid., p. 742, 745. See also p. 560.

56. Ibid., pp. 527, 538. Cf. Trimble's assumption (apparently erroneous) that it was Miles who sent him the 32nd Ohio. Ibid., p. 747.

57. Ibid., p. 1004.

58. Pender's superior, A. P. Hill, reported the 150-yard figure. Ibid., p. 980.

59. Pender's language was "fall back a short distance."

60. James Clark, *The Iron Hearted Regiment* (Albany, N.Y.: J. Munsell, 1865), p. 17.

61. *New York Times*, September 18, 1862, p. 1.

62. WR/OR, series I, vol. XIX, pt. I, p. 527.

63. Ibid., p. 538.

64. Ibid., pp. 980, 984.

65. Ibid., p. 531.

66. F. M. Dowley, *History and Honorary Roll of the 12th Regiment, Infantry, NGSNY* (New York: T. Farrell & Son, 1869), p. 20.

67. WR/OR, series I, vol. XIX, pt. I, p. 531.

68. Ibid. Years later White wrote a similar account of the episode. "The writer, being in command of the forces in this quarter [where the Charlestown Pike crosses Bolivar Heights], ordered the massing of the artillery there and the movement of the regiments holding Camp Hill to the front. These orders, as I afterward learned, were countermanded by Colonel Miles, who deemed it necessary to retain a force [apparently in addition to Maulsby's 1st Maryland (PHB)] near the river-crossing; at all events the order was not executed." J. White, "The Capitulation of Harper's Ferry," in R. U. Johnson and C. C. Buel, *Battles and Leaders of the Civil War*, 4 vols. (New York: The Century Co., 1887: New York: Thomas Yoseloff, 1956), 2: 613.

69. WR/OR, series I, vol. XIX, pt. I, pp. 985, 987.

70. Ibid., p. 997.

71. Ibid., pp. 985, 987.

72. J. F. J. Caldwell, *The History of a Brigade of South Carolinians Known First as Gregg's Brigade* (Philadelphia: King & Baird, 1866), pp. 42–43.

73. Ripley, *Vermont General*, p. 30. Ripley recalled this incident as happening on Saturday, but it had to be on Sunday.

74. WR/OR, series I, vol. XIX, pt. I, p. 980.

75. Ibid., p. 951.

76. WR/OR, series I, vol. LI, pt. II, pp. 618–19.

77. WR/OR, series I, vol. XIX, pt. I, p. 951.

78. D. S. Freeman, *Lee's Lieutenants*, 4 vols. (New York: Charles Scribner's Sons, 1942–44, 1946), 1: 197.

79. In fairness, the reader should know that Jackson was a devout churchman (R. G. Tanner, *Stonewall in the Valley* [Garden City, N.Y.: Doubleday & Co; Inc. 1976], p. 53); yet it is doubtful that this would have stopped him from putting the Good Lord to work for a Good Cause.

Chapter 21. The Brink of Disaster

1. Jackson afterward reportedly said: "I would rather have had them [the Union cavalry] than everything else in the place." Ezra A. Carman, "History of the Civil War, Maryland Campaign, September 1862," Library of Congress, Manuscript Division, Chap. 6, p. 70.

2. Not to be confused with Colonel Hasbrouck Davis of the 12th Illinois Cavalry, who was also present during the siege of Harper's Ferry.

3. U.S. War Department, *The War of the Rebellion: A Compilation of the Official Records of the Union and Confederate Armies*, 128 vols. (Washington, D.C.: G.P.O., 1880 to 1901) [hereafter "WR/OR"], series I, vol. XIX, pt. I, p. 630.

4. Ibid., p. 630. A test crossing ordered by Union General White and Rebel General A. P. Hill after the surrender apparently substantiated Miles's judgment in this respect. Ibid., p. 718.

5. S. B. Pettengill, *The College Cavaliers* (Chicago: H. McAllaster Co., 1883), pp. 77, 81.

6. W. M. Luff, "March of the Cavalry from Harper's Ferry, September 14, 1862," in *Military Essays and Recollections* (M.O.L.L.U.S., Ill., 1894), 2: 38.

7. WR/OR, series I, vol. XIX, pt. I, p. 583.

8. Luff, "March of the Cavalry from Harper's Ferry," p. 38.

9. Pettengill, *The College Cavaliers*, p. 81.

10. Ibid., p. 77.

11. H. Norton, *History of the 8th New York Volunteer Cavalry* (Norwich, N.Y.: Chenango Printing House, 1889), p. 27.

12. WR/OR, series I, vol. XIX, pt. I, p. 584.

13. Ibid.

14. It was actually after dusk by the time the first horsemen started across the pontoon bridge. Luff, "March of the Cavalry from Harper's Ferry, September 14, 1862," p. 39 (purporting to reprint Miles's Special Order no. 120, dated September 14, 1862, verbatim).

15. Ibid. See also Pettengill, *The College Cavaliers*, p. 81; C. A. Newcomer, *Cole's Cavalry; or, Three Years in the Saddle in the Shenandoah Valley*, (Freeport, N.Y.: Books for Libraries Press, 1970), pp. 42–43.

16. Ibid. Colonel Voss's later memory of Miles's order added another reference to Sharpsburg: "Arrived at Sharpsburg, they [the Union Cavalry] will seek to join Gen. McClellan and report to him for duty." Pettengill, *the College Cavaliers*, p. 81.

17. WR/OR, series I, vol. XIX, pt. I, p. 584.

18. It seems to have taken about two hours for the whole column of cavalry to have crossed the pontoon bridge. J. V. Murfin, *The Gleam of Bayonets* (New York and London: Thomas Yoseloff 1965), p. 152. The times of departure reported for certain units range from "after dusk" (12th Illinois Cavalry) to 9:00 P.M. (7th Rhode Island Cavalry and 8th New York Cavalry) to 10:00 P.M. (Cole's Potomac Home Brigade Cavalry). See respectively: Luff, "March of the Cavalry from Harper's Ferry, September 14, 1862," p. 39; "History of the Seventh Squadron, Rhode Island Cavalry," in *State of Rhode Island, Adjutant General's Report* (1865), p. 10; Thomas Bell, "*At Harper's Ferry, Va., September 14, 1862: How the Cavalry Escaped out of the Toils*, 1900, (pamphlet found in U.S.A.M.H.R.C., Carlisle Barracks, Pennsylvania [Civil War Repository]), p. 12; Newcomer, *Cole's Cavalry*, p. 43.

19. Pettengill, *The College Cavaliers* p. 83. See also Bell, *At Harper's Ferry, Va.*, p. 12 (copy in U.S.A.M.H.R.C., Carlisle Barracks, Pennsylvania).

20. Luff, "March of the Cavalry from Harper's Ferry," pp. 41–42.

21. The romantic story of the escape of the Harper's Ferry cavalry is told best in Murfin, *The Gleam of Bayonets*, pp. 147–54 and 191–96.

22. In this connection it is interesting to note that about 9:00 P.M. Sunday one of the Marylanders on Jackson's staff, Kyd Douglas, surprisingly took leave between the battles of Sunday night and Monday morning, ostensibly to visit his family about ten miles away at Shepherdstown, just three miles from Sharpsburg. H. Kyd Douglas, *I Rode with Stonewall* (Chapel Hill, N.C.: Univerity of North Carolina Press, 1940; Greenwich, Conn.: Fawcett Publications, 1965), p. 159.

23. WR/OR, series I, vol. XIX, pt. I, p. 45.

24. Pettengill, *The College Cavaliers*, p. 81, indicates that a Cole lieutenant named Green represented Cole's Cavalry at this meeting.

25. Newcomer, *Cole's Cavalry*, p. 43.

26. Ibid., pp. 44–45.

27. For example: ". . . and at ten o'clock on the night of September 14th, 1862, Cole's Battalion took the advance over the pontoon bridge across the Potomac River, *with their brave Major in the lead* . . ." (Emphasis added). Newcomer, *Cole's Cavalry*, p. 43.

28. Although the writer of the regimental history, C. A. Newcomer, was not present at Harper's Ferry (ibid., p. 32), he secured from Cole the following endorsement on a flyer which is still in the possession of the Maryland Historical Society in Baltimore: "Dear Sir and Comrade (Newcomer): I have with great pleasure read the advance sheets of your work entitled 'Cole's Cavalry; or Three Years In The Saddle In The Shenandoah Valley'! and I am of the opinion that *the book is a faithful and vivid history of the many scenes through which our command passed.* . . ." (Emphasis added.)

29. See scroll list of "Witnesses summoned to appear before the Military Commission now in session in Washington, D.C.," found in National Archives, Record Group 153, Harper's Ferry Court of Inquiry File (KK311). Nonetheless, Cole never testified.

30. Less than two weeks earlier "such a hurrah as the Army of the Potomac had never heard before" had greeted the news that McClellan had been restored to command after Pope's defeat at Bull Run II. "The effect of this man's presence upon the Army of the Potomac—in sunshine or rain, in darkness or daylight, in victory or defeat—was electrical. . . ." J. H. Campbell, *McClellan* (New York: Neale Publishing Co., 1916), pp. 354–55. It was, of course, precisely this popularity with his men which made the Lincoln Administration hesitate so long before finally depriving McClellan of the supreme command and eventually made McClellan the Democratic nominee for President in 1864.

31. WR/OR, series I, vol. XIX, pt. I, p. 586.

32. Washington *Evening Star,* September 18, 1862, p. 1.

33. On Monday morning, after the cavalry had reached Greencastle, Governor Curtin of Pennsylvania wired Secretary of War Stanton: "Colonel Davis says he thinks Colonel Miles will surrender *this morning.* Colonel Miles desires his condition to be made known to the War Department" (Emphasis added). WR/OR, series I, vol. XIX, pt. I, p. 305. See also Washington *Evening Star,* September 16, 1862, p. 2, quoting Miles as saying "he could not hold Harper's Ferry longer than *yesterday morning* unless relieved, rather than *yesterday evening,* as previously alleged" (emphasis added).

34. WR/OR, series I, vol. XIX, pt. I, p. 520 (Wool to Miles, September 5, 1862).

35. Ibid., p. 787 (Halleck to Miles, September 7, 1862).

36. See Miles's conversation with his engineer, Captain Powell, on the night of Saturday the thirteenth (ibid., pp. 766–67) and conversation with Colonel Trimble the afternoon of Sunday the fourteenth (ibid., p. 745). It is not entirely clear, however, whether Trimble in this conversation expressly suggested reoccupying Maryland Heights, as distinguished from urging a general escape in any direction possible.

37. When asked by the Harper's Ferry Commission: "As a military man . . . would not an order to hold Harper's Ferry imply an order to hold the heights which commanded it?," Captain Powell replied "Of course." He also agreed that Maryland Heights commanded Harper's Ferry. Ibid., p. 767.

38. "Report of Maj. Gen. Henry W. Halleck, U.S. Army, General in Chief, of operations September 3–October 24 (1862)," in WR/OR, series I, vol. LI, pt. I, p. 4. (Reprinted in Frank Moore, *The Rebellion Record* [1864] 6: 220.)

39. G. B. McClellan, *McClellan's Own Story* (New York: C. L. Webster & Co., 1886), p. 561.

40. WR/OR, series I, vol. XIX, pt. I, p. 629: "I should suppose that it was not a very good road at any time for artillery . . . but at the rate at which we marched that night, it would have been utterly impossible for the artillery and infantry to have accompanied us, even if the road had been good."

41. WR/OR, series I, vol. XIX, pt. I, p. 559: "The road was very narrow and difficult; infantry could not have kept up with us. The road was too rough for artillery, passing, as it did, frequently over ravines, fields and fences."

42. E. H. Ripley, "Memories of the Ninth Vermont at the Tragedy of Harper's Ferry, September 15, 1862," in *Personal Recollections of the War of The Rebellion* (New York: M.O.L.L.U.S., New York Commandery, 1909), 4: 147.

43. J. G. Walker, "Jackson's Capture of Harper's Ferry," in R. U. Johnson, and

C. C. Buel, *Battles and Leaders of the Civil War,* 4 vols. (New York: The Century Co., 1887; New York: Thomas Yoseloff, 1956), 2: 611.

44. Ibid., p. 745.

45. A general attempt to escape seems to have found its most eager proponents among D'Utassy's officers, particularly Col. Cameron, commanding the 65th Illinois Infantry, who stressed "the want of confidence in Col. Miles, the shortness, almost exhaustion of the ammunition [and] the general impression that seemed to reign through the place that Harper's Ferry would fall" (ibid., p. 635). Particularly vocal was his English-born, professionally trained artillerist, Captain John Phillips, whose disgust with Miles would have important consequences on the morrow. When Phillips failed to get through to Miles (ibid., p. 683), D'Utassy himself attempted, but without success, to win Miles's permission for an escape (ibid., p. 637). Miles's aide Binney reported to the Harper's Ferry Commission that "several regimental officers advised Miles to "surrender or evacuate" (ibid., pp. 538, 584). There is not the slightest evidence, however, to support Binney's assertion that some of the garrison's officers urged "surrender." (Ibid.)

46. "As to his [Miles's] loyalty, there was a universal distrust among the junior officers and men, who judged both from what was done and left undone by a commander in such an important crisis." Ripley, "Memories of the Ninth Vermont at the Tragedy of Harper's Ferry, Sept. 15, 1862," p. 155.

47. WR/OR, series I, vol. XIX, pt. I, pp. 560, 742, 745.

48. Ibid., pp. 985, 987, 997; and J. F. J. Caldwell *The History of a Brigade of South Carolinians Known First as Gregg's Brigade* (Philadelphia: King & Baird, 1866), pp. 42–43.

49. WR/OR, series I, vol. XIX, pt. I, pp. 54, 561.

50. Ibid., p. 562.

51. Ibid., p. 561.

52. Ibid., p. 563. Willard added, however, that he did not believe this could have been done after daylight.

53. Ibid., p. 565.

54. Ibid., pp. 561–62.

55. Ibid., pp. 622, 624.

56. Ibid., p. 624.

57. Ibid., p. 623.

58. Letter from Stephen W. Downey to John G. Barney, dated October 10, 1901, a copy of which is in the present writer's possession. Barney's undated letter to the editor of the *National Tribune* quoted Downey as recommending that the council also "place Miles under arrest."

59. WR/OR, series I, vol. XIX, pt. I, p. 596.

60. Ibid.

61. Ibid.

62. Letter from Stephen W. Downey to John G. Barney, dated October 10, 1901, a copy of which is in the possession of the present writer.

63. WR/OR, series I, vol. XIX, pt. I, p. 45.

64. Ripley, "Memories of the Ninth Vermont at the Tragedy of Harper's Ferry, September 15, 1862," pp. 145–46.

Chapter 22. Surrender (I) As the Commission Saw It

1. J. White, "The Capitulations of Harper's Ferry," in R. U. Johnson and C. C. Buel *Battles and Leaders of the Civil War,* 4 vols. (New York: The Century Co. 1887; New York: Thomas Yoseloff, 1956), 2: 613.

2. Ibid. "Jackson was fulfilling another dream of the officer of artillery: He had his guns precisely where he wanted them [and] he was firing as he desired. . . ." D. S.

Freeman, *Lee's Lieutenants,* 4 vols. (New York: Charles Scribner's Sons, 1942–44, 1946), 2: 197. For specific locations of the Rebel batteries, see U.S. War Department, *The War of the Rebellion: A Compilation of the Official Records of the Union and Confederate Armies,* 128 vols. (Washington, D.C.: G.P.O., 1880–1901) [hereafter "WR/OR], series I, vol. XIX, pt. I, p. 958.

3. WR/OR, series I, vol. XIX, pt. I, pp. 558, 742 (Binney), 742 (Trimble).

4. Ibid., p. 652.

5. WR/OR, series I, vol. XIX, pt. I, pp. 730, 733.

6. As noted earlier, Jackson's left (under Jones) engaged in an elaborate feint against Miles's right (under D'Utassy) but it was never more than a feint.

7. WR/OR, series I, vol. XIX, pt. I, p. 955; White, "The Capitulation of Harper's Ferry," p. 613.

8. WR/OR, series I, vol. XIX, pt. I, p. 742.

9. Ibid., p. 539.

10. Ibid., pp. 666–68.

11. Ibid., p. 748.

12. Ibid., p. 743.

13. Ibid., p. 650 (Rigby) and 654 (Potts).

14. Ibid., p. 651 (Rigby) and 655 (Potts).

15. Ibid., p. 686.

16. Ibid., p. 953.

17. J. G. Walker, "Jackson's Capture of Harper's Ferry," in R. U. Johnson and C. C. Buel, *Battles and Leaders of the Civil War,* 4 vols. (New York: The Century Co. 1887; New York: Thomas Yoseloff, 1956), 2: 610.

18. A. M. Willson, *Disaster, Struggle, Triumph: The Adventures of 1,000 "Boys in Blue"* (Albany, N.Y.: Argus Co., 1870), p. 84.

19. WR/OR, series I, vol. XIX, pt. I, pp. 744–45.

20. E. H. Ripley, "Memories of the Ninth Vermont at the Tragedy of Harper's Ferry, September 15, 1862," in *Personal Recollections of the War of the Rebellion* (New York: M.O.L.L.U.S. [New York Commandery], 1909), 4: 148.

21. WR/OR, series I, vol. XIX, pt. I, p. 549.

22. Ibid., pp. 955, 1004.

23. Ibid., pp. 955, 980, 1004.

24. Ibid., pp. 955, 1004.

25. Ibid.

26. Ibid., p. 584.

27. In fact von Sehlen still had some shrapnel (ibid., p. 664).

28. In fact Phillips still had 40 rounds of canister (for antipersonnel fire). (Ibid., p. 684.)

29. Ibid., pp. 584–85. See also p. 590.

30. WR/OR, series I, vol. XIX, pt. I, p. 688. The two brigade commanders not called were Colonel Ward of the 12th New York Militia, who was back at Camp Hill (ibid., pp. 730, 732) and Colonel Ford of the 32nd Ohio, who had been sick in bed most of the time since his abandonment of Maryland Heights on Saturday (ibid., p. 576). Before the Harper's Ferry Commission, Ward testified that he thought from all he could learn that "at the time we could have held out but *a few hours* longer, if so long. . . . I think it is possible an assault might have been resisted; although, not being in front, it is impossible for me to say. I certainly could have supported the force on Bolivar Heights considerably with artillery from my left" (emphasis added). Ibid., p. 730.

31. Ibid., pp. 598–99.

32. Ibid., p. 744.

33. Ibid., p. 530.

34. S. V. Benet, *A Treatise on Military Law and the Practice of Courts Martial,* 6th ed. (1866), pp. 290–91, 294. Strange as it may seem today, even civilian courts for centuries declined to permit a criminal accused to testify on his own behalf, partly on the theory

that he had too great an interest in fabricating a defense, partly on the theory that he should not have to make a choice visible to the jury. The first American state to remove an accused's disability to testify was Maine, in 1864. See generally 1 *Wigmore on Evidence,* McNaughton's ed. (1961) §579. The Harper's Ferry Commission apparently treated Colonel Ford the same way. In his papers instructing Secretary Chase how to present his petition (for rescission of his dismissal) to President Lincoln, Ford expressly noted that "I was not permitted to testify before the Commission." National Archives, Record Group 153, Harper's Ferry Court of Inquiry, File KK311. Note that General White was permitted to testify as a witness for Colonel Ford (WR/OR, series I, vol. XIX, pt. I, p. 714) and D'Utassy and Trimble were both permitted to testify as witnesses for the Government (ibid., p. 595) and for General White (ibid., p. 741).

35. Ibid., pp. 523, 528, 529, 531.
36. White, "The Capitulation of Harper's Ferry," pp. 612–15.
37. G. E. Waring, "The Garibaldi Guard," in *The First Book of the Authors' Club (Liber Scriptorum)* (New York: The Authors' Club [De Vinne Press], 1893), p. 572.
38. WR/OR, series I, vol. XIX, pt. I, pp. 598–99.
39. Ibid., p. 585.
40. Ibid., p. 666.
41. This was corroborated by White's aide, Curtis, who described the council's "unanimous" decision as being "that there was no beneficial result to be gained by fighting longer; that it was merely sacrificing the men; the position could be held but a very short time, perhaps an hours or two longer, and that [only] at a great sacrifice." (WR/OR, series I, vol. XIX, pt. I, p. 688.)
42. Ibid., p. 744.
43. WR/OR, series I, vol. XIX, pt. I, p. 744.
44. Ibid., p. 744.
45. Ibid., p. 523.
46. Ibid., p. 528.
47. WR/OR, series I, vol. XIX, pt. I, p. 529.
48. Ibid., p. 530.
49. See note on p. 000 (re ammunition supply).
50. See note on p. 000 (re relative manpower).
51. See note on p. 000 (re available artillery).
52. WR/OR, series I, vol. XIX, pt. I, p. 531.
53. It seems possible that White was not even aware that Cole had left, let alone returned, since his battle report refers to Russell's mission to McClellan but omits all reference to Cole's (ibid., p. 526).
54. White, "The Capitulation of Harper's Ferry," p. 615.
55. WR/OR, series I, vol. XIX, pt. 1, pp. 528 and 531 (White); pp. 598–99 (D'Utassy); p. 744 (Trimble).
56. Ibid., p. 592 (Binney); pp. 647–48 (Willmon); p. 689 (Curtis).
57. Ibid., p. 622.
58. Ibid., p. 565.
59. Ibid., p. 573.
60. Ripley, "Memories of the Ninth Vermont at the Tragedy of Harper's Ferry," p. 159.
61. WR/OR, series I, vol. XIX, pt. I, p. 682.
62. Ibid., p. 637.
63. Ibid., p. 638.
64. Ibid., pp. 650–52.
65. Ibid., p. 651.
66. Ibid., p. 654.
67. Ibid.
68. Ibid., p. 664.
69. Ibid., p. 684.

70. Ibid., p. 685.
71. Ibid., p. 749.
72. Ibid.
73. Ibid., p. 761.
74. *Encyclopedia Americana* (1953), s.v. "Wool, John Ellis."
75. WR/OR, series I, vol. XIX, pt. I, p. 793.
76. Ibid., p. 791. See also note, p. 000 above.

Chapter 23. Surrender (II) As the Troops Saw It

1. *New York Times,* September 18, 1862, p. 8. The same correspondent went on, however, to add: "Yet what could be done? Rebel batteries were opened on us from seven different directions and *there was no hope of reinforcements reaching us.*" (Emphasis added.)

2. Report of interview of one Parks by Celeste B. Newcomer at Mancelona, Michigan, May 28, 1905; now in the Harper's Ferry File of the History Department of the National Park Service in Washington, D.C.

3. Benjamin W. Thompson, "Recollections of War Times," p. 22; unpublished Civil War memoir now in Civil War Times Illustrated Collection, U.S.A.M.H.R.C., Carlisle Barracks, Pennsylvania.

4. Reprinted in Washington *Evening Star,* September 18, 1862, p. 1.

5. New York *Daily Tribune,* September 18, 1862, p. 8.

6. U.S. War Department, *The War of the Rebellion: A Compilation of the Official Records of the Union and Confederate Armies,* 128 vols. (Washington, D.C.: G.P.O., 1180–1901) [hereafter WR/OR], series I, vol. XIX, pt. I, p. 585.

7. Ibid., p. 589.

8. A. M. Willson, *Disaster, Struggle, Triumph: The Adventures of 1,000 "Boys in Blue"* (Albany, N.Y.: Argus Co. 1870), pp. 84–85.

9. The 111th and 126th New York infantry regiments had adjoining areas in the middle of Bolivar Heights.

10. B. W. Thompson, "Recollections of War Times," pp. 22–23, in Civil War Times Illustrated Collection, U.S.A.M.H.R.C., Carlisle Barracks, Pennsylvania.

11. WR/OR, series I, vol. XIX, pt. 1, p. 528.

12. Ibid.

13. Ibid.

14. J. G. Walker, "Jackson's Capture of Harper's Ferry," in U. R. Johnson and C. C. Buel, *Battles and Leaders of the Civil War,* 4 vols. (New York: The Century Co., 1887; New York: Thomas Yoseloff, 1956), 2: 616.

15. See map at p.

16. Ibid.

17. W. T. Poague, *Gunner with Stonewall* (Jackson, Tenn.: McCowat-Mercer Press, 1957), p. 44.

18. C. A. Newcomer, *Cole's Cavalry; or, Three Years in the Saddle in the Shenandoah Valley* (Freeport, N.Y.: Books for Libraries Press, 1970), p. 41.

19. No known relation to C. A. Newcomer, the historian of Cole's Cavalry, cited in preceding note.

20. Until 1955 this letter remained in the possession of Mrs. Newcomer's family in Harper's Ferry, where her father founded Storer College. When Harper's Ferry became a National Monument, a copy of the letter was turned over to the National Park Service, which still holds it. A 1962 study by A. L. Sullivan, a National Park Service historian, appended a copy but that writer doubted Parks's story, deeming it unlikely that Phillips would have done such a thing in view of his testimony before the Harper's Ferry Commission that he was out of ammunition other than canister and "considered

that any longer defense ... would have been with a great sacrifice of life as the consequence and we would finally have been overcome." (WR/OR, series I, vol. XIX, pt. I, p. 685.) We have hitherto expressed great doubt about the credibility of Phillips' testimony before the Commission. If, in his rage, Phillips had really ordered Miles's assassination, his overriding concern when called to Washington by the military establishment must have been to avoid any suggestion of trouble with Miles.

21. T. A. Early, *General Jubal A. Early, Autobiographical Sketch and Narrative of the War between the States*, ed. R. H. Early (Philadelphia and London: J. B. Lippincott Co., 1912), p. 137.

22. W. H. Nichols, "The Siege and Capture of Harper's Ferry by the Confederates, September 1862," in *Personal Narratives of Events in the War of the Rebellion* (Providence, R.I.: *The Rhode Island Soldiers and Sailors Society*, 1889), 4: 2: 39.

23. WR/OR, series I, vol. XIX, pt. I, p. 519.

24. W. W. Blackford, *War Years with Jeb Stuart* (New York: Charles Scribner's Sons, 1945), pp. 144–45.

25. Even after the surrender there was a moment when it seemed possible that at least some of the Union garrison might make their escape across the pontoon bridge and destroy it, in which case McLaws would have remained trapped without hope of relief. It was Colonel George Stannard, commander of the 9th Vermont and the man who would break Pickett's charge at Gettysburg just ten months later, who almost performed this feat. One of his young captains wrote later: "When the word reached us that the white flag had gone up, Stannard swore a bitter oath that he would not be sacrificed without one bold struggle for our honor and for our liberty. At his command we rushed by the left down a ravine to the bank of the Shenandoah, thence into town, making for the pontoon over into Maryland, with determination to risk the fire of the batteries on both heights, hoping that, once across, a short struggle would bring us into McClellan's [i.e., Franklin's] lines, then only a few miles away. [A. P.] Hill so rapidly advanced his line of battle, however, that they [the Rebels] were in our camp before we were halfway to the bridge, and being missed from the line, General White, who had assumed command after Miles was mortally wounded, sent one of his own and one of General Hill's aides to intercept us and bring us back. They caught us as we had breathlessly reached the pontoon. In five minutes what would have been left of us would have been in Maryland. At first Stannard refused to obey the orders to return but upon being impressed with the penalties which would be inflicted upon the other troops by his attempt to violate the generous cartel already arranged, he with anguish of heart yielded." E. H. Ripley, *Vermont General* Edited by Otto Eisenschiml. (New York: Devin-Adair Co., 1960), p. 32.

26. WR/OR, series I, vol. XIX, pt. I, p. 791.

Chapter 24.   The Death of Miles

1. Baltimore *Sun*, September 19, 1862, p. 1.

2. E. H. Ripley, "Memories of the Ninth Vermont at the Tragedy of Harper's Ferry," in *Personal Recollections of the War of the Rebellion*. (New York: M.O.L.L.U.S., 1909), 4: 157–58.

3. These two Vermonters gave Miles's exclamation a "treasonable construction" and so did their company commander at the time, although later he was not so sure. E. H. Ripley, "Memories of the Ninth Vermont at the Tragedy of Harper's Ferry," in *Personal Recollections of the War of the Rebellion* (New York: M.O.L.L.U.S., 1909), 4: 157–58.

4. Baltimore *Sun*, September 19, 1862, p. 1.

5. New York *Herald*, September 19, 1862, p. 8, col. 1 (reporting a Frederick dispatch dated September 17, 1862, at 2:00 P.M.).

6. New York *Daily Tribune,* September 20, 1862, editorial page. Greeley's editorial demanded an investigation of the Harper's Ferry fiasco.

7. WR/OR, series I, vol. XIX, pt. I, p. 592.

8. Ibid., p. 593.

9. Baltimore *Sun,* September 19, 1862, p. 1.

10. U.S., War Department, Adjutant General's Office, Washington, D.C., Special Orders #420, Par. 21 (December 30, 1862).

11. New York *Daily Tribune,* September 18, 1862, p. 8.

12. A. M. Willson, *Disaster, Struggle, Triumph: the Adventures of 1,000 "Boys In Blue"* Albany, N.Y.: Argus Co., 1870, pp. 104–5.

Chapter 25.   An Official Verdict

1. H. K. Douglas, *I Rode with Stonewall* Chapel Hill, N.C.: University of North Carolina Press, 1940; Fawcett Publications, Inc., 1965, pp. 161–62.

2. U.S. War Department, *The War of the Rebellion: A Compilation of the Official Records of the Union and Confederate Armies,* 128 vols. (Washington, D.C.: G.P.O., 1880–1901) [hereafter "WR/OR"], series I, vol. XIX, pt. 1, p. 799.

3. S. P. Chase, "Diary of Salmon P. Chase", in *Annual Report of the American Historical Association for the Year 1902,* 2 vols. (Washington, D.C.: G.P.O., 1903), 2: 85.

4. Gideon Welles, *Diary of Gideon Welles (1861–64),* ed. J. T. Morse (Boston and New York: Houghton Mifflin Company, 1911), 1: 140.

5. Ibid., p. 143. See also "Diary of Salmon P. Chase," 2: 88–89.

6. WR/OR, series I, vol. XIX, pt. I, p. 530.

7. Ibid., p. 549.

8. Hunter was a grandson of Richard Stockton, New Jersey's signer of the Declaration of Independence, and his wife was a daughter of John Kinzie, Chicago's first settler. He commanded Lincoln's personal guard during the early months of the Administration. Interestingly, his stay at West Point had overlapped Dixon Miles's by three years.

9. WR/OR, series I, vol. XIX, pt. I, p. 556.

10. Ibid., pp. 762–74.

11. Ibid., p. 794.

12. New York *Daily Tribune,* November 10, 1862, editorial page (4).

13. It is not practical to review more than summarily the long-drawn-out power struggle between McClellan and the Lincoln administration. The general came to power in the summer of 1861 at the age of 35 amidst universal acclamation, when octogenarian Winfield Scott resigned as commanding general after Bull Run I. The young general's popularity remained high for many months while he did an excellent job of organizing and training the new Army of the Potomac. Gradually, however, it appeared to Lincoln that McClellan was constitutionally incapable of leading his army into battle. After long prodding McClellan finally began his Peninsular Campaign against Richmond in the spring of 1862. Lincoln refused, however, to send McClellan a large body of troops guarding Washington. Probably because of that, McClellan eventually failed to take Richmond and was ordered back to northern Virginia. During the summer of 1862 Lincoln installed a Western general, Henry Halleck, as "general in chief" and McClellan's superior. He also brought another general, John Pope, from the West to command a separate Union army in Virginia. When, however, Pope was badly defeated at Bull Run II—whether because of McClellan's refusal to cooperate with him became a hotly contested issue—Lincoln was forced to restore McClellan to power and McClellan proceeded to lead his army against Lee in defense of Maryland, as we have seen here.

14. G. B. McClellan, *Report on the Organization and Campaigns of the Army of the Potomac* (New York: Sheldon & Co., 1864), p. 407.

15. Ibid.

16. Ibid., pp. 406–26.

17. Bruce Catton, *Mr. Lincoln's Army* (New York: Doubleday & Co., 1951; New York: Pocketbooks, Inc., 1964), p. 342.

18. McClellan, *Report on the Organization and Campaigns of the Army of the Potomac*, pp. 435–37.

19. WR/OR, series I, vol. XIX, pt. I, p. 545.

20. Ibid.

21. McClellan, *Report on the Organization and Campaigns of the Army of the Potomac*, p. 438.

22. WR/OR, series I, vol. XIX, pt. I, p. 586.

23. Ibid., p. 722.

24. Ibid., pp. 724–25, 737.

25. Ibid., p. 726.

26. National Archives, Record Group 153, Harper's Ferry Court of Inquiry File (KK 311).

27. See note on p. 000, above.

28. WR/OR, series I, vol. XIX, pt. I, pp. 786–87.

29. Ibid.

30. McClellan, *Report on the Organization and Campaigns of the Army of the Potomac*, pp. 346–53. See also, for example, a dispatch on the evening of Tuesday, September 8, from McClellan to Fitz John Porter: "The army is tonight well posted to act in any direction the moment the enemy develops his movements. I am now in a condition to watch him closely and he will find it hard to escape me if he commits a blunder." WR/OR, series, I, vol. XIX, pt. II, p. 221. In his subsequent report (August 4, 1863) McClellan asserted: "The importance of moving with all due caution so as not to uncover the National Capital until the enemy's plans were developed was, I believe, fully appreciated by me. . . ." WR/OR, series I, vol. XIX, pt. I, p. 41

31. McClellan, *Report on the Organization and Campaigns of the Army of the Potomac*, p. 355.

32. WR/OR, series I, vol. LI, pt. I, p. 4.

33. National Archives, Record Group 153, Harper's Ferry Court of Inquiry File (KK 311).

34. WR/OR, series I, vol. XIX, pt. I, pp. 794–800.

35. The commission also recommended dismissal of Colonel Ford from the service for mismanaging the Union defense of Maryland Heights and dismissal of Major Baird for the "disgraceful behavior" of the 126th New York. WR/OR, series I, vol. XIX, pt. I, pp. 798–99. Ford's dismissal (ibid., p. 803) was shortly thereafter rescinded by President Lincoln on the plea of Secretary Chase, Ford's erstwhile political bedfellow and later enemy, on condition that Ford tender his resignation effective November 8, 1862. See Ford's instructions to Chase on how to present his case to the President in National Archives, Record Group 153, Harper's Ferry Court of Inquiry File (KK 311). For the rescission order see War Department, Adjutant General's Office, General Order #183, dated November 8, 1862. Ford subsequently became superintendent of public printing, a major Washington patronage job, and preached temperance until his death in 1868. A. A. Graham, *History of Richland County (Ohio)* (Mansfield, Ohio: A. A. Graham & Co., 1880), p. 704. Baird, too, was dismissed from the service on November 8, 1862, but his disability was removed June 26, 1863, and he lived through Gettysburg (where Colonel Sherrill was killed) to become colonel of the 126th New York and die in action at Petersburg (Virginia) on June 16, 1864. F. Phisterer, *New York in the War of the Rebellion*, 6 vols. (Albany, N.Y.: Weed, Parsons & Co., 1890; Albany, N.Y.: J. B. Lyon Co., 1912), 4: 3501.

36. WR/OR, series I, vol. XIX, pt. I, p. 799.

37. Ibid.

38. Ibid., p. 800.

39. New York *Daily Tribune,* November 10, 1862, editorial page (4).

40. A. M. Willson, *Disaster, Struggle, Triumph: The Adventures of 1,000 "Boys In Blue"* (Albany, N.Y.: Argus Co., 1870), p. 81.

41. E. Z. Hays, *History of the Thirty-second Regiment Ohio Veteran Volunteer Infantry* (Columbus, Ohio: Cott & Evans, 1896), p. 30.

42. A. W. Corliss, *History of the 7th Squadron, Rhode Island Cavalry* from Adjutant General's Report, 1865, p. 2.

43. M. F. Dowley, *History and Honorary Roll of the Twelfth Regiment, Infantry, NGSNY* (New York: T. Farrell & Son, 1869), p. 20.

44. C. A. Newcomer, *Cole's Cavalry; or, Three Years in the Saddle in the Shenandoah Valley* (Freeport, N.Y.: Books for Libraries Press, 1970), p. 41. Note, however, the following somewhat surprising sequel to the quotation in the text above: "A great injustice has been done Colonel Miles as he was a competent officer and the stigma upon his name should be removed."

45. E. H. Ripley, "Memories of the Ninth Vermont at the Tragedy of Harper's Ferry, Sept. 15, 1862," in *Personal Recollections of the War of the Rebellion,* (New York: M.O.L.L.U.S. [N.Y. Commander] 1909), 4: 136, 155.

46. J. H. Clark, *The Iron Hearted Regiment* Albany, N.Y.: J. Munsell, 1865, pp. 19–20.

Chapter 26.   The Summing Up

1. See, for example, Colonel Cameron's testimony that "he was not excited but he seemed to be stupid. His intellect was dull, all confusion.... It seemed as though everything was mixed up in his mind." *U.S. War Department, The War of the Rebellion: A Compilation of the Official Records of the Union and Confederate Armies,* 128 vols. (Washington, D.C.: G.P.O., 1880–1901) [hereafter "WR/OR"], series I, vol. XIX, pt. I, p. 632.

2. "I never saw him [Miles] except when he was calm and cool, under all circumstances, and seemed equal to all emergencies that might arise, except on Monday morning, the morning of the surrender. I think that then, surrounded as he was on all sides, he seemed a little flustered, and hardly to know how to act.... That is the only time I ever saw him when he seemed to be excited." WR/OR, series I, vol. XIX, pt. I, p. 761.

Index

Adams Express, 142

Alexandria, Va., 59

Alternate Route Forty, 94. *See* National Road

American Party. *See* Know Nothings

Anderson, Maj. Gen. Richard H., C.S.A., 94

Annapolis, Md., 142

Antietam Creek (Md.), possible site for Rebel recrossing of Potomac, 97–98; on Russell's route to McClellan, 155; McLaws summoned by Lee to, 149, 171–72; Lee's decision to fight McClellan at, 87; on route of escaping Harper's Ferry cavalry, 175–76; Harper's Ferry Rebels rejoin Lee at, 207; outcome of battle at affected by surrender of Harper's Ferry, 11–12, 240; Lincoln's reaction to Battle of Antietam, 214; Clara Barton at, 149fn

Astor, John Jacob, 79

Augur, Brig. Gen. Christopher C., U.S.A., 231

Bacon, Lt. Charles G., U.S.A., 190

Baird, Maj. William H., U.S.A., 32, 126, 236

Baker, Col. Lafayette Carlos (Chief of United States Secret Service), 166

Ball, Capt. F., Jr., U.S.A., 232

Baltimore, Md.: headquarters of Middle Department of U.S. Army located at, 42, 199; Miles leads Union troops through in June 1861, 26–27; direct wire and rail communications with Harper's Ferry cut off, 72, 110, 178; indirect wire and rail communication with Harper's Ferry via Cumberland, Md. cut off, 110, 178; quartermaster supplies in Frederick sent to, 51, 226–27; possible attack by Lee on, 87, 91, 146, 217; referred to in Miles's deathbed wanderings, 210; reactions of to Miles's death, 211

Baltimore *American* quoted, 27, 37, 83, 201, 252 n.6, 253 n.8

Baltimore County, Md., 13, 211, 248

Baltimore & Ohio Railroad: target of "bushwhackers," 39; Potomac Home Brigade ("Railroad Brigade") organized to protect it, 271; Downey's 3rd Infantry Regiment (PHB) assigned to patrol it, 96; Miles's jurisdiction over its territory, 39; same expanded, 42, 255; northern lifeline, 39; target of Lee's Maryland Campaign, 91, 94; trains from Baltimore stopped at Frederick, 70. *See also* Garrett, John W. (President of B & O)

Baltimore *Republican,* quoted, 27, 92

Baltimore *Sun,* quoted, 209–10

Banning, Col. Henry B., U.S.A.: first of Miles's troops to encounter invading Rebels, 47; retreats from Point of Rocks to Sandy Hook under orders from Miles, 48–50, 226, 257; warned erroneously by

291

into Harper's Ferry with White on Friday, 108; Downey ordered up Maryland Heights by Miles on Saturday morning, 118–19; Miles's condition then, 119, 222, 256 n.12; Downey reaches Maryland Heights in time for battle, 122, 131, 139, 232; challenges Hewitt retreat order, 124–25, 127–28; Downey and Russell direct continuing action atop Maryland Heights, 129, 133, 140; seeks reinforcements unsuccessfully, 136, 141; after evacuation of Maryland Heights reassigned to defend southern half of Bolivar Heights line, 163; outnumbered and driven back by Pender Sunday afternoon until White brings help, 167–68; Downey urges taking the command from Miles at informal Sunday night conference, 181–82; testifies before Harper's Ferry Commission re need to surrender on Monday morning, 195, and ignorance that relief was at hand, 184. *See also* listing of U.S. Army units at Harper's Ferry: Third Infantry Regiment of Potomac Home Brigade (sometimes called "Third Maryland")

Dranesville, Va., 87

D'Utassy, Capt. Anthony, U.S.A., 44

D'Utassy, Col. Frederick G., U.S.A.: personal background, 58–59; command of Garibaldi Guard, 59; corruption and convictions of crime, 59–60; testimony for Miles at latter's drunkenness trial after Bull Run I, 32–33; assigned to command 1st Brigade at Bolivar Heights, 58, 60; advises Miles on Friday night to withdraw garrison to Maryland Heights, 108–9, 120; offers to retake Maryland Heights, 144; anticipates Rebel attack on Bolivar Heights Sunday morning, 144–45; on Sunday morning sends detachment to recover guns and ammunition on Maryland Heights, 150, 233; Rebel feint holds D'Utas-

sy's 1st Brigade in place Sunday afternoon, 167, and again on Monday morning, 196 fn.; small losses Monday morning, 186; views at surrender council Monday morning, 189–90, 194, 196; enforces Miles's surrender order, 200. *See also* listing of U.S. Army units at Harper's Ferry: Thirty-Ninth New York Infantry

Early, Brig. Gen. Jubal A., C.S.A., 205

Edgecumb County, S.C., 14

Eleventh Maryland Brigade (War of 1812), 13

Elk Ridge Md. (site of Battle of Maryland Heights), 72, 76, 100–104, 107, 114–116, 121, 130, 141, 268 n.4

Emancipation Proclamation, 214

Escape of U.S. Cavalry from Harper's Ferry, 173–78, 228, 235, 281 nn.14, 16, 18, 21, 22

Evans, Dr. John, 52

Evanston, Ill., 52

Ewell, Lt. Gen. Richard S., C.S.A., 20–21, 185, 205

Faithful, Capt. William T., U.S.A., 50–51, 226–27

Falling Waters, Md., 176

"Fighting Parson" (nickname for Russell, Capt. Charles, U.S.A., which see)

Finger Lakes (N.Y.), 104, 116, 118

Ford, Col. Thomas H., U.S.A.: early life, 65; in Mexican War, 65, 67; Ohio lawyer and politician, 67–68, 261 nn.17, 19; organizer of 32nd Ohio Volunteers, 68–69; early Civil War activity, 69, 261 n.36; assigned to defend Maryland Heights, 75–76, 224, 232, 239; conduct of defense of Maryland Heights on Friday, 101–13, 227; same, on Saturday morning, 114–31, 233, 274 n.32; same on Saturday afternoon (including decision to evacuate Maryland Heights),

on Sunday night, 156 fn; McLaws ordered to rejoin Lee at Sharpsburg Sunday night, 171; escapes over Potomac pontoon bridge to Harper's Ferry and then to Sharpsburg after Miles's surrender Monday morning, 179 fn., 206–7

Maginot Line, 163

Manassas, Va., 91

Mancelona, Michigan, 204

"Manor Church". *See* Saint James Episcopal Church

Mansfield, Ohio, 67

Martinsburg, W. Va.: Wool orders White to Martinsburg, 56, 120, 232; White arrives, 81; rumors Rebels will make major attack on Martinsburg, 48, 82, 85; minor attack by Ashby's Cavalry, 83; possibility of capturing 3,000-man garrison attracts Lee, 91; Lee's S.O. #191 includes order for Jackson to seize Martinsburg garrison, 94, 148; Jackson's goal unclear until he crosses Potomac at Williamsport, 98; Rebels cut Harper's Ferry's communications with Cumberland, 110; White marches his Martinsburg garrison into Harper's Ferry, 108, 139

Maulsby, Col. William P., U.S.A., 48, 50–51, 226, 232, 257 n.38, 280 n.68, *See also* listing of United States Army units at Harper's Ferry: First Infantry Regiment of the Potomac Home Brigade

Means, Capt. Samuel, U.S.A., 43, 45, 47, 48, 222

Mexican War, 15–17, 65, 67, 199

Middle Department of U.S. Army, 42, 72, 76, 199

Middletown, Md., 94, 148, 157, 177

Miles, Capt. Aquila, 14, 248 n.1

Miles, Dr. Benjamin Briscoe, 15, 250 n.26

Miles, Col. Dixon Stansbury, U.S.A.: personal background and early career, 13–15, Mexican War service and honors, 15–17, 27, 37–38,

67, 250 n.30; post-Mexican War years, 18–24, 251 n.53; in command of Ft. Fillmore, New Mexico, 18–19; dispute with Territorial Governor, 19–20; leads punitive expeditions against Apache and Navajo Indians, 20–24, 251 n.70; elects to stay with Union Army when Civil War breaks out, despite strong Secessionist feeling in Maryland, 26–28; given command of a new division in McDowell's army, 28; Miles's actions at Bull Run I, 29, 30, 211, 253 n.31; testimony before Court of Inquiry re charge of drunkenness during battle, 29–34, 147, 214; Court's finding of drunkenness, 30–38, compared with assertions of Miles's counsel Reverdy Johnson, 35–37; Marylanders rally around Miles, 37–38; assignment of Miles to Harper's Ferry to command "Railway Brigade" guarding B&O Railroad, 39–40, 255 n.2; Miles superceded by Saxton when Jackson attacks Harper's Ferry in May 1862, 41–42; jurisdiction of Miles's "Railroad Brigade" expanded by Department Commander (Wool), 42; Miles's pulls in outposts as invading Rebels march from Point of Rocks to Frederick, Md., 45–51, 226; orders Frederick supplies destroyed, 50–51, 226–27; poisons Wool's mind against White, 55; wins confirmation of his command at Harper's Ferry from Halleck, who orders Miles to hold out "to the latest moment," 57; Miles allocates defense of Harper's Ferry to four brigades, under D'Utassy (58–60), Trimble (61–64), Ford (65–69) and Ward (78–80); Miles disobeys Wool's order to build blockhouse atop Maryland Heights, 72, 74–75, 262 n.14; refuses Ford a battery for Solomon's Gap, 76, 103; irresponsibly reports various Rebel forces threatening